THE FUTURE IN THE PRESENT

"Over a hundred years ago, Hegel said that the simplest reflection will show the necessity of holding fast . . . the affirmation that is contained in every negation, the future that is in the present. It is one of the signs of the advanced stage of human development that this is no longer a mere philosophical but a concrete question."

C. L. R. James, *Dialectical Materialism and the Fate of Humanity*

C.L.R.James

THE FUTURE IN THE PRESENT

Selected Writings

Lawrence Hill & Co., Westport
Allison & Busby, London

First published in Great Britain 1977
by Allison and Busby Limited
6a Noel Street, London W1V3RB

Reprinted 1980

ISBN 085031 148 9 (hardback)
ISBN 0 85031 149 7 (paperback)

Published in the United States
by Lawrence Hill & Co., Publishers, Inc.
520 Riverside Avenue
Westport, CT 06880

ISBN 0 88208 125x (paperback)
Library of Congress Catalog Number: 77-73129

The publishers gratefully acknowledge the invaluable help they
have received in compiling this selection from David Cork, Michael
Dibb, Robert A. Hill, C.L.R. James, Selma James, John LaRose,
Alan J. MacKenzie, Richard Small.

Contents

"When one looks back over the last twenty years to those men who are most far-sighted, who first began to tease out the muddle of ideology in our times, who were at the same time marxist with a hard theoretical basis, and close students of society, humanists with a tremendous response to and understanding of human culture, Comrade James is one of the first one thinks of."

E. P. Thompson

C. L. R. JAMES: A BIOGRAPHICAL
INTRODUCTION

C. L. R. James — the author of historical studies, a novel, short stories, a play; a seminal figure in black politics on three continents; writer on Hegel and philosophy, and a major innovator in marxist theory and working-class organisation; the author of books and essays on literature, art and sport; and above all a participant, teacher and activist in the events of his time — was born in Tunapuna, near Port of Spain, Trinidad, in 1901, the son of a schoolteacher. He attended Queen's Royal College, the island's major government secondary school, as a scholarship boy, and in the 1920s became a teacher there himself; during this time he played club cricket and began writing fiction.

In 1932 he came to England with the encouragement of an old acquaintance and cricketing opponent, Learie Constantine, whom he was to help to write his autobiography; for a while James lived in Constantine's adopted town of Nelson, Lancashire. He had brought with him his first political book, *The Life of Captain Cipriani*, a pioneer work arguing the case for West Indian self-government which was published that year in Nelson with Constantine's assistance, and later in a shortened version by Leonard Woolf's Hogarth Press in London.

An article by James on cricket in the *Daily Telegraph* brought him to the attention of Neville Cardus, and as a result of this meeting James began to write as cricket correspondent for the *Manchester Guardian*. This, followed by similar employment with the *Glasgow Herald*, was to provide him with a living throughout his first stay in the country. Meanwhile he had become active in British politics and society. Until 1936 he was a member of the Independent Labour Party and chairman of its Finchley branch, and he wrote regularly for the ILP papers *Controversy* and the *New Leader*. In that year he left to help form the Revolutionary Socialist League, along with other trotskyists who had left the ILP, and he was editor of its newspaper *Fight*. At the same time he was editor of *International African Opinion*, the journal of the International African Service Bureau; the members of this organisation included Jomo Kenyatta, and its founder and chairman was George Padmore, whom James had known from childhood and whom he was later to introduce to Kwame Nkrumah. (James was

to write in a letter to Padmore in 1945: "George, this young man
[Nkrumah] is coming to you . . . do what you can for him because
he's determined to throw the Europeans out of Africa." It was
under the auspices of the Bureau that Nkrumah was to go from
London to the Gold Coast in 1947 to begin his preparations for
the revolution which was to initiate a new Africa.) James participated in the movement of the unemployed, and made speaking
tours in England, Scotland and Wales. He was chairman of the
International African Friends of Abyssinia during the Italian invasion, writing many articles on this issue for *The Keys* (the journal
of the League of Coloured Peoples) and agitating among British
workers for solidarity actions. He also played a part in the growth
of the trotskyist movement in France, and was one of the British
delegates to the founding conference of the Fourth International
in 1938. During this period he wrote his famous history of the
Haitian revolution, *The Black Jacobins* (1938), an extensive
history of the Third International, *World Revolution* (1937), and
A History of Negro Revolt (1938), as well as publishing a novel,
Minty Alley (1936). He translated Boris Souvarine's *Stalin* (1939),
the first major exposé of its subject, from the French. He also
wrote and acted in a play, *Toussaint L'Ouverture* (1936), in which
he and Paul Robeson appeared together at the Westminster Theatre.

At the end of 1938 James went to the United States of America
on a lecture tour, and stayed there for the next fifteen years. In
this period his activity developed in two main directions. First of
all, he pioneered the idea of an autonomous black movement
which would be socialist but not subject to control by the leaderships of white-majority parties and trade unions. The record of
his 1938 discussions with Trotsky, in which he laid the basis of
this principle, is still one of the fundamental texts establishing a
black marxism. James took part in wartime sharecroppers' strikes
in the South, and agitated among blacks to oppose the world war.
In the course of this activity he came to the conclusion that not
only did the black movement have autonomy, it was also more
advanced than the rest of the labour movement and would act
as its detonator: this view is summed up in the programme entitled
The Revolutionary Answer to the Negro Problem in the US (1948).
His other main activity (and in fact they interacted) was in the
Socialist Workers' Party, where together with Raya Dunayevskaya
he led a tendency that gradually elaborated an independent
marxism, breaking with its trotskyist background. It extended to
women and youth its idea of the special role of the black movement (this was still the 1940s) and later began to criticise the traditional "democratic centralist" version of the marxist organisation.
This rethinking is recorded in various political documents of the
tendency and in articles in *The New International* during the
1940s; it culminates in two full-length works, *Notes on the Dialectic*
(1948), a study of Hegel's *Science of Logic* and the development
of the dialectic in Marx and his continuators, and *State Capitalism*

and World Revolution (1950). During this period, James had also helped to initiate the first English translation of Marx's *Economic and Philosophic Manuscripts of 1844*. In 1952 he was interned on Ellis Island, and was expelled from the USA in the following year. It was during his internment that he wrote *Mariners, Renegades and Castaways,* a study of the work of Herman Melville.

James spent the next five years in England. He continued to contribute to the political debate in the US through the pages of the Detroit-based journal *Correspondence.* In 1958 he published *Facing Reality,* which presented the ideas worked through in the forties in the light of the Hungarian revolution and the growth of rank-and-file shop stewards'-type movements in Europe and North America. But at the same time he embarked upon a long programme of writing in which he was to re-examine the basis of his assumptions about human culture, and it was with this purpose that on his return to England he began his now classic book on cricket, *Beyond a Boundary* (1963).

The struggle for colonial emancipation in which James had continuously been involved was by now showing some results. In the years before the second world war he had been among the very few who not only foresaw but worked for the independence of Africa, and he maintained and strengthened his links with the Pan-Africanist movement, and with Nkrumah, during his visits to Ghana during the early years of the new régime. *Nkrumah and the Ghana Revolution* (1977) chronicles the events that led up to and ensued from Ghana becoming the first African country to win independence in 1957.

In 1958 James returned to Trinidad, in the run-up to the West Indian independence which he had already been advocating when he left a quarter of a century earlier. He became Secretary of the Federal Labour Party, the governing party of the embryonic West Indies Federation, and he worked with Dr Eric Williams in the Trinidad PNM (People's National Movement), editing and contributing copiously to its newspaper *The Nation.* Over the next three years he wrote two books, *Modern Politics* and *Party Politics in the West Indies,* as well as writing and lecturing on West Indian culture. His partnership with his former student and friend Williams came to an end as a result of the break-up of the West Indies Federation, and more particularly as a result of Williams's rejection of a non-aligned position in favour of the USA and its retention of the Chagauramas Naval Base. *Modern Politics* was banned, and James returned to England in 1962, a few days before Trinidad's independence. He continued to publish from a distance in the Trinidadian press, and returned in 1965 as a cricket correspondent to report the Test series. He was immediately put under house arrest, but his status as one of the founding fathers of West Indian independence ensured an outcry that led to his release. He stayed for several months, during which he founded and edited a newspaper, *We the People,* and initiated the formation of the Workers' and Peasants' Party.

James returned to England in the same year. He has continued to write prolifically on the variety of matters which have concerned him throughout his life, and to take an active part in political life. He initiated the 6th Pan-African Congress in Dar-es-Salaam in 1974, but because of a decision to exclude certain dissident Caribbean movements he declined to attend himself. He has contributed to a number of journals spanning three continents. These include *New Society, New Left Review, Race Today* in Britain; *Black World, Freedomways, Radical America* and *Amistad* in the USA; *Transition* in Africa; *New World* and many occasional publications in the Caribbean. He has been Visiting Professor of Political Science at Northwestern University, Illinois, and is currently Professor of Humanities at Federal City College, Washington; the rest of his time is divided between London and the West Indies. He continues to write on cricket, and is completing his autobiography.

(The Selected Writings of C. L. R. James are being published in three volumes: *The Future in the Present, Spheres of Existence* and *At the Rendezvous of Victory.*)

1

Triumph

[This short story was first published in 1929 in Trinidad, *Vol. 1. James wrote several works of fiction in this period: some short stories, a novel,* Minty Alley, *and a play,* Toussaint L'Ouverture. *James says: "In* The Life of Captain Cipriani *[see no. 2 in this volume] I dealt with the political issues and what the political parties were doing, and with what the middle-class people in general thought about domination by the British system. In 'Triumph' I do something entirely different: I speak about the actual life of the ordinary people, living in the towns . . . People still live that way, but now they are conscious of it and very hostile; in those days, the people in 'Triumph' took it for granted. I was concerned with their immense vitality and the way they met their problems. . . ."]*

Where people in England and America say slums, Trinidadians said barrack-yards. Probably the word is a relic of the days when England relied as much on garrisons of soldiers as on her fleet to protect her valuable sugar-producing colonies. Every street in Port-of-Spain proper could show you numerous examples of the type: a narrow gateway leading into a fairly big yard, on either side of which run long, low buildings, consisting of anything from four to eighteen rooms, each about twelve feet square. In these lived the porters, the prostitutes, carter-men, washerwomen and domestic servants of the city.

In one corner of the yard is the hopelessly inadequate water-closet, unmistakable to the nose if not to the eye; sometimes there is a structure with the title of bathroom, a courtesy title, for he or she who would wash in it with decent privacy must cover the person as if bathing on the banks of the Thames; the kitchen happily presents no difficulty; never is there one and each barrack-yarder cooks before her door. In the centre of the yard is a heap of stones. On these the half-laundered clothes are bleached before being finally spread out to dry on the wire lines which in every yard cross and recross each other in all directions. Not only to Minerva have these stones been dedicated. Time was when they would have had an honoured shrine in a local temple to Mars, for they were the major source of ammunition for the homicidal strife which so often flared up in barrack-yards.

No longer do the barrack-yarders live the picturesque life of twenty-five years ago. Then, practising for the carnival, rival singers, Willie, Jean, and Freddie, porter, wharf-man or loafer in

ordinary life, were for that season ennobled by some such striking
sobriquet as The Duke of Normandy or the Lord Invincible, and
carried with dignity homage such as young aspirants to literature
had paid to Mr Kipling or Mr Shaw. They sang in competition from
seven in the evening until far into the early morning, stimulated
by the applause of their listeners and the excellence and copious-
ness of the rum; night after night the stickmen practised their
dangerous and skilful game, the "pierrots", after elaborate preface
of complimentary speech, belaboured each other with riding whips;
while around the performers the spectators pressed thick and good-
humoured until mimic warfare was transformed into real, and
stones from "the bleach" flew thick. But today that life is dead.
All carnival practice must cease at ten o'clock. The policeman is
to the stick-fighter and "pierrot" as the sanitary inspector to
mosquito larvae. At nights the streets are bright with electric light,
the arm of the law is longer, its grip stronger. Gone are the old
lawlessness and picturesqueness. Barrack-yard life has lost its
savour. Luckily, prohibition in Trinidad is still but a word. And
life, dull and drab as it is in comparison, can still offer its great
moments.

On a Sunday morning in one of the rooms of the barrack in
Abercromby Street sat Mamitz. Accustomed as is squalid adversity
to reign unchallenged in these quarters, yet in this room it was
more than usually triumphant, sitting, as it were, high on a throne
of regal state, so depressed was the woman and so depressing her
surroundings.

The only representatives of the brighter side of life were three
full-page pictures torn from illustrated periodicals, photographs of
Lindbergh, Bernard Shaw and Sargent's "Portrait of a Woman",
and these owed their presence solely to the fact that no pawn-shop
would have accepted them. They looked with unseeing eyes upon
a room devoid of furniture save for a few bags spread upon the
floor to form a bed. Mamitz sat on the door step talking to, or
rather being talked to by her friend, Celestine, who stood astride
the concrete canal which ran in front of the door.

"Somebody do you something," said Celestine with conviction.
"Nobody goin' to change my mind from that. An' if you do what
I tell you, you will t'row off this black spirit that on you. A nice
woman like you, and you carn't get a man to keep you! You carn't
get nothing to do!"

Mamitz said nothing. Had Celestine said the exact opposite,
Mamitz's reply would have been the same.

She was a black woman, too black to be pure Negro, probably
with some Madrasi East Indian blood in her, a suspicion which
was made a certainty by the long thick plaits of her plentiful hair.
She was shortish and fat, voluptuously developed, tremendously
developed, and as a creole loves development in a woman more
than any other extraneous allure, Mamitz (like the rest of her sex
in all stations of life) saw to it when she moved that you missed

none of her charms. But for the last nine weeks she had been "in derricks", to use Celestine's phrase. First of all the tram conductor who used to keep her (seven dollars every Saturday night, out of which Mamitz usually got three) had accused her of infidelity and beaten her. Neither the accusation nor the beating had worried Mamitz. To her and her type those were minor incidents of existence, from their knowledge of life and men, the kept woman's inevitable fate. But after a temporary reconciliation he had beaten her once more, very badly indeed, and left her. Even this was not an irremediable catastrophe. But thenceforward, Mamitz, from being the most prosperous woman in the yard, had sunk gradually to being the most destitute. Despite her very obvious attractions, no man took notice of her. She went out asking for washing or for work as a cook. No success. Luckily, in the days of her prosperity she had been generous to Celestine who now kept her from actual starvation. One stroke of luck she had had. The agent for the barracks had suddenly taken a fancy to her, and Mamitz had not found it difficult to persuade him to give her a chance with the rent. But that respite was over: he was pressing for the money, and Mamitz had neither money to pay nor hope of refuge when she was turned out. Celestine would have taken her in, but Celestine's keeper was a policeman who visited her three or four nights a week, and to one in that position a fifteen-foot room does not offer much scope for housing the homeless. Yet Celestine was grieved that she could do nothing to help Mamitz in her trouble which she attributed to the evil and supernatural machinations of Irene, their common enemy.

"Take it from me, that woman do you something. Is she put Nathan against you. When was the quarrel again?"

"It was two or three days after Nathan gave me the first beating."

Nathan then had started on his evil courses before the quarrel with Irene took place, but Celestine brushed away objection.

"She musta had it in her mind for you from before. You didn't see how she fly out at you. . . . As long as you livin' here an' I cookin' I wouldn't see you want a cup o' tea an' a spoonful o' rice. But I carn't help with the rent. . . . An' you ain't have nobody here."

Mamitz shook her head. She was from Demerara.

"If you could only cross the sea—that will cut any spirit that on you. . . . Look the animal!"

Irene had come out of her room on the opposite side of the yard. She could not fail to see Celestine and Mamitz and she called loudly to a neighbour lower down the yard:

"Hey Jo-jo! What is the time? Ten o'clock a'ready? Le' me start to cook me chicken that me man buy for me—even if 'e have a so'foot. . . . I don't know how long it will last before 'e get drunk and kick me out o' here. Then I will have to go dawg'n round other po' people to see if I could pick up what they t'row 'way."

She fixed a box in front of her door, put her coal-pot on it, and started to attend to her chicken.

Sunday morning in barrack-yards is pot-parade. Of the sixteen tenants in the yard twelve had their pots out, and they lifted the meat with long iron forks to turn it, or threw water into the pot so that it steamed to the heavens and every woman could tell what her neighbour was cooking—beef, or pork, or chicken. It didn't matter what you cooked in the week, if you didn't cook at all. But to cook salt fish, or hog-head, or pig-tail on a Sunday morning was a disgrace. You put your pot inside your house and cooked it there.

Mamitz, fat, easy-going, and cowed by many days of semi-starvation, took little notice of Irene. But Celestine, a thin little whip of a brown-skinned woman, bubbled over with repressed rage.

"By Christ, if it wasn't for one t'ing I'd rip every piece o' clothes she have on off'er."

"Don' bother wid 'er. What is the use o' gettin' you'self in trouble with Jimmy?"

Jimmy was the policeman. He was a steady, reliable man but he believed in discipline and when he spoke, he spoke. He had made Celestine understand that she was not to fight: he wasn't going to find himself mixed up in court as the keeper of any brawling woman. Celestine's wrath, deprived of its natural outlet, burned none the less implacably.

"I tell you something, Mamitz, I goin' to talk to the agent in the morning. I goin' to tell 'im to give you to the end of the month. Is only five days. . . . I goin' to give you a bath. Try and see if you could get some gully-root and so on this afternoon. . . . Tonight I goin' to give you. . . . An' I will give you some prayers to read. God stronger than the devil. We gon' break this t'ing that on you. Cheer up. I goin' to send you a plate with you' chicken an' rice as soon as it finish. Meanwhile burn you little candle, say you' little prayers, console you' little mind. I goin' give you that bath tonight. You ain' kill priest. You ain' cuss you' mudder. So you ain' have cause to 'fraid nothin'."

Celestine would never trust herself to indulge in abuse with Irene; the chances that it would end in a fight were too great. So she contented herself with casting a look of the most murderous hate and scorn and defiance at her enemy, and then went to her own pot which was calling for attention.

And yet three months before Mamitz, Celestine and Irene had been good friends. They shared their rum and their joys and troubles: and on Sunday afternoons they used to sit before Mamitz's room singing hymns: "Abide With Me", "Jesu, Lover of My Soul", "Onward! Christian Soldiers". Celestine and Irene sang soprano and Irene sang well. Mamitz was a naturally fine contralto and had a fine ear, while Nathan, who was a Barbadian and consequently knew vocal music, used to sing bass whenever he happened to be in. The singing would put him in a good mood and he would send off to buy more rum and everything would be peaceful and happy. But Irene was a jealous woman, not only jealous of Mamitz's steady three dollars a week and Celestine's policeman with his twenty-eight dollars at the end of the month. She lived with a cab-man, whose income though good enough was irregular. And he was a married man, with a wife and children to support. Irene had to do washing to help out, while Mamitz and Celestine did nothing, merely cooked and washed clothes for their men. So gradually a state of dissatisfaction arose. Then one damp evening, Mamitz, passing near the bamboo pole which supported a clothes line overburdened with Irene's clothes, brought it down with her broad, expansive person. The line burst, and nightgowns, sheets, pillow-cases, white suits and tablecloths fluttered to the mud. It had been a rainy week with little sun, and already it would have been difficult to get the clothes ready in time for Saturday morning: after this it was impossible. And hot and fiery was the altercation. Celestine who tried to make peace was drawn into the quarrel by Irene's comprehensive and incendiary invective.

"You comin' to put you' mouth in this. You think because you livin' with a policeman you is a magistrate. Mind you' business, woman, min' you' business. The two o' all you don't do nothing for you' livin'. You only sittin' down an eatin' out the men all you livin' wid. An' I wo'k hard an' put out me clo's on the line. And this one like some cab-horse knock it down, and when I tell 'er about it you comin' to meddle! Le' me tell you. . . ."

So the wordy warfare raged, Celestine's policeman coming in for rough treatment at the tongue of Irene. Celestine, even though she was keeping herself in check, was a match for any barrack-yard woman Port-of-Spain could produce, but yet it was Mamitz who clinched the victory.

"Don't mind Celestine livin' with a policeman. You will be glad to get 'im for you'self. An' it better than livin' with any stinkin' so'foot man."

For Irene's cab-man had a sore on his foot, which he had had for thirty years and would carry with him to the grave even if he lived for thirty years more. Syphilis, congenital and acquired, and his copious boozing would see to it that there was no recovery. Irene had stupidly hoped that nobody in the yard knew. But in Trinidad when His Excellency the Governor and his wife have a quarrel the street boys speak of it the day after, and Richard's bad foot had long been a secret topic of conversation in the yard. But it was Mamitz who had made it public property, and Irene hated Mamitz with a virulent hatred, and had promised to "do" for her. Three days before, Nathan, the tram-conductor, had given Mamitz the first beating; but even at the time of the quarrel there was no hint of his swift defection and Mamitz's rapid descent to her present plight. So that Celestine, an errant but staunch religionist, was convinced that Mamitz's troubles were due to Irene's trafficking with the devil, if not personally, at least through one of his numerous agents who ply their profitable trade in every part of Port-of-Spain. Secure in her own immunity from anything that Irene might "put on her", she daily regretted that she couldn't rip the woman to pieces. "Oh Jesus! If it wasn't for Jimmy I'd tear the wretch limb from limb!" But the energy that she could not put into the destruction of Irene she spent in upholding Mamitz. The fiery Celestine had a real affection for the placid Mamitz, whose quiet ways were so soothing. But, more than this, she was determined not to see Mamitz go down. In the bitter antagonism she nursed against Irene, it would have been a galling defeat if Mamitz went to the wall. Further, her reputation as a woman who knew things and could put crooked people straight was at stake. Once she had seen to Jimmy's food and clothes and creature comforts she set herself to devise ways and means of supporting the weak, easily crushed Mamitz.

Celestine's policeman being on duty that night, she herself was off duty and free to attend to her own affairs. At midnight, with the necesary rites and ceremonies, Ave Marias and Pater Nosters, she bathed Mamitz in a large bath pan full of water prepared with gully root, fever grass, lime leaves, *geurin tout, herbe à femmes*, and other roots, leaves and grasses noted for their efficacy (when properly applied) against malign plots and influences. That was at twelve o'clock the Sunday night. On Monday morning at eight o'clock behold Popo des Vignes walking into the yard, with a little bag in his hand.

Popo is a creole of creoles. His name is des Vignes, but do not be misled into thinking that there flows in his veins blood of those aristocrats who found their way to Trinidad after '89. He is a Negro, and his slave ancestors adopted the name from his master. Popo is nearing forty, medium-sized, though large about the stomach, with a longish moustache. He is dressed in a spotless suit of white with tight-fitting shoes of a particularly yellowish brown (no heavy English brogues or fantastic American shoes for him). On his head he wears his straw hat at a jaunty angle, and his manner of smoking his cigarette and his jacket always flying open (he wears no waistcoat) will give the impression that Popo is a man of pleasure rather than a man of work. And that impression would be right. He has never done a week's honest work in his life. He can get thirty dollars for you if you are in difficulties (at one hundred per cent); or three thousand dollars if you have a house or a cocoa estate. During the cocoa crop he lurks by the railway station with an unerring eye for peasant proprietors who have brought their cocoa into town and are not quite certain where they will get the best price. This is his most profitable business, for he gets commission both from the proprietors and from the big buyers. But he is not fastidious as to how he makes money, and will do anything that does not bind him down, and leaves him free of manual or clerical labour. For the rest, after he has had a good meal at about half past seven in the evening he can drink rum until six o'clock the next morning without turning a hair; and

in his own circle he has a wide reputation for his connoisseurship
in matters of love and his catholicity of taste in women.

"Eh, Mr des Vignes! How you?" said Celestine. The inhabitants
of every barrack-yard, especially the women, knew Popo.

"Keeping fine."

"Who you lookin' for roun' this way?"

"I come roun' to see you. How is Jimmy? When you getting
married?"

"Married!" said Celestine with fine scorn. "Me married a police!
I wouldn't trust a police further than I could smell him. Police
ain't have no regard. A police will lock up 'is mudder to get a
stripe. An' besides I ain' want to married the man in the house all
the time, you go'n be a perfect slave. I all right as I be."

"Anyway, I want you to buy a ring."

"Rings you sellin' in the bag? I ain' have no money, but le' me
see them."

Popo opened his bags and displayed the rings—beautiful gold of
American workmanship, five dollars cash and six dollars on terms.
They had cost an Assyrian merchant in Park Street ten dollars
the dozen, and Popo was selling them on commission. He was
doing good business, especially with those who paid two dollars
down and gave promises of monthly or weekly instalments. If later
the merchant saw trouble to collect his instalments or to get back
his rings, that wouldn't worry Popo much for by that time he would
have chucked up the job.

"So you wouldn't take one," said he, getting ready to put away
his treasures again.

"Come roun' at the end o' the month. But don't shut them up
yet. I have a friend I want to see them."

She went to the door.

"Mamitz!" she called. "Come see some rings Mr des Vignes
sellin'."

Mamitz came into Celestine's room, large, slow-moving, volup-
tuous, with her thick, smooth hair neatly plaited and her black skin
shining. She took Popo's fancy at once.

"But you have a nice friend, Celestine," said Popo. "And she has
a nice name too: Mamitz! Well, how many rings you are going
to buy from me?"

Celestine answered quickly: "Mamitz can't buy no rings. The
man was keepin' her, they fall out, an' she lookin' for a husband
now."

"A nice woman like you can't stay long without a husband,"
said des Vignes. "Let me give you some luck. . . . Choose a ring
and I will make you a present."

Mamitz chose a ring and des Vignes put it on her finger himself.

"Excuse me, I comin' back now," said Celestine. "The sanitary
inspector comin' just now, an' I want to clean up some rubbish
before he come."

When she came back des Vignes was just going.

"As we say, Mamitz," he smiled. "So long, Celestine!"

He was hardly out of earshot when Celestine excitedly tackled Mamitz.

"What 'e tell you?"

"'E say that 'e comin' round here about ten o'clock tonight or little later. . . . An' 'e give me this." In her palm reposed a red two-dollar note.

"You see what I tell you?" said Celestine triumphantly. "That bath. But don' stop. Read the prayers three times a day for nine days. . . . Buy some stout, Mitz, to nourish up you'self. . . . 'E ain't a man you could depend on. If you dress a broomstick in a petticoat 'e will run after it. But you goin' to get something out o' 'im for a few weeks or so. . . . An' you see 'e is a nice man."

Mamitz smiled her lazy smile.

Celestine knew her man. For four weeks Popo was a more or less regular visitor to Mamitz's room. He paid the rent, he gave her money to get her bed and furniture out of the pawn-shop, and every Sunday morning Mamitz was stirring beef or pork or chicken in her pot. More than that, whenever Popo said he was coming to see her, he gave her money to prepare a meal so that sometimes late in the week, on a Thursday night, Mamitz's pot smelt as if it was Sunday morning. Celestine shared in the prosperity and they could afford to take small notice of Irene who prophesied early disaster.

"All you flourishin' now. But wait little bit. I know that Popo des Vignes well. 'E don't knock round a woman for more than a month. Just now all that high livin' goin' shut down an' I going see you Mamitz eatin' straw."

But Mamitz grew fatter than ever, and when she walked down the road in a fugi silk dress, tight fitting and short, which exposed her noble calves to the knee and accentuated the amplitudes of her person, she created a sensation among those men who took notice of her.

On Sunday morning she went into the market to buy beef. She was passing along the stalls going to the man she always bought from, when a butcher called out to her.

"Hey, Mamitz! Come this way."

Mamitz went. She didn't know the man, but she was of an acquiescent nature and she went to see what he wanted.

"But I don't know you," she said, after looking at him. "Where you know my name?"

"Ain't was you walkin' down Abercromby Street last Sunday in a white silk dress?"

"Yes," smiled Mamitz.

"Well, I know a nice woman when I see one. An' I find out where you livin' too. Ain't you livin' in the barrack just below Park Street? . . . Girl, you did look too sweet. You mustn't buy beef from nobody but me. How much you want? A pound? Look a nice piece. Don't worry to pay me for that. You could pay me later. Whenever you want beef, come round this way."

Mamitz accepted and went. She didn't like the butcher too much, but he liked her. And a pound of beef was a pound of beef. Nicholas came to see her a day or two after and brought two pints of stout as a present. At first Mamitz didn't bother with him. But des Vignes was a formidable rival. Nicholas made Mamitz extravagant presents and promises. What helped him was that Popo now began to slack off. A week would pass and Mamitz would not see him. And no more money was forthcoming. So, after a while she accepted Nicholas, and had no cause to regret her bargain. Nicholas made a lot of money as a butcher. He not only paid the rent, but gave her five dollars every Saturday night, and she could always get a dollar or two out of him during the week. Before long he loved her to distraction, and was given to violent fits of jealousy which, however, were always followed by repentance and lavish presents. Still Mamitz hankered after Popo. One day she wrote him a little note telling him that she was sorry she had to accept Nicholas but that she would be glad to see him any time he came round. She sent it to the Miranda Hotel where Popo took his meals. But no answer came and after a while Mamitz ceased actively to wish to see Popo. She was prosperous and pretty happy. She and Celestine were thicker than ever, and were on good terms with the neighbours in the yard. Only Irene they knew would do them mischief, and on mornings when Mamitz got up, on Celestine's advice, she looked carefully before the door lest she should unwittingly set foot on any church-yard bones, deadly powders, or other satanic agencies guaranteed to make the victim go mad, steal or commit those breaches of good conduct which are punishable by law. But nothing untoward happened. As Celestine pointed out to Mamitz, the power of the bath held good, "and as for me," concluded she, "no powers Irene can handle can touch my little finger."

Easter Sunday came, and with it came Popo. He walked into the yard early, about seven the morning, and knocked up Mamitz who was still sleeping.

"I t'ought you had given me up for good," said Mamitz. "I write you and you didn't answer."

"I didn't want any butcher to stick me with his knife," laughed Popo. "Anyway, that is all right . . . I was playing baccarat last night and I made a good haul, so I come to spend Easter with you. Look! Here is five dollars. Buy salt fish and sweet oil and some greens and tomatoes. Buy some pints of rum. And some stout for yourself. I am coming back about nine o'clock. Today is Easter Saturday, Nicholas is going to be in the market the whole day. Don't be afraid for him."

Mamitz became excited. She gave the five dollars to Celestine and put her in charge of the catering, while she prepared for her lover. At about half past nine Popo returned. He, Mamitz and Celestine ate in Mamitz's room, and before they got up from the table, much more than two bottles of rum had disappeared. Then Celestine left them and went to the market to Nicholas. She told him that Mamitz wasn't feeling too well and had sent for beef and pork. The willing Nicholas handed over the stuff and sent a shilling for his lady love. He said he was rather short of money but at the end of the day he was going to make a big draw. Celestine cooked. and at about half past one, she, Popo and Mamitz had lunch. Celestine had to go out again and buy more rum. The other people in the yard didn't take much notice of what was an everyday occurrence, were rather pleased in fact, for after lunch Celestine had a bottle and a half of rum to herself and ostentatiously invited all the neighbours to have drinks, all, of course, except Irene.

At about three o'clock Irene felt that she could bear it no longer and that if she didn't take this chance it would be throwing away a gift from God. She put on her shoes, took her basket on her arm, and left the yard. It was the basket that aroused the observant Celestine's suspicions for she knew that Irene had already done all her shopping that morning. She sat thinking for a few seconds, then she knocked at Mamitz's door.

"Look here, Mamitz," she called. "It's time for Mr des Vignes to go. Irene just gone out with a basket, I think she gone to the market to tell Nicholas."

"But he can't get away today," called Mamitz.

"You know how the man jealous and how 'e bad," persisted Celestine. "Since nine o'clock Mr des Vignes, is time for you to go."

Celestine's wise counsel prevailed. Popo dressed himself with his usual scrupulous neatness and cleared off. The rum bottles were put out of the way and Mamitz's room was made tidy. She and Celestine had hardly finished when Irene appeared with the basket empty.

"You see," said Celestine. "Now look out!"

Sure enough, it wasn't five minutes after when a cab drew up outside, and Nicholas still in his bloody butcher's apron, came hot foot into the yard. He went straight up to Mamitz and seized her by the throat.

"Where the hell is that man you had in the room with you— the room I payin' rent for?"

"Don't talk dam' foolishness, man, lemme go," said Mamitz.

"I will stick my knife into you as I will stick it in a cow. You had Popo des Vignes in that room for the whole day. Speak the truth, you dog."

"You' mother, you' sister, you' aunt, you' wife was the dog," shrieked Mamitz, quoting one of Celestine's most brilliant pieces of repartee.

"It's the wo'se when you meddle with them common low-island people," said Celestine. Nicholas was from St. Vincent, and Negroes from St. Vincent, Grenada and the smaller West Indian islands are looked down upon by the Trinidad Negro as low-island people.

"You shut you' blasted mouth and don' meddle with what

don' concern you. It you encouragin' the woman. I want the truth, or by Christ I'll make beef o' one o' you here today."

"Look here, man, lemme tell you something." Mamitz, drunk with love and rum and inspired by Celestine, was showing spirit. "That woman over there come and tell you that Mr des Vignes was in this room. The man come in the yard, 'e come to Celestine to sell 'er a ring, she did promise to buy from 'im long time. Look in me room," she flung the half doors wide, "you see any signs of any man in there? Me bed look as if any man been lyin' down on it? But I had no right to meddle with a low brute like you. You been botherin' me long enough. Go live with Irene. Go share she wid she so' foot cab-man. Is woman like she men like you want. I sorry the day I ever see you. An' I hope I never see you' face again."

She stopped, panting, and Celestine, who had only been waiting for an opening, took up the tale.

"But look at the man! The man leave 'is work this bright Easter Saturday because this nasty woman go and tell 'im that Mr des Vignes in the room with Mamitz! Next thing you go'n say that 'e livin' with me. But man, I never see such a ass as you. Bertha, Olive, Josephine," she appealed to some of the other inhabitants of the yard. "Ain't all you been here the whole day an' see Mr des Vignes come here after breakfast? I pay 'im two dollars I had for 'im. 'E sen' and buy a pint o' rum an' I call Mamitz for the three o' we to fire a little liquor for the Easter. Next thing I see is this one goin out—to carry news: and now this Vincelonian fool leave 'e work—But, man, you drunk."

Bertha, Olive and Josephine, who had shared in the rum, confirmed Celestine's statement. Irene had been sitting at the door of her room cleaning fish and pretending to take no notice, but at this she jumped up.

"Bertha, you ought to be ashame' o' you'self. For a drink o' rum you lyin' like that? Don't believe them, Nicholas. Whole day—"

But here occurred an unlooked for interruption. The cabby, hearing the altercation and not wishing to lose time on a day like Easter Saturday, had put a little boy in charge of his horse and had been listening for a minute or two. He now approached and held Nicholas by the arm.

"Boss," he said, "don't listen to that woman. She livin' with Richard the cab-man an' 'e tell me that all women does lie but 'e never hear or know none that does lie like she—"

There was a burst of laughter.

"Come go, boss," said the cabby, pulling the hot, unwilling Nicholas by the arm.

"I have to go back to my work, but I am comin' back tonight and I am goin' to lick the stuffin' out o' you."

"An' my man is a policeman," said Celestine. "An' 'e goin' to be here tonight. An' if you touch this woman, you spend you' Easter in the lock-up sure as my name is Celestine an' you are a good-for-nothing Vincelonian fool of a butcher."

Nicholas drove away, leaving Celestine mistress of the field, but for the rest of the afternoon Mamitz was depressed. She was tired out with the day's excitement, and after all Nicholas had good money. On a night like this he would be drawing quite a lot of money and now it seemed that she was in danger of losing him. She knew how he hated Popo. She like Popo more than Nicholas, much more, but after all people had to live.

Celestine, however, was undaunted. "Don't min' what 'e say. 'E comin' back. 'E comin' back to beg. When you see a man love a woman like he love you, she could treat 'im how she like, 'e still comin' back like a dog to eat 'is vomit. But you listen to me, Mamitz. When 'e come back cuss 'im a little bit. Cuss 'im plenty. Make 'im see that you ain't goin' to stand too much nonsense from 'im."

Mamitz smiled in her sleepy way, but she was not hopeful. And all the rest of the afternoon Irene worried her by singing ballads appropriate to the occasion.

> "Though you belong to somebody else
> Tonight you belong to me."

> "Come, come, come to me, Thora,
> Come once again and be...."

> "How can I live without you!
> How can I let you go!"

Her voice soared shrill over the babel of clattering tongues in the yard. And as the voice rose so Mamitz's heart sank.

"Don't forget," were Celestine's last words before they parted for the night. "If 'e come back tonight, don't open the door for 'im straight. Le' 'im knock a little bit."

"All right," said Mamitz dully. She was thinking that she had only about thirty-six cents left over from the money des Vignes had given her. Not another cent.

But Celestine was right. The enraged Nicholas went back to work and cut beef and sawed bones with a ferocity that astonished his fellow butchers and purchasers. But at seven o'clock, with his pocket full of money and nothing to do, he felt miserable. He had made his plans for the Easter: Saturday night he had decided to spend with Mamitz, and all Easter Sunday after he knocked off at nine in the morning. Easter Monday he had for himself and he had been thinking of taking Mamitz, Celestine and Jimmy down to Carenage in a taxi to bathe. He mooned about the streets for a time. He took two or three drinks, but he didn't feel in the mood for running a spree and getting drunk. He was tired from the strain of the day and he felt for the restful company of a woman, especially the woman he loved—the good-looking, fat, agreeable Mamitz. At about half past ten he found his resolution never to look at her again wavering.

"Damn it," he said to himself. "That woman Irene is a liar. She see how I am treatin' Mamitz well and she want to break up the livin'."

He fought the question out with himself.

"But the woman couldn't lie like that. The man musta been there."

He was undecided. He went over the arguments for and against, the testimony of Bertha and Olive, the testimony of the cab-man. His reason inclined him to believe that Mamitz had been entertaining des Vignes for the whole day in the room he was paying for, while he, the fool, was working hard for money to carry to her. But stronger powers than reason were fighting for Mamitz, and eleven o'clock found him in the yard knocking at the door.

"Mamitz! Mamitz! Open. Is me—Nicholas." There was a slight pause. Then he heard Mamitz's voice, sounding a little strange.

"What the devil you want!"

"I sorry for what happen today. Is that meddlin' woman, Irene. She come to the market an' she lie on you. Open the door, Mamitz . . . I have something here for you."

Celestine next door was listening closely, pleased that Mamitz was proving herself so obedient to instruction.

"Man, I 'fraid you. You have a knife out there an' you come here to cut me up as Gorrie cut up Eva."

"I have no knife. I brought some money for you."

"I don't believe you. You want to treat me as if I a cow."

"I tell you I have no knife . . . open the door, woman, or I'll break it in. You carn't treat me like that."

Nicholas's temper was getting the better of him, he hadn't expected this.

The watchful Celestine here interfered.

"Open the door for the man, Mamitz. 'E say 'e beg pardon and, after all, is he payin' the rent."

So Mamitz very willingly opened the door and Nicholas went in. He left early the next morning to go to work but he promised Mamitz to be back by half past nine.

Irene, about her daily business in the yard, gathered that Nicholas had come "dawgin'" back to Mamitz the night before and Mamitz was drivin' him dog and lance, but Celestine beg for him and Mamitz let 'im come in. Mamitz, she noticed, got up that morning much later than usual. In fact Celestine (who was always up at five o'clock) knocked her up and went into the room before she came out. It was not long before Irene knew that something was afoot. First of all, Mamitz never opened her door as usual, but slipped in and out closing it after her. Neither she nor Celestine went to the market. They sent out Bertha's little sister who returned with beef and pork and mutton, each piece of which Mamitz held up high in the air and commented upon. Then Bertha's sister went out again and returned with a new coal-pot. Irene could guess where it came from—some little store, in Charlotte Street probably, whose owner was not afraid to run the risk of selling on Sundays. In and out the yard went Bertha's little sister, and going and coming she clutched something tightly in her hand. Irene, her senses tuned by resentment and hate to their highest pitch, could not make out what was happening. Meanwhile Celestine was inside Mamitz's room, and Mamitz, outside, had started to cook in three coal-pots.

Every minute or so Mamitz would poke her head inside the room and talk to Celestine. Irene could see Mamitz shaking her fat self with laughter while she could hear Celestine's shrill cackle inside. Then Bertha's sister returned for the last time and after going into the room to deliver whatever her message was, came and stood a few yards away, opposite Mamitz's door, expectantly waiting. Think as she would, Irene could form no idea as to what was going on inside.

Then Mamitz went and stood near to Bertha's sister; and, a second after, the two halves of the door were flung open and Irene saw Celestine standing in the doorway with arms akimbo. But there was nothing to — and then she saw. Both halves of the door were plastered with notes, green five-dollar notes, red two-dollar notes, and blue dollar ones, with a pin at a corner of each to keep it firm. The pin-heads were shining in the sun. Irene was so flabbergasted that for a second or two she stood with her mouth open. Money Nicholas had given Mamitz. Nicholas had come back and begged pardon, and given her all his money. The fool! So that was what Celestine had been doing inside there all the time. Bertha's sisters had been running up and down to get some of the notes changed. There must be about forty, no, fifty dollars, spread out on the door. Mamitz and Bertha's sister were sinking with laughter and the joke was spreading, for other people in the yard were going up to see what the disturbance was about. What a blind fool that Nicholas was! Tears of rage and mortification rushed to Irene's eyes.

"Hey, Irene, come see a picture Nicholas bring for Mamitz last night! An' tomorrow we goin' to Carenage. We don't want you, but we will carry you' husband, the sea-water will do 'is so'-foot good." Celestine's voice rang across the yard.

Bertha, Josephine, the fat Mamitz and the rest were laughing so that they could hardly hold themselves up. Irene could find neither spirit nor voice to reply. She trembled so that her hands shook. The china bowl in which she was washing rice slipped from her fingers and broke into a dozen pieces while the rice streamed into the dirty water of the canal.

1929

2

The Case for West-Indian Self-Government

[James completed The Life of Captain Cipriani, *his first full-length political writing, before coming to England in 1932. Cipriani, whom he knew well, was a mayor of Port of Spain who had a popular following and had on many occasions taken a stand against the colonial government. The book was first published in 1932 in Nelson, Lancashire, and the following year three chapters —two of them reprinted here—were produced as a pamphlet entitled "The Case for West-Indian Self-Government" (Hogarth Press, London). It is one of the texts on which stands James's reputation as a founding father of West Indian independence.]*

The English in the West Indies

A Colonial Office Commission is now taking evidence in Trinidad, the Windward and the Leeward Islands, with a view to the federation of all or some of them. But in these islands today political unrest is widespread and deep, and Sir Philip Cunliffe-Lister, the Secretary of State for the Colonies, has consented to the request of a deputation that the Commission be allowed to take evidence on the constitutional question. Yet the merits and demerits of constitutions cannot be fairly adjudged without a thorough understanding of the social constituencies they serve. First, then, to give some account of the people who live in the West Indies—in the West Indies, for though the scope of the present Commission is restricted, yet British Guiana (for administrative purposes always considered a part of the West Indies) and Jamaica are closely watching, and the decision of the Colonial Office will powerfully affect opinion and action in these colonies.

The bulk of the population of these West Indian islands, over eighty per cent, consists of Negroes or persons of Negroid origin. They are the descendants of those African slaves who were brought almost continuously to the West Indies until the slave trade was stopped in 1807. Cut off from all contact with Africa for a century and a quarter, they present today the extraordinary spectacle of a people who, in language and social customs, religion, education and outlook, are essentially Western and, indeed, far more advanced in Western culture than many a European community.

The advocates of Colonial Office trusteeship would have you believe that the average Negro is a savage fellow, bearing beneath the veneer of civilisation and his black skin, viciousness and criminality which he is losing but slowly, and which only the virtual domination of the European is able to keep in check. Says Lord Olivier:[1]

> "In the matter of natural good manners and civil disposition the Black People of Jamaica are very far, and indeed, out of comparison, superior to the members of the corresponding class in England, America or North Germany."

Of their alleged savagery:

> "This viciousness and criminality are, in fact, largely invented, imputed and exaggerated in order to support and justify the propaganda of race exclusiveness."

The trustees would have you believe that even when he is not a savage the average Negro is a simple, that is to say, a rather childish fellow. Compare this with Lord Olivier's opinion (among those of a hundred others), that:

> "The African races generally have a subtle dialectical faculty, and are in some ways far quicker in apprehension than the average Caucasian. . . .
>
> The African, whether at home or *even in exile after the great hiatus of slavery*,[2] shows practical shrewdness and aptitude for the affairs of local government. His legal acumen is higher than that of the European."

The last argument of the trustees, even when they have to admit the attainments of the Negro, is that he does not produce sufficient men of the calibre necessary for administering his own affairs. Yet Sir Charles Bruce,[3] after his wide experience, could say:

> "In the meantime, such has been the energy and capacity of the Afro-European population in the Crown Colonies, where they form the bulk of the general community, that there is no department of government, executive, administrative, or judicial, in which they have not held the highest office with distinction, no profession of which they are not honoured members, no branch of commerce or industry in which they have not succeeded."

Today and at any time during the last forty years such posts as Chief Justice, Colonial Secretary, Puisne Judge, Attorney-General, Solicitor-General and Surgeon-General could be filled two or three times over by local men, most of them men of colour. The Civil Services are over ninety per cent coloured, and even in large-scale business, the white man's jealous preserve, numerous coloured men

---

[1] Lord Olivier: Secretary of the Royal W.I. Commission of 1899, Governor of Jamaica (1907-13); Chief Commissioner W.I. Sugar Commission, 1930.

[2] Italics my own.

[3] Served in many Colonies, including the Windward Islands; at one time Governor of British Guiana.

occupy high and important positions.

It has to be admitted that the West Indian Negro is ungracious enough to be far from perfect. He lives in the tropics, and he has the particular vices of all who live there, not excluding people of European blood. In one respect, indeed, the Negro in the tropics has an overwhelming superiority to all other races—the magnificent vitality with which he overcomes the enervating influences of the climate. But otherwise the West Indian people are an easy-going people. Their life is not such as to breed in them the thrift, the care, and the almost equine docility to system and regulation which is characteristic of the industrialised European. If their comparative youth as a people saves them from the cramping effects of tradition, a useful handicap to be rid of in the swiftly-changing world of today, yet they lack that valuable basis of education which is not so much taught or studied as breathed in from birth in countries where people have for generation after generation lived settled and orderly lives. Quicker in intellect and spirit than the English, they pay for it by being less continent, less stable, less dependable. And this particular aspect of their character is intensified by certain social prejudices peculiar to the West Indies, and which have never been given their full value by those observers from abroad who have devoted themselves to the problems of West Indian society and politics.

The Negroid population of the West Indies is composed of a large percentage of actually black people, and about fifteen or twenty per cent of people who are a varying combination of white and black. From the days of slavery, these have always claimed superiority to the ordinary black, and a substantial majority of them still do so (though resenting as bitterly as the black assumptions of white superiority). With emancipation in 1834 the blacks themselves established a middle class. But between the brown-skinned middle class and the black there is a continual rivalry, distrust and ill-feeling, which, skilfully played upon by the European people, poisons the life of the community. Where so many crosses and colours meet and mingle, the shades are naturally difficult to determine and the resulting confusion is immense. There are the nearly-white hanging on tooth and nail to the fringes of white society, and these, as is easy to understand, hate contact with the darker skin far more than some of the broader-minded whites. Then there are the browns, intermediates, who cannot by any stretch of imagination pass as white, but who will not go one inch towards mixing with people darker than themselves. And so on, and on, and on. Associations are formed of brown people who will not admit into their number those too much darker than themselves, and there have been heated arguments in committee as to whether such and such a person's skin was fair enough to allow him or her to be admitted, without lowering the tone of the institution. Clubs have been known to accept the daughter and mother, who were fair, but refuse the father, who was black. A dark-skinned brother in a fair-skinned family is sometimes the subject of jeers and insults and open intimations that his presence is not required at the family social functions. Fair-skinned girls who marry dark men are often ostracised by their families and given up as lost. There have been cases of fair women who have been content to live with black men but would not marry them. Should the darker man, however, have money or position of some kind, he may aspire, and it is not too much to say that in a West Indian colony the surest sign of a man's having arrived is the fact that he keeps company with people lighter in complexion than himself. Remember, finally that the people most affected by this are people of the middle class who, lacking the hard contact with realities of the masses and unable to attain to the freedoms of a leisured class, are more than all types of people given to trivial divisions and subdivisions of social rank and precedence.

Here lies, perhaps, the gravest drawback of the coloured population. They find it difficult to combine, for it is the class that should in the natural course of things supply the leaders that is so rent and torn by these colour distinctions.

For historic and economic reasons, the most important of the other native groups are the white creoles.* The white creole suffers from two disadvantages, one of which he understands, and the other of which he probably does not. The first is climate. It seems that the European blood cannot by itself stand the climate for more than two or three generations. Here and there the third and fourth generation may use wealth, early acquired, to bolster mediocre abilities into some sort of importance, but the West Indies, as the generations succeed each other, take a deadly toll of all those families from temperate climates which make their home permanently there.

The second disability of the white creole is less tangible but equally important. He finds himself born in a country where the mere fact of his being white, or at least of skin fair enough to pass as white, makes him a person of consequence. Whatever he does, wherever he finds himself, he is certain of recognition. But with this power goes nothing beside personal responsibility. Englishmen govern the country. The result is an atmosphere which cramps effort. There is not that urgent necessity for exceptional performance which drives on the coloured man of ambition, and the white creole suffers accordingly. But this is not a disease which is easily seen by those who suffer from it, nor is the disease, even when diagnosed, one for which the patient is likely to take the remedy.

Into this community comes the Englishman to govern, fortified

---

* Many of the West Indian islands are cosmopolitan, and East Indians form about twelve per cent of the total population, though concentrated in Trinidad. But there is no need to give them special treatment, for economically and educationally they are superior to the corresponding class in India, and get on admirably with the Negroes.

(sometimes) by university degrees; and of late years by a wide experience in dealing with primitive peoples in Africa.

His antecedents have not been helpful. Bourgeois at home, he has found himself after a few weeks at sea suddenly exalted into membership of a ruling class. Empire to him and most of his type, formerly but a word, becomes on his advent to the colonies a phrase charged with responsibilities, but bearing in its train the most delightful privileges, beneficial to his material well-being and flattering to his pride. Being an Englishman and accustomed to think well of himself, in this new position he soon develops a powerful conviction of his own importance in the scheme of things and it does not take him long to convince himself not only that he can do his work well — which to do him justice, he quite often does — but that for many generations to come none but he and his type can ever hope to do the work they are doing.

On his arrival in the West Indies he experiences a shock. Here is a thoroughly civilised community, wearing the same clothes that he does, speaking no other language but his own, with its best men as good as, and only too often, better than himself. What is the effect on the colonial Englishman when he recognises, as he has to recognise, the quality of those over whom he is placed in authority? Men have to justify themselves, and he falls heavily back on the "ability of the Anglo-Saxon to govern", "the trusteeship of the mother country until such time" (always in the distant future) "as these colonies can stand by themselves", etc. etc. He owes his place to a system, and the system thereby becomes sacred. Blackstone did not worship the corrupt pre-Reform constitution as the Colonial Office official worships the system of Crown Colony government.

"Patriotism," says Johnson, "is the last refuge of a scoundrel." It is the first resort of the colonial Englishman. How he leaps to attention at the first bars of "God Save the King"! Empire Day, King's Birthday, days not so much neglected in England as ignored, give to his thirsty spirit an opportunity to sing the praises of the British Empire and of England, his own country, as its centre. Never does he seem to remember that the native place of the majority of those to whom he addresses his wearisome panegyrics is not England, but the colony in which they were born, in which they live, and in which they will in all probability die.

This excessive and vocal patriotism in the colonial Englishman is but the natural smoke of intensified fires burning within. That snobbishness which is so marked a characteristic of the Englishman at home, in the colonies develops into a morbid desire for the respect and homage of those over whom he rules. Uneasily conscious of the moral insecurity of his position, he is further handicapped by finding himself an aristocrat without having been trained as one. His nose for what he considers derogatory to his dignity becomes keener than a bloodhound's, which leads him into the most frightful solecisms.

In Grenada in 1931 there was a very orderly demonstration by all classes of the community against a decision of the Governor. One man who with his family had been invited to Government House for some social function took part in it. The Governor cancelled the invitation, but informed him that the cancellation did not apply to his wife and daughter who could come if they wanted to.

It is not surprising that the famous English tolerance leaves him almost entirely. At home he was distinguished for the liberality and freedom of his views. Hampden, Chatham, Dunning and Fox, Magna Carta and Bill of Rights, these are the persons and things (however misconceived) which Englishmen, undemonstrative as they are, write and speak of with a subdued but conscious pride. It is no accident, the Whig tradition in English historical writing. But in the colonies any man who speaks for his country, any man who dares to question the authority of those who rule over him, any man who tries to do for his own people what Englishmen are so proud that other Englishmen have done for theirs, immediately becomes in the eyes of the colonial Englishman a dangerous person, a wild revolutionary, a man with no respect for law and order, a self-seeker actuated by the lowest motives, a reptile to be crushed at the first opportunity. What at home is the greatest virtue becomes in the colonies the greatest crime.

The colonial Englishman it is fair to say retains some of the admirable characteristics which distinguish his race at home, but he is in a false position. Each succeeding year sees local men pressing him on every side, men whom he knows are under no illusions as to why he holds the places he does. Pressure reduces him to dodging and shifting. Thus it is that even of that honesty which is so well-recognised a characteristic of the English people — but I shall let an Englishman speak: "It is difficult," says Mr Somervell, the historian, "for white races to preserve their moral standards in their dealings with races they regard as inferior." Should Englishmen of fine sensibility stray into the Colonial Service they find themselves drawn inevitably into the circle of their colleagues and soon discover that for them to do otherwise than the Romans would be equivalent to joining a body of outsiders against their own. Thus it is that in the colonies, to quote an English official in the West Indies, "such large and intelligent classes of Englishmen come to have opinions so different from those for which the nation has ever been renowned at home." . . .

The Legislative Council

The deliberations of an Executive Council are secret. The body in which public interest centres is the advisory Legislative Council, which undoubtedly wields great influence, if not power. The Legislative Council of Trinidad is typical and will best serve as an example. This Council consists of three sections. The first is that of the official members, twelve in number, chosen by the Governor from

among the various heads of departments. The second consists of
the unofficial members, thirteen in number, partly nominated and
partly elected. The third section is not the least important of the
three — the Governor, who is in the chair. It will be seen how
potent for misgovernment is each of these three sections.

The official section, composed mainly of heads of departments,
comprises a solid block of Englishmen with a few white creoles,
generally from some other colony. These officials are for the most
part strangers to the community which they govern; in Trinidad
there have been five Attorney-Generals during the last dozen years.
Their position is secure, and their promotion depends not on the
people over whom they rule, but on a Colonial Office thousands
of miles away. It is not difficult to imagine their bureaucratic
attitude. There have been official members of the Trinidad Legislature who over a period of years have sat in the Council, saying
nothing, doing nothing, wasting their own time and the time of the
public. There is a further unreality, because whenever the Governor
wishes he can instruct the officials all to vote in the same way. And
the Council becomes farcical when two members of a committee
appointed by the Governor receive instructions to vote against their
own recommendations. Here today and gone tomorrow, these heads
of departments, in clubs and social gatherings mix chiefly with the
wealthy white creoles, whose interests lie with the maintenance of
all the authority and privileges of the officials against the political
advancement of the coloured people. Their sons and daughters
intermarry with the white creoles and get employment in the big
business houses. From all this springs that alliance so clearly fore-
shadowed by Cornewall Lewis, "We represent large interests," said
the Attorney-General in a recent debate, and every West Indian
knows the interests which he and the other officials represent. The
local government is the Chamber of Commerce, and the Chamber
of Commerce is the local government.

The unofficial members "representing the people" form the
second group, and since 1925 they have consisted of six members
nominated by the Governor and seven members elected by the
people. Formerly the Governor nearly always appointed white men
representing business interests. He might as well have appointed
a few more heads of departments for all the representation the
people got from them.

But it has been the policy of the government for some years past
to appoint a few Negroes to these positions. These have usually
been Negroes of fair, and not of dark skin. And that type of man,
whether on the Council or in the other departments of government, is often a more dangerous opponent of the masses of the
people than the Europeans themselves.

In its broader aspect this is no new thing in politics. There is,
first of all, the natural gravitation of all men towards the sources
of power and authority, and, on far larger stages, parties of
privilege have not yet ceased to hire mercenaries to do what would

be less plausibly and effectively done by themselves. The West Indian Islands are small and the two easiest avenues of success are the help of the government or the help of the white people. It is, therefore, fatally easy for the nominee to rationalise his self-seeking by the reflection that after all, in such a legislature, he can achieve nothing that the government sets its mind against.

There is yet another consideration no less powerful than the foregoing. These West Indian colonies offer, especially to those no longer young, little in the way of organised amusement, and individuals are thrown back almost entirely on society for recreation. Mr Julian Huxley, after four months' extensive travel in Africa, has written:

> "Of a large and important section of white people in Africa, officials as well as settlers, it is not unfair to say that *The Tatler*, *Punch*, a few magazines, detective stories and second-rate romantic novels represent their intellectual and cultural level."

The case in Trinidad is precisely the same, and indeed the shallowness, the self-sufficiency and the provincialism of English colonial society has long been a by-word among cultivated persons. But it keeps itself to itself and thereby becomes exclusive. It is the wealthiest class, lives in the best houses, has the best clubs, organises the best amusements. For the fair-skinned Negro who does not seek much, that society seems a paradise.

But when that is said, though much is said, all is not said. There is first of all the Governor. There have been recent Governors whom the people despised, and rightly. Of one and his entourage it could be said that he represented the butler, his wife the house-keeper, and his ADC the groom. But His Majesty's Representative is sometimes a man of parts, his wife a person of elegance. And whatever qualities they may have are naturally enhanced by the

> "... power
> Pre-eminence, and all the large effects
> That troop with majesty."

Now and then among the officials one finds a really brilliant man. Of late, members of the Consular Body, and some of the Professors of the Imperial College of Tropical Agriculture, have contributed their fair share to local society. Distinguished visitors often lend both tone and colour to the social dullness of local life. Any unusual social talent of local origin, if it is white, will usually find its way to the top. Thus around the Governor centre a few small groups which, though they will vary in value from time to time, yet whatever they are, are by far the best that the islands can show, for the coloured people, though possessing in themselves the elements of a society of some cultural value (their range of choice being so much wider), are so divided among themselves on questions of colour, based on varying shades of lightness or darkness, that they have been unable to form any truly representative social group or groups. The result is that many a man conscious of powers above the average, and feeling himself entitled to move in the best society the island affords, spends most of his leisure time and a small fortune in trying to get as near to the magic centre as possible, in itself a not too mean nor too contemptible ambition. The serious flaw in the position of the local man of colour is this, that those to whose society and good graces he aspires are not only Englishmen, but Englishmen in the colonies, and therefore constitutionally incapable of admitting into their society on equal terms persons of colour, however gifted or however highly placed (unless very rich). The aspirant usually achieves only a part of his aim. The utmost sacrifice of money, influence, and dignity usually gains him but a precarious position on the outer fringes of the society which he hopes to penetrate, and he is reduced to consorting with those fairer than himself, whose cupidity is greater than their pride. Others who feel themselves above this place-at-any-price policy stand on their dignity and remain at home, splendidly isolated. Thus it is nothing surprising to find on the Legislative Council three or four coloured men, each a little different in colour, who are more widely separated from one another than any of them is from a white man, and whose sole bond of unity is their mutual jealousy in their efforts to stand well with the governing officials.

These matters would not concern us here except for their unfortunate reaction on the political life of the community.

Not only nominations to the Council but all appointments in the service are made by the government, and the government can, and usually does, point to the number of coloured men it has appointed. But either by accident or design it rarely appoints black men. The appointment of these fair-skinned men seems to depend to a large extent on the way, whether openly or covertly, they dissociate themselves from their own people. But those same arts a place did gain must it maintain. The result is that a more or less intelligent and aspiring minority occupy a position in which they do more harm than good, for to the Colonial Office and the ordinary observer, being men of colour, they represent the coloured people, while the government and the white creole know that when it comes to a crisis these, their henchmen, are more royalist than the king. Some people have endeavoured to see in this a characteristic weakness of the coloured people and a grave reflection on their capacity for leadership. It is not so. Disinterested service actuated by nothing more than a sense of responsibility to one's own best convictions is a thing rare among all nations, and by necessity of less frequent occurrence in a small community of limited opportunities. These men are not so much inherently weak as products of the social system in which they live. Still, whatever the cause of their conduct, its effect is disastrous. Particularly as the government will appoint a dark Negro to a position of importance only when it cannot get a fair one. In this way it builds up in the service a group of men who, however distasteful to Englishmen themselves, are at one with them in their common antipathy to the black. Despising black men, these intermediates, in the Legislative Council and out of it, are forever climbing up the climbing wave, governed by one dominating motive—acceptance by white society. It would be unseemly to lower the tone of this book by detailing with whom, when and how Colonial Secretaries and Attorney-Generals distribute the nod distant, the bow cordial, the shakehand friendly, or the cut direct as may seem fitting to their exalted Highnesses; the transport of joy into which men, rich, powerful, and able, are thrown by a few words from the Colonial Secretary's wife or a smile from the Chief Justice's daughter. But political independence and social aspiration cannot run between the same shafts; sycophancy soon learns to call itself moderation; and invitations to dinner or visions of a knighthood form the strongest barriers to the wishes of the people.

All this is, and has been, common knowledge in the West Indies for many years. The situation shows little signs of changing. The type of constitution encourages rather than suppresses the tendency. But the day that all fair-skinned Negroes realise (as some do today) that they can only command respect when they respect themselves, that day the domination of the coloured people by white men is over. If the white men are wealthy, they will have the influence of wealthy men. If they are able they will have the influence of able men. But they will cease to have the influence of wealth or ability, not because they are wealthy or able, but simply because they are white.

If we neglect the elected members for the time being (a form of attention to which they are well accustomed) there remains now only the Governor in the chair.

At first sight it may seem that the Governor in the chair occupies a merely formal position, but on closer observation it becomes immediately obvious that his position there is as mischievous as those of the other two sections of a Crown Colony legislature. The Governor of a Crown Colony is three things. He is the representative of His Majesty the King, and as such must have all the homage and respect customary to that position. But the Governor is also the officer responsible for the proper administration of the government. The Governor-General of South Africa, like the other Governors-General, is not responsible for the government of the country. The responsible persons are the prime ministers of those countries. In Trinidad the Governor is Governor-General and Prime Minister in one. But that makes only two. When the Governor sits in the Legislative Council he is chairman of that body. The unfortunate result is that when a member of the Council rises to speak he is addressing at one and the same time an incomprehensible personage, three in one and one in three. A member of the House of Commons can pay all due respect to His Majesty the King, submit himself to the proper authority of the

Speaker of the House, and yet express himself in uncompromising terms about any aspect of government policy which appears to him to deserve such censure. In a Crown Colony legislature that is impossible. The Governor, being responsible for the administration, is liable to criticism directed against his subordinates. It is natural that he should, it is inconceivable that he would, do otherwise than defend those who assist him in carrying on the affairs of the colony. But should a Governor make an inconvenient admission as the head of the government he immediately assumes one of his other alibis. And in the Council as it is constituted and with the Governor holding the power that he holds, there are never lacking members always on the alert to jump to the defence of the dignity of His Majesty's representative or the respect due to the President of the Chamber, quite neglectful of the responsibility of the head of the administration. In December 1931 one nominated member in the course of his address on a Divorce Bill referred to the part the Governor had played in bringing forward that piece of legislation so unpopular with a certain section:

> "It is a pity that Your Excellency did not publish these despatches earlier, so that the public might have known the part Your Excellency has played in respect to this matter. I have no doubt that now the despatches have been published and the atmosphere has been clarified, it will be realised that Your Excellency's share of the responsibility for the presentation of this Bill is absolutely nil.
>
> If I may say so without offence, it would appear that you are regarded by the Colonial Office merely as a servant of the centurion. . . . It must be very humiliating indeed to any responsible officer to find himself in the position in which Your Excellency must find yourself. . . ."

Now that speech erred, if it erred in any way, on the side of temperance. The speaker was forcible, but, nominated brownskinned Negro in a Crown Colony Legislature, his tone was so respectful as to be almost humble.* But not so in the eyes of one member. No. For him the Governor had been insulted. Nor did he wait for a government official to say so. He (himself a brownskinned Negro) began his own address with a flood of compliment to the Solicitor-General (a white man) for the able way in which he had argued for the Bill and then turned his hose on the Attorney-General (another white man) and complimented him on the able way he had argued against the Bill. Then he switched off to the address of his brother Negro and nominated member: "He referred to the Governor of this Colony in a way ill befitting any member of this Council. . . ."

---

*Alas! It did not save him. He has been omitted from the new nominations.

Nor was he yet satisfied that enough sacrifices had been offered on the altar of the Governor's dignity. Before his speech was finished he found opportunity to make another salaam: "I was pained to listen to his statement in almost flippant language that the Governor of this Colony was the servant of the centurion."

Instances may be multiplied. In his triple position the Governor in the chair exercises a disproportionate influence. His presence is a constant check to free expression of opinion. And a Legislative Council in which a man cannot freely speak his mind is a place fit for academic debates and not for the discussion of the affairs of government.

It is not difficult to imagine the result of all this in the working of the constitution. The government, already so overwhelmingly strong, is without effective criticism or check, and being composed of men who are governing not for the sake of governing, but because they have to make a living, it is not strange that it should be as slack and regardless as it usually is. "Public life is a situation of power and energy. He trespasses upon his duty who sleeps upon his watch and may as well go over to the enemy." There, Burke, as ever, master of political statement, distils for the politician a first principle.

It is the lack of this active vigilance which robs our politics of any reality. Far from being alert guardians of the public weal, the favourite formula of most of these members is: "I beg to congratulate the government." Should an official make a speech of no more than mediocre ability, each one, at some time in his own speech, "begs to congratulate the honourable member". Always they seem to be bowing obsequiously, hat in hand, always the oily flattery, the ingratiating smile, and criticism offered on a silver salver. A person gaining his first impression of politics from a reading of some of these debates would conclude not that it was the sole business of the government to govern properly, but a favour that was being conferred upon the people. It must not be imagined that some of these members have been ciphers of no value on the Legislature. Sometimes they possess great ability or force of personality. They are men of the world enough to know that if to assert themselves too much is a mistake, it would be equally a mistake to assert themselves too little. But they can never have that full weight in public matters which comes from a man like Captain Cipriani, who speaks from his well-known and settled convictions, or from a respected Colonial Secretary who is stating the case from the government point of view. Sometimes they find themselves inadvertently on the wrong side, and it is interesting to see them wriggle out. "Can the government see its way to . . . ?" "No." "Couldn't the government . . . ?" "No. . . ." "I still think I am right, however, though I beg to congratulate the honourable member who explained the government's position. It is clear that the government is quite right, too. I beg to congratulate the government. The government will hear nothing more of this from me."

One concrete example must be given of the attitude of these nominated representatives of the people.

From the time that the Imperial College of Tropical Agriculture started its work in Trinidad there were well-founded complaints of discrimination against coloured men. When in April 1930 there came up before the Legislative Council a grant to the Imperial College of £8,500 a year for five years, Captain Cipriani asked the government for a definite assurance that there would be no discrimination. If not, he would oppose the vote. Here for once the underlying reef was showing above the surface, plain, stark, and not to be denied.

The debate continued.

> *Mr O'Reilly* (who had had a brother there): ". . . I do not follow my honourable friend in suggesting that there has been any discrimination at the College. . . ."
>
> *Sir Henry Alcazar:* ". . . I do not propose to address you on the question of discrimination. . . ."
>
> *The Colonial Secretary* (reading a statement from the Principal of the Imperial College of Tropical Agriculture): "I am at a loss to know how the idea has occurred that there is a differentiation over coloured students. . . ."
>
> *Dr McShine:* "Your Excellency, I also supported the desire to have some assurance from the College that the discrimination did not exist or that it was exaggerated, and I am glad to have the explanation, the statement of fact that it is not so. . . ."
>
> *Mr Kelshall:* "I think that we ought in looking at this subject, to take a long view. . . . But I have the utmost confidence in the Head of the College — Mr Evans — a broad-minded Englishman of the right sort . . . and I do not believe there is at present any ground for complaint in regard to discrimination among the students. . . ."
>
> *Mr Wortley* (the Director of Agriculture): "I do feel strongly that the reason is not that the College does not wish them, but that for one reason or another the Trinidadians do not wish to go to the College. In other words, other professions and other openings attract them more. . . ."

It remained for the Governor to conclude in the same strain:

> ". . . We cannot dictate to private companies what appointments they should make, but it appears to me to be very foolish if companies operating in the country do not appoint people that live there, and prefer to go elsewhere to fill appointments. If I can help in this matter I shall certainly do so." (Applause.)

So far the public debate. But what were the actual facts? Mr Gaston Johnston (a coloured man), who was present, did not say anything in the House, but when the meeting was over he told Captain Cipriani that Father English, the Principal of St Mary's

College, had received a letter from Mr Martin Leake, the previous Principal of the Agricultural College, in which Mr Leake had asked Father English to discourage young men of colour from coming to the Imperial College, because although he, the Principal, had nothing against them, the white students made it unpleasant, which caused a great deal of difficulty.

"My God, Johnston, you mean to say you knew that and not only did not say so yourself, but did not tell me?"

"No, for if I had told you, you would say it and cause a lot of trouble."

Captain Cipriani knew, as every other member of Council knew, the true state of affairs at the College. When he went to England in the July following, he brought the matter to the notice of the Colonial Office. The Colonial Office official listened to him and then took up a copy of *Hansard*.

"Captain Cipriani, you complain of discrimination. Now, isn't Mr O'Reilly a coloured man? Yes. Now listen to what he says. . . . Isn't Sir Henry Alcazar a coloured man? Now listen to what he says. . . . Isn't Mr Kelshall a coloured man? . . . Isn't Dr McShine a coloured man, And this is what he says. . . . Now, Captain Cipriani, what have you come here making trouble about?"

Now one can understand the position of the white men who spoke in this debate. One can understand Mr Wortley feeling so strongly that Trinidadians did not go to the Imperial College because they preferred other avenues, for it is an important part of the business of the government official to deprecate any sug- gestion of colour discrimination, and, whenever the opportunity arises, to throw as much dust as possible. The same motives obviously actuated the Governor. How else is it possible to account for his apparent ignorance of the fact that the oil companies would as soon appoint a Zulu chief to some of their higher offices as a local man of colour, whatever the qualifications he had gained at the Imperial College? We can even pass over the irreconcilable conflict of evidence between Mr Evans and his immediate prede- cessor. Englishmen or white men stand to gain nothing by talk about race discrimination; and on a short-sighted view they stand to lose a great deal. But in this debate, as in every other, what is so pitiful is the attitude of these so-called representatives of the people, who so often hold the positions that they do hold because of their colour. The majority of them hate even more than white men any talk about colour. For if they stand up against colour discrimination they will be noted by the government as leaders of the people, and then good-bye to some of their dearest hopes; while for some it will mean facing in public the perfectly obvious but nevertheless dreadful fact that they are not white men.

That is the Trinidad Legislature. There is no room nor should there be need to go any farther into details of the course of legislation.

The reader may want to know more of that pitiful remnant, the elected members, who form usually about a third of the various legislatures. The usual colour prejudices often divide them; and in any case it takes a man of the courage and strength of Captain Cipriani to hurl himself continuously against the solid phalanx arrayed against him. But the real hopelessness of the situation is best to be seen in Grenada and Dominica. In each of these smaller islands, where the population is more homogeneous and more closely-knit, the local Government has achieved the astonishing feat of uniting both nominated and elected members against itself. In Grenada, both these groups, defeated by the official majority, retired from the Council. Warmly supported by the whole population they have returned, but certainly not to shed tears of happy reunion on the shoulders of the government. In Dominica all the unofficials, nominated and elected, have refused to go back and though writs have been issued for a new election no one will stand. When, after a time, one man accepted nomination by the government the people burnt his house down. It is in this way that empires prod their citizens into violence and sow the seeds of their own dissolution. Yet though the writing on the wall stretched from Burma to Cyprus, there are those who will not read.

When will British administrators learn the lesson and for the sake of future cordial relations give willingly and cheerfully what they know they will have to give at last? How do they serve their posterity by leaving them a heritage of bitterness and hate in every quarter of the globe? Solution of the problem there is but one—a constitution on democratic lines. This does not necessarily mean a form of government modelled plastically on the English or Dominion systems. Ceylon shows one way, Malta another. The West Indian legislators have their constitution ready. That is not a matter for debate here. But there will only be peace when in each colony the final decisions on policy and action rest with the elected representatives of the people. Hard things are being said today about parliamentary democracy, but the West Indian colonies will not presume to reject it until England and the dominions show them the way. The high qualification for membership of the Council must go. The high franchise for the power to vote must go. That tight-rope dancer, the nominated member, must vanish forever, and the representatives of the people thrown back upon the people.

No one expects that these islands will, on assuming responsibility for themselves, immediately shed racial prejudice and economic depression. No one expects that by a change of constitutions the constitution of politicians will be changed. But though they will, when the occasions arise, disappoint the people, and deceive the people and even, in so-called crises, betray the people, yet there is one thing they will never be able to do—and that is, neglect the people. As long as society is constituted as it is at present that is the best that modern wage-slaves can ever hope to achieve.

For a community such as ours, where, although there is race

prejudice, there is no race antagonism, where the people have reached their present level in wealth, education, and general culture, the Crown Colony system of government has no place. It was useful in its day, but that day is now over. It is a fraud, because it is based on assumptions of superiority which have no foundation in fact. Admirable as are their gifts in this direction, yet administrative capacity is not the monopoly of the English; and even if it were, charity begins at home, especially in these difficult times. The system is wicked, because to an extent far more than is immediately obvious it permits a privileged few to work their will on hundreds of thousands of defenceless people. But most of all is the system criminal because it uses England's overflow as a cork to choke down the natural expansion of the people. Always the West Indian of any ambition or sensibility has to see positions of honour and power in his own country filled by itinerant demigods who sit at their desks, ears cocked for the happy news of a retirement in Nigeria or a death in Hong Kong; when they go and others of the same kind take their places, while men often better than they stand outside rejected and despised. And even were the Colonial Office officials ideally suited to their posts the situation would not be better, but worse than it is. For the more efficient they are, the more do they act as a blight upon those vigorous and able men whose home is their island, and who, in the natural course of events, would rise to power and influence. Governors and governed stand on either side of a gulf which no tinkering will bridge, and political energy is diverted into other channels or simply runs to waste. Britain will hold us down as long as she wishes. Her cruisers and aeroplanes ensure it. But a people like ours should be free to make its own failures and successes, free to gain that political wisdom and political experience which come only from the practice of political affairs. Otherwise, led as we are by a string, we remain without credit abroad and without self-respect at home, a bastard, feckless conglomeration of individuals, inspired by no common purpose, moving to no common end.

"Self-government when fit for it."

That has always been the promise. Britain can well afford to keep it in this case, where evidence in favour is so overwhelming and she loses so little by keeping her word.

1933

3

Stalin Ruins the Chinese Revolution

[World Revolution 1917-36 (*Secker and Warburg, 1937*) was an extensive study of the history of the Third International. Written when James's involvement in the trotskyist movement was at its most active, this was the first full-length statement in Britain of the attitudes of the communist opposition. Antipathy to stalinism was as yet very much a minority stance on the left, but as this chapter from the book shows, James's attitude was based on a thorough and at that time quite unique piece of research into the actual facts about Stalin's bungled and criminal policies towards the Chinese revolutionaries.]

China remained comparatively untouched by European civilisation until less than a century ago, but even in those early days Britain was already too small for British capitalism, and between 1839 and 1860 the British bombarded Chinese ports and massacred the Chinese people to ensure the continuance of the opium traffic, one of the main sources of revenue to British India. Besides the profits of this lucrative trade they extorted millions of pounds as indemnities, seized Hong Kong and territory on the mainland, and opened Chinese ports to British trade by force. In 1842 the Treaty of Nanking limited the Chinese tariff to five per cent ad valorem, to prevent Chinese industry developing behind a high tariff wall. This they maintained by brute force until 1925 when, under the menace of the revolution, the first small breaches were promised. In the war of 1857 the British government, again at the point of the bayonet, added to the usual indemnity, seizure of territory, etc, a British Inspector General of Customs. The steady drain of silver from China for the purchase of opium, the ruin of Chinese handicraft industry, the breakdown of the Manchu government under the blows of the British navy, the corruption of the Chinese official class by the opium smuggling, undermined the foundations of the once great but now outpaced civilisation of China.

. In the middle of the century a serious rebellion broke out in the South, held power in the Southern provinces for eleven years, and then failed. The British at Hong Kong sided with the rebels, and the other powers followed their lead. But as the movement disintegrated the foreign powers, chiefly Britain, deserted it and (after first defeating the Manchu dynasty and bringing it under its financial control) gave assistance against the rebels. By 1870 there were other rivals to Britain in the field. Russia and France stole large territories, the

British seized Burma. China was still a market, and between 1851 and 1855 the excess of imports over exports from China was over £175,000,000. But the late eighties were the crisis years for European capitalism, when for the export of goods was gradually substituted the export of capital. Africa was for the time being divided, but Africa was not enough. The Chinese people had now to give concessions and accept loans in order to buy iron and steel from Europe. They had no choice in the matter. The British government on occasion offered them the choice of British loans or British shells.

In 1894 the scramble entered its most dangerous but inevitable phase. Japanese capitalism tried to annex a portion of China, but the annexation clashed with British and other European interests. Russia and France intervened and checked her "in defence of their own interests". Japan was too weak to assert her rights (it is a different story today). Yet she got a treaty port and £34½m indemnity. To pay this, British and other European banks lent China £48m. God spoke to the American President,* and in 1892 America seized the Philippine Islands and entered the race. This organised banditry threw an ever-increasing load on the millions of peasants out of whose produce came the taxes to pay these loans. As far back as 1856 Karl Marx, basing himself always on the economic unity of modern capitalism, had seen that the devastating influences of this unceasing plunder of China would end in revolution, destroy a great market for European capitalism, and thus precipitate the revolution of the European proletariat. In its essential outlines the analysis is today as sound as when it was made. But the rottenness of the Manchu dynasty was propped up by the military and financial support given it by the European governments, and the Chinese native bourgeoisie, mainly commercial, could not provide the forces for the liberation of China. As in Russia, it was the entry of capital, and the consequent creation of a native proletariat organised and disciplined by large-scale production, that was to provide a means for the destruction of foreign capitalist domination in China.

It was this process which Lenin saw so clearly in 1908, the inevitable intensification of the export of capital, and the consequent growth of the international revolution. He based on it his calculations for world revolution, described in his book *Imperialism*. It is the unshakeable foundation of the permanent revolution. Small though the Chinese or Indian proletariat might be, as in Russia it would have as allies the hundreds of millions of peasants, sucked dry enough before by Oriental feudalism, but now driven to ruin by the burden which capitalist exploitation placed upon them.

The growing Chinese bourgeoisie, now increased by the export

---

* He (Mackinley) has told us himself. See Lenin's *Imperialism, the Last Stage of Capitalism*.

of European capital, found itself hampered by the reactionary Manchu government.

The first spontaneous uprising of the Chinese masses had been easily canalised into the anti-foreign Boxer rebellion at the end of the nineteenth century. But after that failure the Chinese bourgeoisie saw its main enemy in the Manchu dynasty. The Chinese bourgeoisie planned to build a railway with Chinese capital, Chinese material and Chinese labour. European capital stepped between and lent the money to the Chinese government, and a year later, in 1911, the revolution broke out. Sun Yat-sen, dreaming of a republic and a regenerated China, was made president. But Yuan Shih-k'ai from the North, hitherto a supporter of the Manchus, but with large forces at his disposal, ousted Sun from the position of president. The Chinese liberal bourgeois who were supporting Sun were afraid he might go too far, and thus, even before 1914, had shown their counter-revolutionary nature. Sun Yat-sen formed the Kuomintang or People's Party, but once again foreign capital came to the assistance of reaction and made a large loan to Yuan Shih-k'ai, who crushed the revolution, first in 1913, again in 1915, and died just as he was about to restore the monarchy. Meanwhile industrialisation of China under both European and native capital steadily increased, with the corresponding growth of native bourgeoisie and proletariat and the increasing misery of the peasantry.

The war accelerated all the processes at work in China. Japanese capitalism seized the opportunity to enforce exorbitant demands on China. Sun Yat-sen formed a revolutionary government in South China, traditionally the revolutionary section of China in revolt. Despite some manoeuvring, his main enemy was now foreign capital which had established itself firmly in large concessions, Shanghai the chief, whence it controlled the economic life of the country and drained its blood away, supported reaction and conducted itself to all Chinese, rich and poor, with studied insolence. Yet the insulted Chinese bourgeois was under the domination of foreign capital, and Sun, though no communist, by 1923 had realised that Chinese reaction, reinforced by foreign capitalism, could not succeed without the assistance of workers and peasants. By 1923 China was in political chaos. Each huge province, from ancient times economically autonomous, was under the control of a Tchun or feudal military leader, who concentrated into his hands both civil and military power, taxed the peasants for the upkeep of his private armies, and engaged in ceaseless warfare with other Tchuns. The ablest and most powerful of these exercised some sort of overlordship of subsidiary groups and enjoyed the support of the capitalist countries whose interests predominated in the particular regions he controlled. Thus in Manchuria Japan supported Chang Tso-lin, while Britain supportted Wu Pei-fu, chief marauder over many provinces in Northern China, and Sun Ch'uan-fang in Central China. Sun Yat-sen's government in South China seeking to

call a constituent assembly for all China, was constantly attacked
by militarists supported by British and Japanese capitalism. He
appealed to America for assistance, but America was interested
in the Chinese market, not in the aspirations of the Chinese people,
and Sun turned at last to the Soviet Union. Russia stood high in
Chinese favour for Lenin had given back all that tsarist Russia had
stolen. In 1923 Sun met Joffe, the Russian representative in
Shanghai. The Soviet Union promised him assistance in the struggle
to free China from imperialism, and its tool and ally, Chinese
militarism. Sun Yat-sen reorganised his party. He declared that
the sole aim of the old members was to get rich and obtain posts
as high officials, and that the workers and peasants were the only
real forces of revolution. But he did not, in the Bolshevik manner,
organise a party based on a single class; whence the ultimate ruin
of all he hoped for. His reorganised Kuomintang was still a hotch-
potch, a few big capitalists, the nationalist bourgeoisie, the petty-
bourgeoisie, and the workers and peasants. His programme promised the nine-hour day to one, high tariffs to another, reduction
of rents to a third, land from the state for landless peasants and
tenant-holders, the right of self-determination for the various
nationalities, democracy, all lumped together under the one term
—socialism. A determined revolutionary and undoubtedly a great
leader, even at the very end of his life, he was only able to leave
to his party a programme that Ramsay MacDonald could have
drawn up for him without any difficulty in half an hour.

But Lenin, too, in 1919 had been devoting himself to the problem
of China and the colonial countries of the East, and in 1920 he
presented theses on the Eastern Revolution to the Second Congress
of the Third International. Lenin saw the Chinese revolution as
part of the international proletarian revolution. Without the continued exploitation of the colonial people capitalism in Europe
would collapse. His practical proposals were, as always, based on
the independent proletarian movement, intransigence in programme
and organisation, flexibility in the formation of the United Front.

He knew that the workers and peasants alone could liberate
China. But he knew that the chief danger to their activity was
exactly such a Popular Front type of Government as the Kuomintang, which would end inevitably by betraying. He therefore called
for "determined war" against the attempt of all those quasi-
communist revolutionists to cloak the liberation movement in the
backward countries with a communist garb. "The exclusive purpose" of the Communist International in all backward countries
was to educate the communist movements in those countries, however small, to "the consciousness of their specific tasks, i.e. to the
tasks of the struggle against the bourgeois democratic tendencies
within their respective nationalities." It was by fighting against
their own bourgeoisie that the workers and the peasants would
drive out the imperialists. The Communist International would
establish temporary relations and even unions with the revolution-

ary movements in these countries. But it must never amalgamate with them, "always preserving the independent character of the proletarian movement even though it be still in its embryonic state."

In China the peasant question was far more acute than it had been in Russia before 1917. Consequent on the whole Russian experience, therefore, the most inexperienced Bolshevik could formulate the second step after the organisation of the proletarian party. "Above all, we must strive as far as possible . . . to give the peasant movement a revolutionary character, to organise the peasants and all the exploited classes into the soviets." Lenin wrote this in 1920. In three years the Chinese proletariat had passed even more rapidly than the Russian proletariat before 1905 to the stage where it was mature for revolution. We have to trace this process in some detail, for early in 1923 it was not only already clear that the Chinese revolution was on its way, but obvious also that the theory of the permanent revolution and Lenin's organisational principles could carry it to success.

The post-war crisis, the resumption of industry in the West, hit Chinese industry severely. There had been small strikes in 1912, and the beginning of a labour and socialist movement before the war; an attempt had been made to form a trade union in Hong Kong in 1915. But the Chinese workers who had served in the war brought back with them experience of labour organisation. In September 1919, the Chinese Returned Labourers' Association was organised in Shanghai to fight for better wages, the right to hold meetings, the right to make public speeches for promoting the welfare of the workers. The more backward the country, the closer the relation between economics and politics.

After the war the Japanese attempted to hold Shantung and in May 1919, a score of students attacked the residences of pro-Japanese ministers in Peking and were arrested. When the news reached Shanghai, labour leaders declared a strike which spread rapidly even to the public utilities. In a few days the Peking government was compelled to remove the offending ministers and release the agitators. In 1920 the Overseas Labour Union appeared in Canton. Hundreds of pre-war publications dealing with syndicalism, socialism, anarchism and all phases of the labour movement were being published. On 1 May 1920, in Peking, Canton and Shanghai, Chinese workers celebrated the workers' anniversary. On 12 January 1922, the Chinese Seaman's Union of Hong Kong presented its third petition for an increase in wages, and demanded an answer within twenty-four hours. 1,500 men struck the next day. On 1 February the British Governor of Hong Kong declared the Chinese Seamen's Union an unlawful assembly. The reply was a sympathetic strike of 50,000, a symbolic general strike, representing every trade in the island. The strike lasted for nearly three months, when the seamen won a wage increase of twenty to thirty per cent. The young Communist Party of China organised in Canton the first

Chinese Congress of Trades Unions with 170 delegates. Medieval Chinese Tchuns and post-war European capitalism recognised a common enemy. In the autumn of 1922 the British police fired on Chinese workers and killed several of them. In February 1923, Wu Pei-fu, the British Tchun, banned a railwaymen's conference. On the 6th a conference took place between the foreign consuls, Wu Pei-fu's military representatives, and the directors of the Peking-Hankow railway. The next day troops in big railway stations opened fire on the crowds of railwaymen. In Hankow alone sixty were killed. The result was a railway strike of 20,000 men. The workers were ready to resist, but parliamentarians in Peking pressed for an investigation, placatory resolutions were passed, the edge of the workers' attack was blunted, and the strike was called off. At once the repression began; arrests, executions, the closing down of workers' papers, the driving of the trade union movement into illegality. Like the Russian workers, the Chinese workers were learning the close connection between economics and politics in a country with a backward or disorganised economy.

It was at this time, in the spring of 1923, that Lenin, writing his last article, spoke with supreme confidence of the coming revolution in the East. China he knew would unloose India. For in addition to the insoluble contradictions of their internal economy, the Russian revolution had given all these millions a concrete example, more potent than a hundred years of propaganda. But after that spring Lenin never worked again, and at once, in the autumn of 1923 Stalin, Zinoviev and Kamenev in Moscow again revealed their lack of principle and their ingrained opportunism by sending the Chinese Communist party into the Kuomintang — the first and most criminal error. Trotsky, as so often in those days fighting alone for Lenin's ideas, voted against. Had Lenin been sitting as chairman such an entry could never have taken place. It is in this way that men make history. In that autumn Borodin and other advisers went to Canton and opened a military school at Whampoa to train and organise the Kuomintang army. For the average bourgeois observer such a collaboration was well worth to Stalin even the temporary subordination of the communist movement. It is here that the wide gulf between Menshevism and Bolshevism opens at once. Always when faced with such a choice Lenin chose the proletarian way. He did under certain circumstances advocate the temporary subordination of a revolutionary organisation, not large enough to be a party, to a centrist organisation; to a social democratic, or worse still, a bourgeois organisation, never. The sketch we have given of the Chinese proletariat between 1920 and 1923 shows that to the discerning eye the movement was mature. Stalin, an organic Menshevik and profoundly ignorant of international affairs as well as of marxism, instinctively chose the other way, and Zinoviev and Kamenev followed. The test lies not in argument but in history.

In January 1924, the reconstituted Kuomintang held its first meeting in Canton. Sun Yat-sen agreed to admit the communists into its ranks. But they entered not as a party, only as individuals, and had to swear to abide by the rules of the Kuomintang. The only conceivable justification for such a step was to consider it as a highly dangerous manoeuvre.* The Chinese communists might possibly, under a strong and supple leadership, have worked under cover of the Kuomintang for a certain period of time and then, having spread their influence, left demonstratively on some political issue understandable to the masses, and resumed their organisational and programmatic independence. They could make a temporary agreement for some specific objective even with the liberal bourgeoisie, tenaciously guarding their independence. No one in 1923 could have foreseen that under Stalin's orders they were going to cling desperately to the Kuomintang for four years until hacked off by the swords of Chiang Kai-shek's soldiers.

For the moment, however, the communists, taking advantage of their new position, began with energy to help the proletariat in its task of organising itself.

At the beginning of 1925 Feng Yu-hsiang, a nationalist leader, defeated the pro-British Wu Pei-fu, drove him out of Peking, and proclaimed his army the army of national liberation. The nationalist movement awoke. In Shanghai some worker delegates, elected to negotiate with the management in a dispute, were dismissed. The other workers protested, and the Anglo-Indian police, being summoned, fired on them, seriously wounding five. The Shanghai workers rose against this brutality. They did not know it at the time, but they were beginning the Chinese revolution. That is the way a revolution often comes, like a thief in the night, and those who have prepared for it and are waiting for it do not see it, and often only realise that their chance has come when it has passed. The protest movement was fed not only from the immediate arrogance and rapacity of the foreigner. It was the whole history of China which was soon to express itself through this channel. The Chinese workers and peasants had reached one of the breaking points of their history. Inside and outside the foreign concessions the Chinese workers, men, women and children, suffered from some of the most inhuman conditions of labour that obtained in any part of the globe, twelve hours and more seven days a week, no time for meals, not sanitary conveniences in the older factories, foreign and native, overseers with loaded rifles to keep discipline, and all for a few pence a day. National liberation rested on the solid foundation of millions of workers, seeking a way out of intolerable conditions.

What had been a small dispute about wages and a protest against administrative injustice, became overnight a political weapon for

---

* Lenin's thesis to the Second Congress should be read in full, in order to understand how clearly he saw the main business of the Chinese proletarian party to be opposition to the bourgeois leadership.

the liberation of China. The four months and a half between 1 May and the middle of September showed like clockwork the class forces which would struggle for mastery in the coming revolution. "Down with the imperialists" was the slogan of the day. The Chinese government in Shanghai thought it was dealing with a riot, and demonstrations and meetings were met with the killing and wounding of scores of people. The allies of Chinese reaction, foreign imperialism, of necessity rushed to aid in the repression. On 4 June the allied imperialists, whose gunboats are always in Chinese harbours to protect property and rights and interests, landed a party and occupied the university and other buildings in the city. The Shanghai proletariat replied with the general strike. Nearly a quarter of a million workers came out and paralysed the city, and as the mass force of the Shanghai proletariat showed itself, it drew in its wake (exactly as in France in June 1936) the petty bourgeois students, the artisans and the small traders, and, in the special conditions of China as a country struggling for national independence, even some of that treacherous brood, the liberal Chinese bourgeoisie. A special committee was formed, the Committee of Labour, Education and Commerce, which along with delegates from the trade unions had representatives from students' associations, the small shopkeepers and even some of the bourgeoisie. But the trade unions predominated and, far more clearly than in Russia, from the very start the Chinese proletariat was leading the nation. All classes seemed to support the strike. But in an industrialised country all classes never make a revolution, and as the strike developed, the necessity for Lenin's life-long principle, the proletarian organisations and party retaining their independence, emerged with startling clearness. After one month the Chinese bourgeoisie, who had never been very ardent, ceased to support the strike. During July and August the petty bourgeoisie, the intelligentsia, the students, wobblers from the very intermediate position they hold in society, began to weaken: nothing but immediate success and continued vigorous action can ever keep these to the proletarian movement. Aid from the international proletariat would have helped, but only the Third International agitated, collected money, made donations. The Second International, those perpetual preachers of self-determination, did nothing. The International Federation of Trades Unions behaved likewise. The British General Council, at this period consorting with the Russians in the Anglo-Russian Committee, refused even to answer telegrams of appeal from the Chinese unions, Realising their limitations the Shanghai leaders in good time fell back to the defensive. Some of their most pressing economic demands were satisfied, the strike was called off and the Shanghai workers retired in good order and with a living, vital experience to help them in the future.

But so ripe was China that the Shanghai strike had acted as a detonator. There had been over a hundred sympathetic strikes in various towns, and out of one of these developed the Hong Kong and Canton strike, demonstrating the fighting power and endurance of the proletariat in the manner that so constantly surprises even the most sanguine revolutionaries.

On 23 June a demonstration of protest against the Shanghai shooting took place in Canton. British police from the Anglo-French concession fired on the demonstration, killing and wounding scores of people. As in Shanghai the Chinese proletariat replied with a general strike, and their comrades in Hong Kong joined. The Chinese bourgeoisie in Canton rallied to the strikers, and supported them, owing to the long revolutionary tradition in Canton and the much more important fact that the strike was accompanied by a boycott of British goods. From all the Chinese communities in the Philippine Islands, East Indies and America, money poured in. The British tried to prevent Chinese money coming into Canton, but failed; in Hong Kong they unloosed all the forces of repression to break the strike. The Hong Kong workers were unshakeable. In thousands they began to leave Hong Kong for Canton. Estimates vary, but one Chinese writer claims that from start to finish about a hundred thousand Chinese left the island for Canton. There a strike committee was formed. The strikers organised propaganda meetings, study courses and lectures, they drew up regulations for workers and submitted them to the Canton Kuomintang government, they confiscated and stored contraband goods which British merchants tried to smuggle in, they captured, tried and imprisoned blacklegs, they organised pickets along the entire frontier of Kwangsi province to keep out British ships and British goods from Hong Kong. They formed a workers' guard which led the picketing, fought against smugglers and fought with the Kuomintang government against counter-revolutionary Tchuns. The strike ruined British trade with China. Between August and December 1924, the British ships entering Canton numbered between 160 and 240 each month. For the corresponding period in 1925 the number was between 27 and 2.

British capitalism lost half a million pounds per day. In 1926 the British Empire lost half its trade with China, and three-quarters of its trade with Hong Kong. After fifteen months the British began to give way and sought to placate the workers, handling recalcitrant Britishers very roughly. No government can continue to fight against strikers who will not even stay to be imprisoned or shot at. After one year the strike continued as powerful as ever, the Communist Party of China playing a leading part, and the spirit of the workers all over China rose steadily. Trades union membership, which in May 1924 was 220,000, reached 540,000 in May 1925, and in May 1926, over a million. In Shanghai alone during the 1925 strike it had reached 280,000. And this unprecedentedly rapid industrial organisation of the workers was expressing itself in many strikes that were primarily political, which meant that the workers were looking to solve their industrial difficulties by the social revolution.

The Communist Party, 800 in 1925, by January 1926 was 30,000, and to this powerful proletarian movement could be added the overwhelming revolutionary force of the starving Chinese peasantry. In Kwangtung, a province typical of the South, seventy-four per cent of the population held nineteen per cent of the land. In Wiush in Central China, 68.9 per cent of the poor peasantry held 14.2 per cent of the land. In Paoting in the North 65.2 per cent held 25.9 per cent of the land. Of the Chinese population, on a rough estimate, sixty-five per cent were driven by the most consistent and powerful revolutionary urge in all historical periods — the hunger of starving peasants for land.

The fundamental task of the Communist Party was basically the task of the Bolshevik Party in Russia — to link the proletarian movement with the peasant, organising the peasants into Soviets for the forcible seizure of the land. In no other way but on the basis of the proletarian and peasant revolution could China then or now achieve national independence. Sun Yat-sen had learnt that by hard experience, though he shrank from drawing the full conclusions. He had hoped somehow to bring the revolutionary masses into the struggle led by the nationalist bourgeoisie. The thing is impossible. Now since the great strikes when it was clear that the Chinese proletariat was challenging the bourgeoisie, it was inevitable that at the first opportunity the Chinese bourgeoisie would join with imperialists and militarists and crush the revolution.

The farther East the bourgeoisie the more cruel and treacherous. The powerful French bourgeoisie in 1789 had joined with the counter-revolution; how much less likely was the weak Chinese bourgeoisie, far weaker than the Russian, to ally itself with a proletariat which had shown its power. That was the whole theoretical prognosis of the Bolshevik Party, amply confirmed by the course of the Russian revolution. After 1917 the main strategic line of the Chinese revolution could only be as follows. The Chinese revolution would begin as a bourgeois-democratic revolution, but only as an immediate slogan. While the Communist Party of China would not oppose this slogan, it would be aware that for a backward country with an advanced proletariat (we shall see it in Spain) the bourgeois-democratic régime is impossible. The revolution would conquer as the dictatorship of the proletariat, or not at all. The Communist Party had already shown that it knew how to link industrial with political demands. It had to strive to popularise the idea of soviets among the peasantry on the simple slogan — the land for the peasants — and, as the party which urged the seizure of the land, would ultimately have the firm support of the peasantry for its political demands. Guarding its own independence, the Communist Party would boldly raise the slogan of national independence based on the revolutionary demands of the proletariat and the peasantry. If the movement developed (there could have been no doubt of this after the Hong Kong strike, and in Hupeh in 1926 the peasants were already seizing the land), the anti-imperialist pretence of the Chinese bourgeoisie would be exposed and the Chinese petty bourgeoisie, the traders, the students and some of the intellectuals would be swept in the wake of the proletarian movement, and follow the proletariat as leader of the national revolution. A Congress of Soviets would appoint a provisional revolutionary government, and call a constituent assembly, arranging the franchise to secure the predominance of the poor. In this assembly the Chinese proletariat, organised in the Communist Party and in the trade unions, would occupy a dominating position. According to the strength of the movement and the dangers of the revolution, the dictatorship of the proletariat might be established immediately. But either the bourgeoisie would establish their dictatorship; or conversely the proletariat would establish theirs. It was this strategic line which would guide the Communist Party, already superior in the towns. It would jealously maintain its independence as the party of the proletariat and, if it could draw the hundreds of millions of peasants behind it, it would be the most powerful political force in the country. There was the danger of foreign intervention, but nothing would bind revolutionary China so firmly together as the sight of the Chinese bourgeoisie, but yesterday lovers of their country, attacking China along with the hated imperialists. China could stand a blockade far more easily than Russia. A Soviet China linked to a Soviet Russia, supported by the far-flung Third International, would alter the whole relationship of the capitalist and revolutionary forces in the far East. Such a bloc would not only throw British and Japanese economy into the gravest disorder, but would unloose movements in India, Burma, and even Egypt and the near East which would set the whole structure of capitalism rocking. The movement might perhaps not develop so powerfully but there was a chance that, at least in a substantial part of China, the revolution might hold power and use it as a base for future extension. At worst it might be totally defeated. The proletariat was ready. But the boldness of its slogans, the strength of its attack would depend on the strength of the peasant movement it could develop.

Even if it failed, as the Russian revolution of 1905, the Chinese proletariat would have acquired an invaluable experience, the more advanced elements in the peasantry would have had time to recognise with which party their future lay, and the party, with tried and experienced leaders, would be able to prepare for the inevitable return of the revolutionary wave as the Russian party prepared for the new revolution on the basis of 1905. Such is the theory and practice of the permanent revolution. Lenin, alive and well in Moscow, would from day to day have analysed the development of events and through the Chinese Communist Party would have made the road clear for the Chinese masses. The Chinese proletariat had, by 1926, shown what it was capable of. Starting in 1929, nearly a hundred million peasants were to show for five heroic years how ready for revolution was the Chinese peasantry. It was not only the objective conditions which were so favourable. The Russian revolution and the Communist International exercised an enormous subjective influence. The Chinese workers and peasants knew broadly what the Russians had done, and wanted to do the same. They trusted the Chinese Communist Party which they knew to be guided by the now world-famous leaders in Moscow. And yet it was the communist leadership in Moscow which led the revolution in China to disaster. Step by step Stalin mismanaged it with such incompetence and dishonesty that, one year after the final defeat in December 1927, the name of the International stank in Shanghai and Canton.

In April 1927, the party had nearly 60,000 members, including 53.8 per cent workers; by July the percentage of workers in the party was seventy-five. On 8 November, 1928, a circular of the Central Committee stated: "The party does not have a single healthy party nucleus among the industrial workers." In 1930 not two per cent were workers. In 1935 at the Seventh Congress of the Communist International the secretary admitted that they had failed to make progress in organising the industrial workers. The blight that Stalin and Bukharin cast on the Chinese revolution in 1925-27 is still upon it.

Stalin had had as little to do with international politics as with economics. Now in his important position as Lenin's successor he continued the role he had begun in October 1924, when he prophesied the imminent revolution in Europe. In May 1925, the month in which the Shanghai strike began, he spoke at the University of the Peoples of the East and expounded his leninism for the revolutionary movement in the Orient. There he put forward, for such countries as Egypt and China, what is from the leninist point of view the most singular of all Stalin's conceptions, surpassing even the relegation to the dust-heap of basic capital. He proposed a two-class party, a party of workers and peasants "after the model of the Kuomintang". Not all the red professors in Russia could find him any quotations from Lenin to support this doctrine, and the speech is remarkable as one of the few in the collected volumes which is not interspersed with "Lenin said".

> "They will have to transcend the policy of the united nationalist front, and adopt the policy of forming a revolutionary coalition between the workers and the petty bourgeois. This coalition may find expression in the creation of a single party whose membership will be drawn from among the working class and the peasantry, after the model of the Kuomintang. But such a party should be genuinely representative of the two component forces, the communists and the revolutionary petty-bourgeois. This coalition must see to it that the half-heartedness and duplicity of the great bourgeoisie shall be laid bare, and that a resolute attack shall be made upon imperialism. The formation of such a party,

composed, as we have seen, of two distinct elements, is both necessary and expedient, so long as it does not shackle the activities of the communists, so long as it does not hamper the agitational and propagandist freedom of the communists, so long as it does not prevent the proletariat from rallying round the communists, so long as it does not impair the communist leadership of the revolutionary forces. But the formation of such a party is neither necessary nor expedient unless all these conditions are forthcoming; otherwise the communist elements would become absorbed into the bourgeois elements and the communists would lose their position as leaders of the proletarian army."*

In that muddled blundering paragraph lay the germ of all the muddles and blunders which were to come. It is difficult to say where he got the idea of a party representating two classes from. It was due most probably to a misunderstanding of the phrase "the revolutionary democratic dictatorship of the proletariat and the peasantry". That there can be only one proletarian or Communist Party, that a peasant may become a member of a Communist Party only by adopting the proletarian policy of the Communist Party, that a peasant party would be a separate entity led by the proletarian party, as the Social Revolutionaries formed a minority party in the Soviet Union between November 1917 and July 1918, that to talk about a party "composed, as we have seen, of two distinct elements" in which communists would not be shackled by peasants, was the very antithesis of all that Lenin had fought for, was in complete opposition to what the Communist International stood for, was, in fact, the most dangerous nonsense, especially in the mouth of the leader of the international proletariat. To point out all this, of course, was trotskyism.

Given Stalin's obstinacy and the servility of his subordinates, we can see today that from that moment the Chinese revolution was doomed. For Stalin and Bukharin the revolution, according to leninism, was a bourgeois-democratic revolution against the foreign imperialists, and therefore was to be carried out by the bourgeoisie organised in the Kuomintang and the nationalist army of the Canton government which Borodin was training. The business of the proletariat and the peasantry, therefore, was to do nothing which would impede the bourgeoisie and the Kuomintang in their struggle. Not for nothing had they spent the previous two years abusing the permanent revolution and all its teachings as the main vice of trotskyism. After the imperialists had been driven into the sea by the united nation, by all classes, except the biggest of the bourgeoisie, then the proletariat and peasantry would turn upon the bourgeoisie and conquer. This in 1925, after 1905 and 1917, after over twenty years of reading and expounding Lenin.

The two-class party Stalin envisaged on the model of the

---

* *Leninism*, Vol. I, p. 278.

Kuomintang quickly developed into the four-class party of the
Kuomintang.

The Kuomintang, whatever Sun Yat-sen[1] and his wife might
think, was a government party ruling a large extent of territory
in Southern China. By 1925 its membership consisted of about
a quarter of a million, big bourgeoisie, factory-owners, petty bourgeoisie, professional men and petty traders, landowners, gentry,
rich peasants and also, after the reorganisation by Sun Yat-sen,
working men and poor peasants. But the proletariat was being
organised in trade unions under the leadership of the Communist
Party. We have watched its steady growth. And the Kuomintang,
as organised, could from its very nature have nothing to do with a
revolutionary seizure of land by the poor peasants. There might
be a right wing and a left wing (in January 1926, there were 168
lefts to 45 rights, and 65 centrists out of 278 delegates), but such a
party could never lead a revolutionary proletariat and a revolutionary peasantry. Why should it? Not only in Lenin's thesis at
the Second Congress, but also in supplementary theses presented
at the Fourth Congress in 1922, the proletarian parties in the
colonies had been warned against such parties, and in both sets
of theses the Kuomintang had been mentioned by name as one of
the specially dangerous. Trotsky therefore continued to demand
that the Communist Party leave the Kuomintang. Whatever remote justification there might have been for its being in before,
now that the revolution had begun, at all costs it must come out. It
might be driven underground for a time. So had been the Bolshevik
Party. The rise of the revolution would bring it out again with re-
newed force. Stalin and Bukharin condemned this as trotskyism,
and bound the Communist Party and the Chinese revolution to the
Kuomintang.

During 1925 the left wing of the Kuomintang had been following Sun Yat-sen's directions, and like good liberals displayed much
sympathy for the workers' movements.[2] They had organised peasant leagues to fight against the Ming Tuans, a sort of fascist
militia in the countryside. But they warned the peasants against the
seizure of land. That would come after, duly arranged by law.
But even the formation of these peasant leagues had been causing dissatisfaction among the right elements in the party.

The Executive Committee, however, was left, and the Executive
Committee ruled between congresses. Stalin and Bukharin, through
Borodin, supported the left against the right, that is to say supported the petty-bourgeois traders and small capitalists against
their greater brethren. The Political Bureau of nine members was
left. Wang Ching-wei (the same who was Prime Minister to Chiang
Kai-shek until a few months ago — a bullet caused his retirement)
was head of the party and of the Canton government. He was

[1] He died in March 1925, and later, as the Chinese bourgeoisie was revealed
in its true colours, Madame Sun became a communist.
[2] As has been pointed out, the Social Democrats do more; they even
organise and lead it.

absolutely left, and Borodin, the Russian representative, was high in favour with Wang Ching-wei. Borodin, with Wang's support, drafted programmes for Kuomintang conferences which sounded revolutionary enough, and the Chinese Communist Party worked and grew within the shelter of the left Kuomintang. But as the Shanghai strike began and unloosed the hundreds of thousands of striking workers on Canton itself, the Chinese bourgeoisie and landowners grew frightened and demanded the expulsion of the communists. The communists had now either to leave and fight for the revolution according to Lenin, or stay and fight for it according to the left Kuomintang. Stalin chose the left Kuomintang, and Borodin organised a plan of campaign to suit.

In the North Chang Tso-lin, the pro-Japanese war-lord, had established a dictatorship in Peking, and gathered some other military chiefs to oppose the nationalists in the South. Borodin and the left wing therefore outlined the national revolution as follows. In the coming spring the nationalist forces in the South under Chiang Kai-shek would set out from Canton in the extreme South, raise the banner of revolution, conquering anti-nationalist Tchuns, uniting with those who wished a liberated China, and end by defeating Chang Tso-lin and taking the ancient capital of Peking. Chiang Kai-shek was willing to lead this revolution but he did not wish to go marching off to Peking and leave·a radical Kuomintang government under the influence of Borodin behind him. Yet his party needed the temporary support of the International. It applied for membership as a sympathising party. The stalinists agreed, as usual Trotsky alone dissenting. To the two plenums of the Executive Committee held in February and again in November, Chiang sent fraternal delegates. He and Stalin exchanged portraits. But on 20 March 1926, while Borodin was out of Canton, Chiang Kai-shek coalesced with the right Kuomintang, staged a coup d'état, seized power and forced Wang Ching-wei, and other radical members of the Kuomintang to fly from the country. He had acted too early. He had control of the army, but the nationalist movement was too weak as yet to progress without mass support. There was a sharp reaction against Chiang, and in May left and right wing were reconciled. But Chiang Kai-shek became head of the party in place of Wang Ching-wei, and at the May plenum in 1926 he laid down harsh terms. The Communist Party was pledged not to criticise the anti-class struggle doctrines of Sun Yat-sen. It was compelled to give a list of its members in the Kuomintang to Chiang Kai-shek (so that he could put his hands on them when he wanted them). It was forbidden to allow its members to become heads of any party or government department. In all important committees its members were limited to one. Members of the Kuomintang were forbidden to join the Communist Party. Borodin, under Stalin's orders, agreed to all these conditions. In return Chiang Kai-shek expelled some of the members of the right wing. (They went to Nanking to await him there.)

Thus at the moment when the revolution needed the leadership of the Communist Party Stalin tied it hand and foot. Marxism apart, Chiang Kai-shek stood revealed. Stalin, however, follows his policies to the end and never gives away to trotskyism. The news of this coup d'état would have reinforced Trotsky's insistence that the Communist Party leave the Kuomintang at once. Stalin proved his own policy correct by his favourite method of argument. He suppressed the news. When news of the coup d'état eventually leaked out, the *International Press Correspondence* of 8 April 1926, called it a "lying report". In the 6 May issue of the same journal Voitinsky, one of the Russian delegation under Borodin, called it "an invention of the imperialists". Thus encouraged, Chiang made all strikes in Canton illegal, Borodin agreeing.

With his rear tolerably safe from revolution, Chiang set out in July to the North, ostensibly to fight the militarists. He carried with him printing presses and a huge propaganda apparatus, developed and run by communists, who put forward Chiang's slogans. Believing him to be the leader of the revolution, the masses rushed to his support and the anti-nationalist armies crumbled. As he gained confidence Chiang suppressed trade unions, the peasant leagues and the communists. His support fell away. He recalled the communists, who came willingly, again did propaganda for him, using the prestige of the October revolution and the Soviet state in the service of Chiang Kai-shek, the leader of the revolution. Where the Bolsheviks in Russia had called for soviets and the confiscation of the land, the communists now agitated for better working conditions and a twenty percent reduction in rent. That was all Chiang would allow them to do. Chiang resumed his triumphant progress. By September the Yangtze valley was in his hands, and Stalin and Bukharin and the Internationalist Press were delirious with joy. By October his army had captured the important triple town of Hankow, Wuchang and Hanyang, known as Wuhan. The Kuomintang government was moved from Canton to Wuhan, and before it left Canton it called off unconditionally the Hong Kong and Canton strike. This had lasted with undiminished vigour for sixteen months and in all its aspects it is the greatest strike in history. In Canton also the Kuomintang provincial left wing was replaced by the right, the famous workers' guard was disarmed, revolutionary workers were arrested, workers were forbidden to agitate among the peasantry, anti-English demonstrations were prohibited, and the gentry or small landowners in the villages encouraged. The Communist Party leadership submitted to everything. And as the news of all this leaked through to Russia, in Moscow the internal struggle between Stalin's leninism and trotskyism was now extended to Stalin's Kuomintang policy.

In July 1926, Radek, a member of the opposition, rector of Sun Yat-sen University in Moscow, wrote to the Politbureau of the CPSU and asked for answers to a series of questions so that he might bring his lectures into harmony with the policy of the International in China. The questions were awkward. What was the attitude of the party to the military dictatorship of Chiang Kai-shek initiated after the coup d'état of March 1926, and supported by Borodin? What work was the Kuomintang doing among the peasantry? A manifesto had been issued by the Central Committee of the Chinese party, part of which ran: "We must carry on a minimum of class struggle, and when the policy of the Communist Party is designated as Bolshevik, it is not a matter of Bolshevism but of Bolshevism in the interests of the whole nation." Did Stalin approve of this as leninism?

Radek received no reply. He wrote a second letter in July. There was no reply. He wrote again in September. Still no reply. Stalin and Bukharin dared not as yet say openly that they were responsible for the instructions to the Communist Party of China to do nothing which would accelerate any conflict with Chiang Kai-shek. But in November 1926, after the Seventh Plenum of the ECCI (at which a fraternal delegate from Chiang Kai-shek took part), the executive issued a manifesto. Stalin had proposed a two-class party; Martynov, one of his henchmen, made the Kuomintang into a three-class party. Now this manifesto defined the revolutionary movement as a bloc of four classes, comedy in the mouths of liberal bourgeois seeking to deceive the masses, but a shameful crime coming from Lenin's International not three years after his death:

> "The proletariat is forming a bloc with the peasantry (which is actively taking up the struggle for its interests), with the petty urban bourgeoisie and a section of the capitalist bourgeoisie. This combination of forces found its political expression in corresponding groups in the Kuomintang and in the Canton govern-actively taking up the struggle for its interests' with the petty urban bourgeoisie and a section found its political expression in corresponding groups in the Kuomintang and in the Canton government. Now the movement is at the beginning of the third stage on the eve of a new class combination. In this stage the driving forces of the movement will be a bloc of still more revolutionary nature — of the proletariat, peasantry and urban petty bourgeoisie, to the exclusion of a large section of the big capitalist bourgeoisie. This doesn't mean that the whole bourgeoisie as a class will be excluded from the arena of the struggle for national emancipation, for besides the petty and middle bourgeoisie, even certain strata of the big bourgeoisie may, for a certain period, continue to march with the revolution."

What pen wrote this we cannot say. But there can be no mistake about the originator of these ideas. It was the same who called the struggle between Lenin and Trotsky a storm in a tea-cup, and urged support of the Provisional Government in 1917.

On the future Chinese government Stalin had travelled far since the two-class party:

"The structure of the revolutionary state will be determined by its class basis. It will not be a purely bourgeois democratic state. The state will represent the democratic dictatorship of the proletariat, peasantry and other exploited classes. It will be a revolutionary anti-imperialist government of transition to non-capitalist (socialist) development."

All of which means that the Kuomintang would govern henceforth.

Boldly the manifesto came out for the agrarian revolution:

"The national government of Canton will not be able to retain power, the revolution will not advance towards the complete victory over foreign imperialism and native reaction, unless national liberation is identified with agrarian revolution."

This sounded grand enough, but it was only one of the flourishes which Stalin habitually uses as a preface to the blackest reaction. The next paragraph was many flights lower:

"While recognising that the Communist Party of China should advance the demand for the nationalisation of the land as its fundamental plank in the agrarian programme of the proletariat, it is necessary at the present time, however, to differentiate in agrarian tactics in accordance with the peculiar economic and political conditions prevailing in the various districts in Chinese territory."

This meant simply that the views on property of Chiang Kaishek and the Kuomintang leaders of the revolution were to be respected. What, therefore, was the revolutionary programme? It had to be a programme that Borodin and Chiang could carry out peacefully together:

"The Communist Party of China and the Kuomintang must immediately carry out the following measures in order to bring over the peasantry to the side of the revolution."

And the first of a long list of demands was:

(a) To reduce rents to the minimum.

Stalin and Bukharin were asking the peasants of China to make a revolution in order "to reduce rents to the minimum".

Not once was the word Soviet mentioned, and the manifesto took good care to exclude every possibility of the organisation of one. "The apparatus of the National Revolutionary Government provides a very effective way to reach the peasantry. The Communist Party must use this way." The Kuomintang therefore was to make the peasant revolution.

Chiang had severely limited the participation of the communists in the organisation of the Kuomintang. Stalin and Bukharin, having hidden this from the International, with their tongues in their cheeks proceeded as follows:

"In the newly liberated provinces state apparatuses of the type of the Canton government will be set up. The task of the communists and their revolutionary allies is to penetrate into the apparatus of the new government to give practical expression to the agrarian programme of national revolution. This will be done by using the state apparatus for the confiscation of land, reduction of taxes, investment of real power in the peasant committees, thus carrying on progressive measures of reform on the basis of a revolutionary programme."

They then dealt the now traditional blow at trotskyism:

"In view of this and many other equally important reasons, the point of view that the Communist Party must leave the Kuomintang is incorrect."

The manifesto showed that they knew quite well the nature of the Kuomintang government in Canton: "Since its foundation the real power of the Canton government has been in the hands of the right-wing Kuomintang (five out of the six commissars belong to the right wing)." But they called on the communists to enter this government to assist the revolutionary left wing against the right. As if four revolutionary classes were not enough they envisaged five.

"The Communist Party of China must strive to develop the Kuomintang into a real party of the people—a solid revolutionary bloc of the proletariat, peasantry, the urban petty bourgeoisie and the other oppressed and exploited classes which must carry on a decisive struggle against imperialism and its agents."

Stalin and Bukharin might talk about bourgeois-democratic revolution and the democratic dictatorship of proletariat and peasantry and the remaining classes which made up the five, but the Kuomintang Canton government with five right-wingers out of its six commissars was quite good enough for them:

"The Canton government is a revolutionary state primarily owing to its anti-imperialistic character."

The industrial programme of the revolution was to be:
"(a) Nationalisation of railways and waterways.
(b) Confiscation of large enterprises, mines and banks having the character of foreign concessions.
(c) Nationalisation of land to be realised by successive radical reform measures enforced by the revolutionary State."

For twelve years before 1917 the Bolsheviks had tirelessly preached the simple slogans, the democratic republic, the eight-hour day, the land for the peasants. Yet with the Chinese proletariat already in action and millions of hungry peasants ready to fight, this was the programme and policy imposed on them with all the authority of the October revolution and the Communist International. This cruelly deceptive and dangerous document went to Borodin and the Communist Party of China, through them to demoralise the ardent but trusting Chinese masses and lead scores of thousands into the death-trap of the Kuomintang.

But it was all that Borodin and the Communist Party could do to hold back the Chinese masses. By January 1927, the membership of the CP was nearly 60,000; the Young Communist League of China was 35,000, and the organised workers, 230,000 in 1923, were now 2,800,000, a greater number than in the Russia of October 1917. However much Stalin might wish to hold them down in order not to displease Chiang Kai-shek, the masses, in Canton and Wuhan could feel on their backs the blows of reaction. In the Southern provinces by March 1927, ten million peasants had been organised in the peasant leagues. In Hupeh the peasants were already seizing the land on a large scale. Furthermore, Chiang Kai-shek's treachery, made so clear in March, was now becoming open to the masses. In the early months of 1927 he was carrying on negotiations with the Japanese and the pro-Japanese reactionary war-lords; and the Communist Party knew it. The nearer he got to Shanghai the more he threw off the thin mask. Since December he had been in open conflict with Borodin, Galen and other communists. But their only strength lay in the mass movement, and this they had, by Stalin's manifesto, to subordinate to the Kuomintang.

Suddenly the masses broke away. On 3 January the workers and petty bourgeoisie of Hankow were holding a meeting near the British concession. The British authorities got into conflict with them and the masses spontaneously occupied the concession, organised a workers' guard and maintained control. The revolution in the South flared up again, and so powerful a wave of nationalist sentiment flowed through the country that even the Japanese supporter, Chang Tso-lin in Peking, found it politic to speak of the return of the concessions. Chiang Kai-shek, now at Nanking, then as today a stronghold of reaction, afraid of the militant workers in the South, demanded that the government seat should be transferred to Nanking. But the left Kuomintang, between whom and Chiang there had always been almost open hostility, insisted that according to a resolution passed in Canton the government should remain at Wuhan. For weeks there existed practically two Kuomintang governments, two central committees, two political bureaux. Chiang, not yet ready to come out openly against the International, praised trotskyism because the trotskyists were demanding the withdrawal of the party from the Kuomintang.* In the Russian delegation three young communists (all anti-trotskyists), Nassonov,

---

* Stalin's representatives in Shanghai stated explicitly Chiang's treacherous reason for so doing.

Fokin and Albrecht, were chafing at the suicidal policy of Borodin. The bold action of the Chinese proletariat at Hankow had given Borodin an opportunity. The left Kuomintang rallied round him and stiffened its resistance to Chiang Kai-shek. But Borodin, shackled by Stalin, did not know what to do. To the masses holding Hankow neither Borodin nor the Chinese party gave any directives. Instead they rebuked the workers who had formed the guard and were keeping order in Hankow.

Nassonov, Fokin and Albrecht urged Borodin to leave Shanghai and go to Wuhan to rally the left Kuomintang, initiate a broad mass campaign on the rising militancy of the masses, explain that the quarrel over the government seat was not personal but political, and demand openly from Chiang Kai-shek a clear and distinct political declaration. Borodin stuck to Stalin's manifesto.

Chiang took the offensive, and he and the bourgeois and imperialist press brought the struggle against Borodin into the open. On 21 February Chiang delivered a pogrom speech against the party, and the conflict could no longer be hidden. Borodin and the party remained silent before the bewildered masses. Urged to unloose the peasant movement against Chiang, they declared that the peasants did not want land.

In Shanghai the revolutionary proletariat, roused to fever-heat by the victories and approach of Chiang Kai-shek, the leader of the revolution, received the news that Chiang had defeated Sun Ch'uan-fang, the reactionary feudal general who dominated Shanghai and the surrounding area. The joy of the workers broke out on 18 February into a spontaneous general strike in which three hundred thousand workers joined. A section of the petty bourgeoisie shut up their shops and joined in the strike, the fleet came over to the side of the workers and the strike developed into an armed uprising. A detachment of Sun Ch'uan-fang's troops in the city broke under the strain. Some began to loot and pillage, others wanted to join the nationalist revolution. But the Chinese Central Committee, which did not expect the strike, deliberated as to whether the rising should take place or not, even while it was taking place. No directives were issued. The slogans were "Down with Sun Ch'uan-fang" and "Hail the Northern Expedition", "Hail Chiang Kai-shek". Not one anti-imperialist slogan was issued in Shanghai, the centre of foreign imperialism in China. The movement collapsed.

Nassonov, Fokin and Albrecht, seeing the revolution being destroyed by those who were supposed to lead it, sent to Moscow a long and bitter complaint against the leadership of Borodin and the leaders of the Chinese Communist Party:

> "The slogan of the democratic national assembly, which we had advanced shortly before the strike, was conceived of as a new means of combinations at the top, and was not launched among the masses. As a result, we let slip an exceptionally favourable historical moment, a rare combination of circumstances, where

power lay in the streets but the party did not know how to take it. Worse still, it didn't want to take it; it was afraid to.

"Thus, the right tendency, which has already contaminated the party for a year, found a crass and consummate expression during the Shanghai events, which can only be compared with the tactics of the German Central Committee in 1923 and of the Mensheviks during the December uprising in 1905. Yet there is a difference. It lies in the fact that in Shanghai the proletariat had considerably more forces and chances on its side and, with an energetic intervention, it could have won Shanghai for the revolution and changed the relationship of forces within the Kuomintang.

"It is not by accident that the leadership of the Chinese Communist Party committed these errors. They flowed from the right wing conception of the revolution, the lack of understanding of the mass movement and the complete lack of attention towards it."[*]

But the right wing conception of the revolution which had contaminated the party for a year had come from Stalin. Stalin dealt with the protest against his policy in the usual manner. He suppressed the letter, recalled Nassonov in disgrace and banished him to America.

While the Shanghai proletariat fought, Chiang Kai-shek, but two days' march outside the city, would not enter. He waited while the soldiers of the reaction · "bled" the workers. (The military governor of Shanghai was later to receive a command in Chiang's army.) Instead Chiang spread terror in the outlying provinces. Nassonov and his friends had written their despairing letter on 17 March, in the belief that the Shanghai proletariat was crushed for some time to come. But on 21 March the workers of Shanghai again rose spontaneously, and this time drove out the Northern forces. Millions of workers all over the globe have suffered at the hands of the Stalin-dominated International, but none so much as the valiant proletariat of Shanghai. For three weeks they held the city. By this time the masses knew that Chiang Kai-shek meant mischief, for his army had stood outside the gates for several days while they fought with the reactionaries inside. The majority of the workers wished to close the gates to Chiang and fight him. But Stalin's orders were rigid. Mandalian, a communist official in Shanghai at the time, has written that the orders to the workers were "not to provoke Chiang" and "in case of extreme necessity to bury their arms," and Bukharin, in his *Problems of the Chinese Revolution*, has confirmed this. From Chiang's army itself came a warning of the coup that Chiang was preparing. His army was not homogeneous, and contained elements devoted to the revolution. Certain sections of Chiang's army entered the city but took no action. The first division was led by Say-O, who had been promoted from the ranks, and he and his division were in sympathy with the mass movement. Chiang Kai-shek knew this and hated

---

[*] *Problems of the Chinese Revolution*, by L. Trotsky.

Say-O. While the main army stood outside the gates of Shanghai, Chiang called Say-O to headquarters, received him coldly and proposed that he leave the city and go to the front. Say-O sought the central committeee of the Chinese Communist Party and told them that he would not go back to Chiang Kai-shek because he feared a trap. He was willing to remain in Shanghai and fight with the workers against the counter-revolutionary overthrow which Chiang was preparing. Ch'en Tu-hsiu and the leaders of the Chinese party told him that they knew the overthrow was being prepared, but that they did not want a premature conflict with Chiang Kai-shek. Say-O therefore led his division out of the city.* But the split in the Kuomintang ranks and the coming treachery of Chiang were now no secret and were openly discussed even in the imperialist press. The Chinese party holding fast to Moscow, reassured the doubting Shanghai workers.

On 6 April Stalin addressed a meeting in Moscow, and the meeting unanimously adopted a resolution condemning trotskyism and endorsing the line of the Chinese Communist Party:

> "This meeting considers the demand that the Communist Party of China leave the Kuomintang to be equivalent to the isolation of the CP of China and the proletariat from the national movement for the emancipation of China and further considers this demand to be absolutely false and erroneous."

All over the world the Communist International, drugged by the stalinist policy and the stalinist lies, was waiting for the victory of Chiang Kai-shek. On 23 March the Communist Party of France held a great meeting in Paris at which appeared Cachin, Sémard and Monmousseau. They sent a telegram to Chiang Kai-shek:

> "The workers of Paris greet the entry of the revolutionary Chinese army into Shanghai. Fifty-six years after the Paris Commune and ten years after the Russian, the Chinese Commune marks a new stage in the development of the world revolution."

But the Shanghai workers knew that Chiang was a traitor. The British and Americans bombarded Nanking and killed seven thousand Chinese and the imperialists were openly inciting Chiang against the workers. To allay feeling, therefore, Communist Party and Kuomintang issued a joint manifesto in Shanghai on 6 April. In all the misleading literature of the stalinist International this

---

* This narrative Trotsky, who is our authority here, claims was told to the sixteenth session of the XV Congress of the CPSU, 11 December 1927, by Khitarov, home from China. Stalin had the most damaging passages deleted from the minutes and Trotsky quotes the pages, 32 and 33, ot the chief omissions. The fanatical obedience of the leadership was due to the prestige of Stalin as representative of the Russian revolution and the strong backbone of control from above in the International. We shall see it even more strikingly and with more disastrous consequences in Germany, 1930-33.

manifesto is perhaps the most criminal:

"The national revolution has reached the last basis of imperialism in China, Shanghai. The counter-revolutionaries both inside and outside China are spreading false reports in order to bring our two parties in opposition to each other. Some say that the Communist Party is preparing to form a worker's government, to overthrow the Kuomintang and to recover the concessions by force of arms. Others say that the leaders of the Kuomintang intend to make war on the Communist Party, to suppress the labour unions and to dissolve the workers' defence organisations.

Now is not the time to discuss the origin of these malicious rumours. The supreme organ of the Kuomintang declared at its last plenary session that it has not the least intention of attacking the Communist Party or of suppressing the labour unions. The military authorities in Shanghai have declared their complete allegiance to the central committee of the Kuomintang. If differences of opinion exist they can be amicably settled. The Communist Party is striving to maintain order in the freed territories. It has already completely approved of the tactic of the National Government not to attempt to force a return of the concessions by armed force. The trades council of Shanghai has also declared that it will make no attempt to enter the concession by violence. At the same time it declared that it fully approved of the co-operation between all oppressed classes through the formation of a local government. In face of these facts, there is *no basis whatever for these malicious rumours.*"

On 12 April Chiang Kai-shek, having concluded his arrangements with the imperialists, launched the terror on the Shanghai workers. Chiang's long-sword detachments marched through the streets, executing workers on the spot: some of the strikers in the Railway Department were thrown into the furnaces of the locomotives. Communist Party, trades union movement, all workers' organisations, were smashed to pieces and driven into illegality. The Chinese counter-revolution, backed by imperialism, reigned triumphant in Shanghai, while Stalin and Bukharin in Moscow led the whole Communist International in an ear-piercing howl of treachery.

Shanghai might be lost, but one thing had to be saved—Stalin's prestige against trotskyism. In the following month at the Eighth Plenum of the ECCI, Stalin exposed the mistakes of the opposition:

"The opposition is dissatisfied because the Shanghai workers did not enter into a decisive battle against the imperialists and their myrmidons. But it does not understand that the revolution in China cannot develop at a fast tempo. It does not understand that one cannot take up a decisive struggle under unfavourable conditions. The opposition does not understand that one cannot take up a decisive struggle under unfavourable conditions. The opposition does not understand that not to avoid a decisive struggle under unfavourable conditions (when it can be avoided), means to make easier the work of the enemies of the revolution."

For the eighth plenum Stalin and Bukharin insisted that the communists should remain within the Kuomintang and should now support the left Kuomintang and the Wuhan government as leaders of the revolution. Wang Ching-wei was substituted for Chiang Kai-shek. Borodin in China was sending urgent messages to Stalin telling him that the Kuomintang leaders in Wuhan were determined to prevent the growing agrarian revolution even at the cost of a split with Moscow. From Stalin's point of view the only thing was to hold the agrarian revolution in. For him now the left Kuomintang government at Wuhan, with two communists in it and supported by Feng Yu-hsiang, (the Christian general)[1] was now the revolutionary government, and its head, Wang Ching-wei, was immediately baptised leader of the Chinese revolution.

It is at this stage that the personal responsibility of Stalin (and Bukharin) assumes international proportions. They could have changed the policy then. It is true that Stalin had the power he held because he was the ideal representative of the bureaucracy. But a change of policy did not in any way involve the internal position of the bureaucracy. Proof of this is that in a few months the policy was violently changed. But Stalin's stubborn ignorance and political blindness held the revolution down.

Seven years before Lenin had said China was ripe for soviets. Now, in May 1927, after two years of revolution, Stalin rejected outright the policy of soviets for which the left opposition pressed. "Now can we say that the situation in Russia from March to July 1917 represents an analogy to the present situation in China? No, this cannot be said. . . . The history of the workers' soviets shows that such soviets can exist and develop further only if favourable premises are given for a direct transition from the bourgeois-democratic revolution to the proletarian revolution."[2]

Trotsky, though conscious that against the stalinised International arguments were useless, led the attack of the left opposition with undiminished vigour and courage.

"Stalin has again declared himself here against workers' and peasants' soviets with the argument that the Kuomintang and the Wuhan government are sufficient means and instruments for the agrarian revolution. Thereby Stalin assumes, and wants the International to assume, the responsibility for the policy of the Kuomintang and the Wuhan government, as he repeatedly assumed the responsibility for the policy of the former 'National Government' of Chiang Kai-shek (particularly in his speech of 5 April, the

---

[1] He made his soldiers sing Methodist hymns every day, and say grace at meals. America, it was stated, backed him.
[2] Minutes of the Plenum, German edition, Hamburg-Berlin, 1928, p. 66. See Third International after Lenin, by L. Trotsky, p. 840.

stenogram of which has, of course, been kept hidden from the International). . . .

The agrarian revolution is a serious thing. Politicians of the Wang Ching-wei type, under difficult conditions, will unite ten times with Chiang Kai-shek against the workers and peasants. Under such conditions two communists in a bourgeois government become impotent hostages, if not a direct mask for the preparation of a new blow against the working masses. We say to the workers of China: the peasants will not carry out the agrarian revolution to the end if they let themselves be led by petty-bourgeois radicals instead of by you, the revolutionary proletarians. Therefore, build up your workers' soviets, ally them with the peasant soviets, arm yourselves through the soviets, shoot the generals who do not recognise the soviets, shoot the bureaucrats and bourgeois liberals who will organise uprisings against the soviets. Only through peasants' and soldiers' soviets will you win over the majority of Chiang Kai-shek's soldiers to your side."*

The plenum adopted a resolution against trotskyism:

"Comrade Trotsky . . . demanded at the plenary session the immediate establishment of the dual power in the form of soviets and the immediate adoption of a course towards the overthrow of the left Kuomintang government. This apparently ultra-left but in reality opportunist demand is nothing but the repetition of the old trotskyist position of jumping over the petty-bourgeois, peasant stage of the revolution."

Barring a note which said that the line of the CI had been quite correct, no accounts of this May plenum were ever published until a year after, long after the opposition had been expelled and had made some of the documents public. For even while the plenum was sitting the generals seized power in the province of Honan, a month later Feng Yu-hsiang allied himself with Chiang Kai-shek, and before another month Wang Ching-wei, the new leader of the revolution, and the Wuhan government had come to terms with Chiang Kai-shek and put to the sword the workers' movement in Wuhan. Even more bitter than that of the workers of Shanghai was the experience of the peasants in the revolutionary district of Changsha, an important revolutionary centre near to Wuhan. The Kuomintang army in Changsha consisted of only 1,700 soldiers, and the peasants around had armed detachments consisting of 20,000 men. When the peasants heard that the counter-revolutionary generals had started to crush the national movement they gathered round Changsha, preparing to march on the city. But at this point a letter came from the central committee of the Chinese Communist Party. Faithful to their instructions from the great revolutionists in Moscow, they told the

---

* *Problems of the Chinese Revolution,* pp. 102 and 103.

peasants to avoid conflict and to transfer the matter to the revolutionary government in Wuhan. The district committee ordered the peasants to retreat. Two detachments failed to get the message in time, advanced on Wuhan itself and were there destroyed by the soldiers of Wang Ching-wei.

The pitiless exposure of the false policy in China only intensified Stalin's attacks against the policy of the opposition at home and confusion in the ranks of the opposition gave Stalin and Bukharin the opportunity to win ideological victories. In the early stages of the Chinese revolution, Zinoviev, as president of the Communist International, had lent himself to Stalin's leninism. When the Zinoviev-Trotsky bloc was formed, Trotsky's uncompromising stand for the immediate withdrawal from the Kuomintang which he had maintained since 1923 was voted down by Zinoviev, and Trotsky was compelled for the sake of discipline to moderate his demand for the immediate withdrawal. Stalin and Bukharin knew quite well the differences between Trotsky and Zinoviev, but seized on this divergence and made great play with it against the opposition, while Chiang Kai-shek and Wang Ching-wei massacred tens of thousands of deluded Chinese workers and peasants. After Wuhan the Trotsky wing won over the Zinoviev wing and came out unequivocally for the withdrawal from the Kuomintang. Stalin still refused.

The proletariat had been totally defeated in Shanghai and Wuhan. The peasant movement, which was to show its force a year later, was still hobbled by the stalinist policy. As always, this was the time chosen by Stalin to make a sharp turn to the left. Soviets, inadmissible in May, were in July proclaimed the immediate task. Prestige, however, had to be maintained. The first thing to do was to throw the blame on the leadership in China, which was condemned root and branch. Bukharin did the dirty work and let loose a stream of abuse on them. A new representative was sent to replace Borodin. Telegrams from Moscow called a hasty conference. A new leadership was set up and the course set for mass revolt. The left opposition raised a protest at the cruel massacres and disillusionment which would inevitably follow. They were now violently abused as liquidationists. On 9 August a joint session of the central committee and of the CPSU made the following declaration: "The Chinese revolution is not only not on the ebb, but has entered upon a new higher stage. . . . Not only is the strength of the toiling masses of China not yet exhausted, but it is precisely only now that it is beginning to manifest itself in a new advance of the revolutionary struggle." On this dreadful orientation the defeated revolution was pounded to pieces. Rising after rising, doomed in advance to failure, destroyed some of the finest and bravest of the Chinese revolutionaries. On 19 September, after two risings had been crushed, the Kuomintang was abandoned at last. But Moscow still preached the rising of the revolution to a higher stage and inevitable victory.

All in China who opposed this policy were driven ruthlessly out of the party. In Moscow the left opposition were jeered at as counter-revolutionary. This was the leninism that led to the ill-fated Canton insurrection in December 1927, when, without preparation, without a sign as yet of a mass peasant rising, with thousands of Kuomintang soldiers in and near Canton, the Communist International encouraged the workers to seize the city which they held for two or three days. The insurrection had been timed to coincide with the fifteenth congress of the Russian party, where Stalin was expounding the mistakes of the opposition. Over seven thousand workers paid with their lives for this last stalinist adventure. From first to last a hundred thousand Chinese workers and peasants lost their lives making the Kuomintang revolution.

Some communists, who escaped from the Canton Commune with other remnants of the revolutionary movement, insurgent peasant-bands and ex-Kuomintang soldiers, raised the countryside in Central China and formed Soviet China. With the proletarian movement dead the Chinese peasant soviets were bound to be defeated, but it took Chiang Kai-shek six years to do it and demonstrated what could have been accomplished in China by a combination of proletariat and peasantry. The remains of the Red Army are now wandering somewhere in North China. While Red China lasted, the Communist International, in writings and speeches, trumpeted. Not so Stalin. With the defeat of the revolution his open role as revolutionary strategist came to a final end. In the second volume of his collected speeches there is only one direct reference to the revolution. It is in the best stalinist vein, and deserves consideration. It is one of those revealing statements which explain so many things in the history of Soviet Russia. "It is said that already a Soviet government has been formed there. If that is true, I think it is nothing to be surprised at. There can be no doubt that only the Soviets can save China from final collapse and beggary."* Thus the leader of the international proletariat in his political report to the sixteenth congress. But not only on revolution in China has he been silent. Never since has he openly taken upon himself the responsibility for the policy of the International. He could send the opposition to Siberia and pass innumerable resolutions condemning their policy and justifying his own, which would have been successful but for the mistakes of the leadership in China. But nothing could wipe away his responsibility for the hideous failure there, and he would not run that risk again.

What explanation can be given of the policy in China between 1923 and 1927? Bukharin's share in it may be neglected. Stalin has used one after the other of the old Soviet leaders as his mouthpiece and then cast them aside if the policy failed. The policy was

---

* *Leninism*, Vol. II, p. 318.

his. What lay behind it? Not conscious sabotage.

That was to come later. Stalin spent enormous sums in China. He knew that a successful Chinese revolution would enormously strengthen Russia in the Far East, the failure would leave Russia in the position she is in today, with the Chinese Eastern Railway lost, threatened by both China and Japan. He wanted a Chinese revolution, but he had no belief in the capacity of the Chinese masses to make one. This man of steel, fierce Bolshevik, etc., is first and foremost a bureaucrat (and is therefore the representative man of the Russian bureaucracy). Like Blum, Citrine, Wels, Leipert, Otto Bauer and the other Mensheviks, he believes in the bourgeoisie far more than he believes in the proletariat. He was prepared in 1917 to support the Russian bourgeoisie rather than depend upon the international proletariat. In 1925-1927, despite all facts and warnings, he stuck to Chiang Kai-shek and Wang Ching-wei. The consequences, however, did not lead him to recognise error. It had the opposite result. The bureaucracy now not only in theory but in fact turned its back on the revolution. Henceforward the International had one exclusive purpose—the defence of the USSR.

1937

4

Revolts in Africa

[*In 1938, Raymond Postgate commissioned from James* A History of Negro Revolt *(later republished in the USA as* A History of Pan-African Revolt*). James says: "Such a book had never been done before. I gathered a lot of material in it, and really I'm astonished now at how much there was that I didn't know. But the book has the virtue that there were all sorts of problems — like the struggles of women, market women in Africa and so on — that went into it, aside from the historical things like the Haitian revolution and the blacks in the American Civil War. . . . The book has a peculiar history. Postgate's name got the book sold in book-stores all over the country. When they found out what was in it some of them carefully hid it. There were places we went to where we found they had hidden it — they put it under a lot of other books, but when you asked for it they would say, yes, we have it."*

The chapter reproduced here was the first account of early revolts in the African colonies, and is one of the products of James's work with George Padmore in the International African Service Bureau.]

For four centuries the African in Africa had had to suffer from the raids of the slave dealers and the dislocation of African civilisation which had been caused thereby. America continued with the slave-trade until the end of the Civil War, but whereas in 1789 San Domingo alone was taking forty thousand slaves a year, between 1808 and 1860 the Southern states of North America took only two hundred thousand. Other nations of Europe and the Arabs on the East coast continued the trade. Actual colonies, however, were comparatively few in Africa. There was, of course, Cape Colony and the districts beyond, and colonies in West Africa which were on the whole little more than trading stations. In the middle of the nineteenth century Disraeli referred to colonies as damned millstones around the necks of the British people. As we have said, it is unlikely that more than one tenth of Africa was in European hands. But in the 1880s began the intensive rivalry of European imperialisms for colonies as the sources of raw materials, for markets and spheres of influence. By the end of the nineteenth century, less than one tenth of Africa remained in the hands of Africans themselves. This rapid change could not fail to produce a series of revolts, which have never ceased.

Before we consider the actual revolts, it is necessary to see, briefly, what the Negro is revolting against. European colonisation is broadly speaking of two types, the first, as in South Africa, the two Rhodesias and Kenya, where it is possible for Europeans to settle and remain; the second in British West Africa, where the European is for the most part official and trader, does not look upon the colony as his home and does not settle there in large numbers.

In areas like the Union of South Africa, the Rhodesias and Kenya, the white settlers have to force the native to leave his own work and interests in order to labour for them in mine or plantation. The method they adopt is to tax him by means of a poll tax. The Negro, though perhaps quite comfortably placed according to his own wishes and needs, must have money to pay this tax, which compels him therefore to seek employment with European masters, on whatever conditions these choose to lay down. Hence the wages of fourpence a day in Kenya and fifteen shillings a month in the copper mines of Rhodesia. The Europeans also take the best land and herd the natives in areas which are not only difficult to cultivate but too small for their most elementary needs. In the Union of South Africa, for instance, about two million whites own about eighty per cent of the land, while over six million natives own ten per cent. The rest is Crown Land, that is to say, at the disposal of the white government. Obviously this state of affairs can only be maintained by a social and political régime based on terror.

The natives are made to carry passes which they must produce on request; a pass if they are out later than nine o'clock, a pass to show that their tax has been paid, a pass from their employer, finger-prints for identification—in the Union of South Africa there are a dozen passes of one kind or another which the Negro may have to carry. A Negro who has a profession is given an exemption pass which absolves him from the necessity of carrying these other passes. But any native policeman is able to ask him for this exemption pass, and arrest him on the spot if it is not produced at once. Negroes, whatever their status, whatever their appearance, are debarred from frequenting all public places of business or entertainment frequented by whites. In places like the post office, there are two counters, one for whites and one for blacks.

What does the native get in return? After four hundred years of European occupation, there are not half-a-dozen native doctors in South Africa. Over three-quarters of the native population is almost entirely without education. The education supplied to the rest is officially admitted to be of the poorest quality. Far from making a gradual, if slow, political progress, the natives of the Cape have recently been deprived of the franchise, a relic of more liberal days. They are debarred by law from being even skilled labourers, as tyrannical and demoralising a piece of legislation as has been passed in any country during the last hundred years.

In the mines they receive one-eighth of the wages of the white miner. In ancient territories like the Union of South Africa, or in more modern areas as Rhodesia and Kenya, the method is exactly the same, with slight local variations. While politicians in Britain speak of trusteeship, South African white leaders and officials in Rhodesia and Kenya periodically state quite unequivocally that Africa is to be run for the benefit of the whites and the Negro must make up his mind to know his place and keep it.

In West Africa the situation is somewhat different. There, over large areas, the Negroes were guaranteed their land by law, at a time when it seemed unlikely that Europeans would ever need it. European capital, of course, dominates. But the racial discrimination is not nearly so acute as in the South and in the East of Africa, and the conflict between the Negroes and their rulers is more strictly economic and political than it is in the Cape or Kenya.

French Equatorial Africa and the Belgian Congo form two areas to some degree different from those described above. In a French colony, a Negro who by education or military service becomes a French citizen, is given all privileges, and is governed by the laws which apply to white men. He can become a high official in the government service, or a general in the French army. During the war Pétain's Chief of Staff at Verdun was a Negro. Commandant Avenol, who was in charge of the air defence of Paris from 1914 to 1918 with ten thousand men under him, including British and white American aviators, was a Martinique Negro. At the present moment the Governor of Guadeloupe is a black man. These men, it is true, are from the old West Indian colonies. But there are Africans in the service, and it is admitted that promotion is open to them on practically the same terms as whites. There have been Africans, deputies in the Chamber, who have become Cabinet Ministers. After the war the French issued a serious warning to Americans in Paris who tried to introduce American race prejudice, and it is noteworthy that these Americans who cannot tolerate the sight of a Negro in an American restaurant, learnt in Paris to admit him and his white girl friends into an American bar: Briand told them that he would close down the bar if they didn't. This is a valuable feature of French civilisation and disposes of many illusions, carefully cultivated in America and Britain, about Negro incapacity and racial incompatibility. But imperialism remains imperialism. During the last twenty years the population of French Congo has declined by more than six millions, and the French have as black a record in Africa as any other imperialist nation.

In the Belgian Congo the Negro has certain privileges; for example, he is allowed to ocupy important posts on the railways, which is forbidden to him in South Africa. Thus Negroes run trains to the border of the Belgian colonies where South African whites take them over. Yet the Belgian attitude is less liberal than the French. No African who has spent more than six months abroad is allowed to return to the Congo, and the severity of the forced labour regulations is such that when the company which owns the sugar plantations of Moabeke built a railway, almost the entire male population of the district was worked to death. This is in no way exceptional. French and Belgians have an evil reputation in the Congo for cold-blooded cruelty. As in the days of slavery in the West Indian colonies, the European colonising nations claim superiority to each other. But an African in Eritrea is no worse off under Italian Fascism than an African in the Congo under democratic Belgium, or a Rhodesian copper miner.

Let us begin with revolts in one of the oldest colonies on the West Coast, Sierra Leone. The Negroes in the actual colony are some of the most advanced in education and should be grouped with those of the West Indies rather than with those in Central or Eastern Africa. Freetown, the capital, for instance, was until recent years a municipality. The hinterland is, however, a protectorate where the less developed Africans are governed by the method of indirect rule.

At the end of the last century there were two Negro communities, one with its own press, barristers-at-law, doctors and other intelligentsia, and on the other hand the natives in the interior, the new Africa and the old. These two communities were divided. Those with generations of British education had an outlook similar to that of the majority of Negroes in the West Indies: they regarded the African tribes as barbarous and uncivilised. The African tribes looked upon these Europeanised blacks as black white men. In 1898 a revolt burst out in the protectorate. The natives resented the paying of the poll tax and the Mendi, a famous fighting tribe, had a special grievance of their own: they objected to corporal punishment. So much did they oppose it, that they would not send their children to the missionary schools where the missionaries sometimes beat them. The tribes completely wiped out some battalions of West Indian blacks who were sent against them, and it is claimed by Negroes who were in Sierra Leone at the time that certain white battalions were also completely destroyed. The great massacres of government soldiers took place at Sherbro and Mofeno. The revolt was of course put down, many hundreds of natives being killed. The insurgents killed not only white and black soldiers and every missionary they could put their hands on, but also certain of the Europeanised blacks as well. They looked upon all of these as members of one exploiting, arrogant group. The war, however, has marked the beginning of a change.

The conflict of capital and labour is intensified by the fact that capital is usually white and labour black; this in a continent where the whites have always sought to justify their economic exploitation and social privilege by the mere fact of difference of colour. The class conflict, bitter enough in countries where the population is homogeneous in colour, has an added bitterness in Africa, which has been strengthened by the growth of nationalism among the post-war intelligentsia. The politically conscious minority increasingly realise that their future is with the developing Africans rather than with the European traders. Further, they are Africans in Africa — not the descendants of Africans, as in the West Indies. The result is a growing solidarity between the blacks, chiefly workers in the colony and the more untutored Africans in the protectorate. Black politicians in the colony attribute the ill-feeling in 1898 to white propaganda aimed at dividing potential allies, and they have common ground in that they are Negroes in a continent where to be black is to be inferior. It is against this background that we must see more recent movements in Sierra Leone and Gambia.

In 1919 there was a railway strike in Sierra Leone. The railway workers attempted to get other workers to join with them and were joined by over two thousand police striking for higher wages. In 1926 there was another railway strike and the workers again attempted to make the strike general and to win over the police. The strikers showed an extraordinary militancy. They removed the rails in front of the manager's train. The attacked it with sticks. They removed or loosened the rails on curves or steep banks and at the approach to a bridge, pulled down telegraph poles and cut wires to prevent telegraphic communication with the protectorate. In the words of the Governor, "it was a revolt against the state by its servants". The municipality supported the strike and the native press hinted at rebellion, whereupon the Governor suppressed the municipality. We have here a very sharp division between the African labourers and the employers in industry, mostly white.

In Gambia, a colony which is usually grouped with Sierra Leone, the seamen are organised and in 1929 a sailors' strike lasted forty days and then grew into a general strike. At the same time, the farmers, hostile over the low prices paid for their products, carried on strenuous agitation. The people were fired upon and nearly fifty were wounded. After three weeks of the general strike, the Colonial Secretary addressed a letter to the Union seeking arbitration. The government finally combined with the employers to defeat the strike. This was not a revolt, but shows the capacity for organised action which has developed in these older colonies, while an outbreak which took place in Sierra Leone in February 1931 shows the possibility of revolts infinitely more dangerous than any that have hitherto taken place. Hundreds of Negroes from the protectorate, led by an armed battalion of fifty men, invaded the Kambia district. The leader was Hahilara, a Negro Moslem leader who had converted thousands of natives to Mohammedanism, with which he united anti-imperialism. Hahilara called upon the peasants to refuse to pay taxes and to drive away the British officials. He demanded that all Crown Lands in the protectorate should be confiscated and divided among the landless peasants. This was social revolution. Hahilara's agitation had widespread support. The government attempted to arrest him, but the Negroes threatened to kill all Europeans who entered their territory. Government soldiers invaded the territory, and Hahilara was defeated and killed. But Captain H. J. Holmes, the officer commanding the British troops, was also killed. Hundreds of native huts were burnt to the ground and the rising was suppressed.

Yet perhaps the most significant feature of the revolt was the attitude of the Negro press in the colony, which emphasised the grievances of the insurgents in the protectorate. Sympathy among the intellectuals of Sierra Leone for the natives was widespread and the Sierra Leone workers were solid with the tribesmen. Should there be at any time a movement of the organised and educated blacks in the colony with a widespread peasant revolt in the protectorate, it would be difficult to prevent the Negroes of Sierra Leone and Gambia from gaining possession of the colony, though whether they would be able to keep it would depend upon events in other and wider spheres.

In Nigeria, a colony similar in social structure to Sierra Leone and Gambia, the crisis which began in 1929 produced the extraordinary women's revolt in which over fifty women were killed and over fifty wounded. The fall of prices for agrarian commodities placed the finances of the colony in difficulties, and the Government attempted to recuperate its falling revenues by an increase in direct taxation. Indirect rule works for the most part through chiefs, many of whom are merely instruments of the British government. The chiefs were instructed to impose a tax upon the women whereupon the slumbering discontent broke out. Thousands of women organised protest demonstrations against the government and its chiefs and at Aba, the capital of the Eastern Province, the women who sold in the market, faced with the possibility of a tax which would destroy their small profits, organised a revolt. The writer is informed by Africans from Nigeria that the actual happenings in Aba have been suppressed in all official reports. The women seized public buildings and held them for days. The servants refused to cook for their white masters and mistresses and some of them made the attempt to bring the European women by force into the markets to give them some experience of what work was like. These saved themselves only by precipitate flight, some of them with only the clothes they had on their backs. A detachment of soldiers suppressed the revolt, shooting at the black women as they tried to escape across the river. Martial law was proclaimed and the Governor called a meeting of the African editors in Lagos and threatened them with imprisonment if they published news of what was happening at Aba. That is why written evidence is confined to the official reports. A local committee of investigation was appointed and issued a report which was approved by the Legislative Council. Mr Drummond Shiels, the Labour Under-Secretary of State for the Colonies, in answer to a question in the House of Commons replied that "the Colonial Office was satisfied that the officials on the spot acted in the best interest of the country". But the publication of the report was the signal for a widespread agitation throughout the colony. Mass meetings denounced it. The workers threatened to refuse to pay taxes; demanded a new commission, and redress of their economic and political grievances. The government was forced to appoint another commission. The Negroes threatened to boycott it unless Africans were appointed and the government was forced to appoint two. This commission admitted economic grievances and suggested measures of reform. The Governor, however, imposed a fine of £850 on the town of Aba. Such was the resentment aroused that the political officers appealed to the Governor to withdraw the fine, and again the Governor had to capitulate.

The strength and vigour of the movement were a shock to the Europeans. Sir Frank Baddeley, the Colonial Secretary of Nigeria, found that the revolt was the work of the agents of Moscow. *The Times* correspondent, however, gave a more sober estimate:

> "The trouble was of a nature and extent unprecedented in Nigeria. In a country where the women throughout the centuries have remained in subjection to the men, this was eventually a woman's movement, organised, developed and carried out by the women, without either the help or commission of their menfolk, though probably with their tacit sympathy."

The risings in Sierra Leone and Gambia are of a dual type. While the Negroes in the protectorates when driven to action think in terms of social revolution, those in the towns, like the majority of workers in Europe or America, aim at redress of immediate grievances, violent though their methods may be. Trade unions, the municipalities, the African press, have all given the movement its organised force, but of necessity make it more conservative.

In Eastern and Central Africa, more primitive territories, we have had during the last thirty years a series of risings of an entirely different type. In the years before the war, the tribes simply threw themselves at the government troops and suffered the inevitable defeat. Such risings could not go on. They were too obviously suicidal. In 1915, however, we have a new type — a rising led not by a tribal chief but by a Negro who has had some education. Such education as the African is given is nearly always religious, so that the leader often translated the insurrection into religious terms.

The Chilembwe rising in Nyasaland in 1915 was of this character. The first Europeans to arrive in Nyasaland were missionaries sent out by the Church of Scotland. Soon after, many of them left the mission for the land which they had acquired from the native chiefs. They set up as coffee planters, converting the natives jointly to Christianity and to cheap labour. By 1915, these plantations had passed into the hands of syndicates whose sole object was to make the maximum profit. Within these plantations which covered an area of three hundred square miles and employed tens of thousands of Negroes, the companies permitted no school, no hospital and no missions.

A Negro, John Chilembwe by name, was sent to America by a small mission nearby. After having had a good education, he returned to his native land. He could find no position in any mission, so he built a church of his own with money raised from his fellow blacks. Most of the white men in Africa hate Africans who are educated and wear European clothes. His own treatment at the hands of the white planters and missionaries and his readings of the Bible, especially the story of the national struggle of the Jews in the Old Testament, inspired Chilembwe to lead a revolt against the European oppressors ("the Philistines").

Support for the revolt came mainly from the workers on the estate and according to plan, the five European heads of the estate were killed. Their wives and children, however, met with great kindness. The blacks spent money to get eggs and milk for the white children, and banana leaves were held over their heads to protect them from the sun on their journey away from the estate.

The Europeans, frightened for their lives, ran to the military camps. But Chilembwe did not go very far. Just after he had preached a sermon in the church, with the estate manager's head on the pulpit, white police and soldiers appeared. The rebels took to the jungle, but were rigorously hunted down. Among those captured alive, about twenty were hanged, and all the rest sentenced to life terms. Chilembwe himself, old and nearly blind, was shot down in the long grass with the other leaders.

Six years after, in 1921, the greatest of the religious type of revolt occurred in the Belgian Congo, and shook the whole colony. The leader was Simon Kimbangu, a carpenter and a convert to Christianity. In the spring of 1921 he had a dream in which he was directed to go out and heal the sick. Kimbangu's influence immediately became very great among the native Christian converts. He appealed to the natives to leave the mission churches, controlled by their European masters, and to set up their own independent church organisation under his guidance. To every African such a movement is an instinctive step towards independence and away from the perpetual control of Europeans. Negroes flocked in large numbers to Kimbangu, chiefly from the Protestant but from some of the Catholic missions as well. They declared they were tired of paying money to European churches.

The government at first watched the movement uneasily but with tolerance. But the prophet's policy was soon seen to be detrimental to European interests in its implications. The natives left the plantations to listen to the prophet, in much the same way as the Negro slaves in the West Indies a century before had been wont to plead religion and religious meetings as a convenient excuse for leaving the plantations at all times and without permission. The Negroes followed Kimbangu in such large numbers that industry was disorganised. Key plantations, upon which government depended for the food for native employees in public utilities, were deserted. There was apprehension lest the natives should attempt to seize the lower Congo railway, which was indispensable to the colony. The fixing of Wednesday instead of Sunday as the day of rest created further dislocation. Worse still, as in all religious movements, minor "prophets" sprang up in the wake of the master, all professing to work miracles, but all more extreme than the prophet himself. Their preachings tended to become more and more anti-European. Wealthy natives in Kinshasa gave the movement financial and ideological support. Native students from all British and French colonies joined the movement and spread radical doctrines among the rank and file. The movement became so threatening that in June 1921 the Belgian government ordered Kimbangu's arrest.

Like a true prophet, Kimbangu escaped and this served only to strengthen his hold upon the masses. He stayed in one village and was visited by thousands of his followers, yet remained free until September, a striking testimony to his own influence and the strength and solidarity of his organisation.

He was eventually tried by court-martial in October. It was held that Kimbangu's organisation had aimed at overthrowing the Belgian régime, and that religion was only a means of inciting the population. Kimbangu was sentenced to death, his lieutenants to sentences of imprisonment varying from one year to life-time, while a girl, Mandobe, described as the most revolutionary woman in the Congo, received two years. The Negroes reacted with great violence. Strikes immediately broke out everywhere, to such an extent that European traders at Thysville petitioned the King that Kimbangu should be publicly hanged. The Africans threatened that Kimbangu's death would be followed by a general massacre of the whites and the Home government commuted Kimbangu's sentence to life imprisonment and deported many of the minor leaders. The movement has been crushed but the natives continue to expect the reappearance of their "Messiah" and with it the departure of Europeans from the country.

We can conveniently deal here with the revolt of Africans in Kenya under the leadership of Harry Thuku. Harry Thuku, officially described as a man of base character, was very young, in his early twenties. He was a sort of petty clerk, and therefore had a little education, but he did not agitate in the name of God. He protested against high taxation, forced labour and other grievances. His propaganda touched even the smallest village and the state of an African colony is usually such that any strong leadership wins immediate support. The Thuku movement spread with great rapidity. It was estimated that at one meeting in Nairobi over twenty thousand workers were enrolled.

Such a movement was too dangerous to be tolerated, and the Governor ordered mobilisation of the native regiment, the King's African Rifles, to suppress it.

The government supplemented force with trickery. It persuaded the chiefs to sign a proclamation appealing to the masses to return to work, and pledging the government to reduce taxation and raise wages. This drove a wedge into Thuku's organisation. The more timid accepted these promises, the movement subsided and Thuku was arrested. The arrest at once brought the masses out again, ready for a general strike. Crowds swarmed round Thuku's prison demanding his release. The soldiers were ordered to fire upon the crowd, and more than a hundred and fifty were killed. The Negroes, however, were not intimated. The government circulated a rumour that Thuku would be transferred to another prison. This put the crowd on the wrong trail while Thuku was removed to a more remote and safer place. Hundreds were arrested, heavy fines were imposed, which in view of the low wages of the colony could only be liquidated by months of unremitting and unremunerative toil. All associations were declared illegal, and Thuku himself was shipped to Kismay on the Somali border, without trial.

The Kimbangu movement took place in 1921. The Belgians, however, feared that there would be repetitions of the Kimbangu movement in a more extreme form. They were not mistaken. Indeed conditions in the Congo seemed to produce an especially bitter and conscious type of revolt without any religious trimmings.

The difficulty here is to get accounts written in any detail. The British send out their punitive expeditions against revolting tribes and do not necessarily mention them in the annual colonial reports. But if the revolt awakens public interest, a commission will investigate and make a report. This report will frequently class violently with the accounts of participants, eye-witnesses, correspondents of newspapers, native and European, and persons living in the colony at the time. The French and Belgians, however, publish little of this kind, and it is only indirectly that one can gain official confirmation of the vast revolts which have shaken the Belgian Congo since the days of Kimbangu. Thus, in the summer of 1932, M. Vandervelde, at one time Prime Minister of Belgium, spoke of the outrages in Belgian colonial administration and the revolts of the natives. In the course of his speech he said that lest he might make a mistake he had departed from his usual custom and was reading a part of his speech from notes. He told in detail the course of one revolt.

Three agents, sent to recruit workers in a Negro village, found only the women. The men, warned of their coming, had fled. The agents made the women kill cattle to feed them, then raped some of them. Some days after one of the Negroes, as is the custom in the Congo, demanded compensation. He was refused and lost his temper. He threw himself upon the white and bit him in the breast. This savage behaviour gained him a severe flogging from his masters, who had him whipped until he bled, then handed in an indictment against him. An investigation began, but the natives fell on the official and cut him to pieces. Followed the inevitable punitive expedition to restore law and order and the damaged prestige of the whites. The officer in command found that the natives had fled into the bush. To continue with the expedition meant that they would remain there and many children would starve to death. The Governor was adamant. "We must," he telegraphed, "carry out an act of authority and defend the prestige of the government before the population." The instruction was carried out. The natives fought back. They had only lances and other primitive weapons, but they fought for weeks. They died, says M. Vandervelde, in hundreds. But Lukutate, a native worker from Elizabethville, writing in the *Negro Worker* of July 1932, states that they died in thousands. Whole tribes, not knowing the effects of modern weapons, attacked the soldiers almost empty-handed. They starved in the forests. Some died under the whip, others were shot without trial in front of the women and children so as to warn them that blacks must never make rebellion against their white masters.

M. Vandervelde's account tallies very closely with that written by the Congo native. The files of the *Negro Worker* give many accounts of these revolts, and *The Life and Struggles of Negro Toilers*, by George Padmore, contains a great deal of co-ordinated information which is not easily obtainable elsewhere.

In 1924 there was a revolt in French Congo, lasting several days and suppressed by the French military authorities. In 1928, however, another revolt broke out, more class-conscious and better organised than the last. This lasted four months. The natives, despite the fewness of their arms, inflicted a number of defeats on the French troops, capturing a large section of the infantry. The fighting capacity of the revolutionaries, despite their handicaps, amazed even their enemies. The French shot all suspects, and whipped old men and women publicly in the villages as a warning. But by April 1930 the natives were rebelling again. A white French revolutionist and several natives were arrested at Brazzaville, capital of the Middle Congo, and sentenced to three years' imprisonment for attempting to organise a trade union. The natives, hearing of the sentence, went on strike and demonstrated before the court. The police attempted to break up the demonstration, but were attacked with stones. The soldiers were called out and without warning opened fire. The unequal fight continued until the natives were inevitably defeated. But the natives wounded the Governor of the Middle Congo, the troops had to occupy the native quarters of Brazzaville, and for days all business in the town was at a standstill.

This movement had definite communist tendencies. What the authorities fear most is a combination of the workers in the towns and the peasants in the interior. Such a movement, however, has not yet taken place. The size of the territory, the differences of language, make such organisation a task of great difficulty. Yet railways are linking the different portions of the territory, and in both French and Belgian Congo, French is becoming a *lingua franca* among those natives who get the chance to learn a little. Between 1921 and 1932 the whole temper of revolt in these territories has risen steadily. Since the war each succeeding revolt has been more fierce, more concentrated than the last.

Nor has the mandatory system made any essential difference. Ruanda-Urundi, formerly a part of German East Africa, is now mandated territory under the Belgian government. Land alienation, or more precisely, taking away the natives' land, forced labour in the Katanga copper mines, all these typical features resulted in such a dislocation of local production that the fields were not tilled and in 1929 a famine broke out in the district of Ruanda. Under the whip of hunger, the natives rose in revolt and the movement spread from Belgian Ruanda to British Uganda, where the tribes on the frontier also took up arms. The daughter of the King of Ruanda was one of the leaders of the revolutionaries, who made their first strike at Gatsolon. There they killed a group of Belgian soldiers, officials, and native chiefs who were friendly with these whites. Belgian troops armed with modern weapons were brought to the scene, and against them the natives, armed only with spears and knives, battled for weeks. The masses of natives fled from the double scourge of famine and machine-guns. Where they fell, some of the bodies, still living, were devoured by wild animals. As was inevitable, the revolt was beaten down. The leaders fled through the swamps until they reached the Uganda frontier. There the British arrested them and handed them over to the Belgians. Over a thousand tribesmen were shot and a Belgian regiment and a British detachment of the East African Rifles were stationed in Kiforte, the centre of the revolt.

The difference between the native under Belgian imperialism plain and simple, and Belgian imperialism carrying out the mandate of the League of Nations, is that the Belgian government presents a report at Geneva on the working of the mandate. The native, however, is not likely to know this.

The post-war period in South Africa has given us at least two clearly-marked types of Negro revolutionary activity, the Bondelzwarts revolt and the Industrial and Commercial Workers' Union. The Bondelzwarts revolt belongs in spirit to the early tribal revolts, that of the tribes beating their heads against a wall.

The Bondelzwarts are a tribe of Hottentots inhabiting the extreme southern portion of South-West Africa. They have actually never been fully conquered by Europeans, and their history is full of struggles against the Germans. After their last rebellion against the German Government, the leaders of the tribe, Jacobus Christian and Abraham Morris, were compelled to leave the territory and reside in the Cape Province. When the Germans were defeated during the war, Jacobus Christian asked the new authorities for permission to enter. He was refused. But in 1919, disregarding the government's order, he returned to his native country. In April 1922, Abraham Morris, the other exiled leader, also returned home with a group of followers. On entering the territory he handed over his gun to the police, as required by the law. But the magistrate was not satisfied with that and, considering him a dangerous character, sent the police to arrest him and five of his followers. Morris resisted the arrest, and the people threatened to use violence on his behalf. When called upon to assist the police, all headmen refused, and the people working on the neighbouring farms abandoned their work and began to assemble at Haib, the headquarters of Jacobus Christian.

On 12 May, Major van Coller with a police force was sent to effect the arrest of the "five criminals". He sent a message to Jacobus Christian to come and see him at Dreihoek, but, seeing the trap, Christian refused. The discontent of the people suddenly crystallised around their leader's arrest. Patrols of armed Hottentots forcibly collected arms from isolated European farmers, and at one farm, as the administration later stated, "European women were forced to prepare and pour out coffee for the Hottentots".

On 16 May, Jacobus Christian sent a statement to the Administrator stating that the five men would immediately report to the magistrate on condition that he received an assurance, in writing, from the Administrator, that no further steps would be taken against his people. This the Administrator refused to do, and both sides prepared for an armed struggle. Haib, the headquarters of the Bondelzwarts, was placed under martial law by Jacobus Christian. Armed pickets guarded all the roads and passers-by were subjected to the scrutiny of these guards. When Major van Coller, being unable to make Christian come to Dreihoek, was compelled to go to see him at Haib, he, a major of the South-West African police, was stopped by armed pickets who allowed him to go to see the leader only after close examination. In his report he afterwards stated that the Bondelzwarts were all assembled and "judging from their dispositions they are prepared to meet an armed force. They gave attentive hearing and showed no hostility towards us, but there was visible demurrence when they were told that arms and ammunition were to be surrendered."

The struggle broke out on 26 May, 1922. The forces of the rebels were very poor. The tribe had only six hundred men capable of bearing arms, and these six hundred had only about one hundred rifles. Against this ill-armed force, the South African Government sent 445 well armed men, equipped with artillery, machine-guns, mechanical transport, and two aeroplanes. Yet the fighting lasted for nearly two weeks. The Bondelzwarts at first evaded big battles and tried to elude the Government forces. But they were surrounded and one big battle was fought in the mountains. Only the use of aeroplanes, something new and unexpected to the black warriors, compelled them to surrender. The number of killed will probably never be known. This was essentially a tribal revolt of the old pre-war type. But the resistance reached a pitch of calm determination to fight and die rather than give in, which makes it one of the most significant of African risings.

The Bondelzwarts revolt was an anchronism in 1922. The Union of South Africa is marked by a new type of political action — not the instinctive revolt of primitive tribes, but the militant action of the proletariat in the towns. Far more than in Sierra Leone and Gambia, South African industry has brought the natives together in factories, mines and on the docks, and the circumstances of their employment tended to drive them towards industrial organisation in the modern manner. There is also the influence of the Russian revolution. The South African Communist Party was founded only in 1924, but it had its origins in a previous organisation which was already in existence in 1920. It directed its propaganda chiefly to the natives. But whereas in Sierra Leone and Gambia the Negro intelligentsia of the left for the moment are more vocal than effective, the South African system allows very few of these to exist and drives even the few that are there into militant opposition. From these post-war conditions and the economic and political crisis of 1919 sprang the Industrial and Commercial Workers' Union of South Africa.

It was formed in 1919 by a Nyasaland native, Clements Kadalie, and the organisation began with only twenty-four members. Without any help in finance, experience or encouragement, suffering persecution and arrest, these built a movement which matured in strikes, demonstrations and battles with the police, while white South Africa watched its incredible growth with alarm. Kadalie, as a native of Nyasaland, could easily have been deported, but somehow he escaped this fate and drove his movement forward.

The first sign of the ICU's real strength was the Port Elizabeth strike of 1920. The Port Elizabeth workers, mainly unskilled labourers, had demanded and obtained an increase of sixpence a day. In February 1920, a branch of the ICU was formed in Port Elizabeth. This demanded a further increase of sixpence a day and as a consequence of fresh agitation, the workers obtained it. But this did not satisfy them and, on the advice of Kadalie, the President of the ICU, they advanced a demand for a minimum daily wage of ten shillings for unskilled male workers and seven shillings and sixpence for adult females. Meetings were held all over the district by the ICU, at which workers were called upon to insist on this demand even to the point of a strike. This ICU agitation had a tremendous effect. Feeling was running high and the influence of Kadalie was increasing. At one meeting, the feelings of the workers were so aroused that some made a physical attack on Dr Rubusama, also a Negro, who was known to be opposed to Kadalie. Dr Rubusama was only rescued by Kadalie who, on seeing his danger, immediately intervened.

The police, in the meanwhile, were looking for an excuse to

arrest Kadalie. This attack on Dr Rubusama was used as a pretext. Rubusama made an affidavit concerning the attack on him, and Kadalie was arrested on 23 October 1920, without a warrant.

When news of the arrest became known, the workers congregated in the nearest square. A meeting was held and a deputation was sent to the police to ask for the release of Kadalie on bail. The chief of police refused. When the deputation returned with this news the meeting resolved to send an ultimatum to the police: unless Kadalie was released by five o'clock, they would release him themselves. The South African native was openly challenging not only white employers but the actual forces of the state.

The whole police force was armed. The railway police were called out. In addition, European volunteers were armed and stationed in front of the police station where Kadalie was detained. By five o'clock the demonstration numbered three thousand people.

The mounted police were ordered to charge, but they were unhorsed. An attempt was made to disperse the crowd by means of a water-hose. But the masses replied with stones and other missiles. At this stage two shots were fired and the crowd began to retreat. It was at this moment, while the crowd was running, that the police opened fire upon it. The official Commission of Inquiry stated:

> "It is established beyond doubt that immediately after the first shots were fired, the crowd stampeded in all directions, and that a rapid and sustained fusillade was directed on the retreating crowd from the police station for sixty seconds, as alleged by some witnesses, or two minutes as alleged by others. One civilian admitted firing 15 shots; another as many as 13 shots, with the most fatal results, viz.: 1 European and 23 natives or coloured males were killed or died of wounds. Native and coloured males wounded, 45; females, 1. European females wounded, 4. Total casualties, 76. Only two of these were shot immediately in front of the steps, the others fell in different parts of the street away from the police station, as far as Castle Street, 100 yards distant."

Obviously the police were seizing the opportunity to smash the workers' organisation once and for all. The net result, as so often, was to increase its strength.

So powerful a force did the ICU become among the Bantu and coloured people that Hertzog, a future Prime Minister of South Africa, thought it profitable to seek the support of the ICU in the Cape Province. He sent a very cordial letter to Kadalie, enclosing a donation to the ICU, saying that he was sorry that he could not do more.

Of course, immediately Hertzog gained power, he persecuted the ICU even more fiercely. But the movement continued to grow, and in 1926 it reached its peak. In that year it had a membership of 100,000. Teachers were leaving the profession to become agents of the ICU. In remote villages of South Africa one could find a representative. Many who had not joined rallied to it in time of difficulty.

It will be difficult to overestimate what Kadalie and his partner, Champion, achieved between 1919 and 1926. Kadalie was an orator, tall, with a splendid voice, and at his meetings he used to arouse the Bantu workers to great heights of enthusiasm. At the conclusion of the speech his hearers were usually silent for some seconds before they were able to begin the applause. Champion was the very opposite of Kadalie in everything. More backward in outlook than Kadalie, who was aware of the working-class movement as an international force, he saw very little beyond Zululand, or Natal, and he was more organiser than orator.

The real parallel to this movement is the mass uprising in San Domingo. There is the same instinctive capacity for organisation, the same throwing up of gifted leaders from among the masses. But whereas there was a French revolution in 1794 rooting out the old order in France, needing the black revolution, and sending out encouragement, organisers and arms, there was nothing like that in Britain. Seen in that historical perspective, the Kadalie movement can be understood for the profoundly important thing it was.

After 1926 the movement began to decline. It could not maintain itself for long at that pitch without great and concrete successes. It was bound to stabilise itself at a less intense level. Kadalie lacked the education and the knowledge to organise it on a stable basis — the hardest of all tasks for a man of his origin. There was misappropriation of the funds. He saw the necessity for international affiliation. But though the constitution of the organisation condemned capitalism, he would not affiliate to the Third International. The white South African workers refused his offer of unity, for these, petty-bourgeois in outlook owing to their high wages and the social degradation of the Negro, are among the bitterest enemies of the native workers. Kadalie came to Europe, affiliated the ICU to the International Federation of Trade Unions and sought the help of left-wing Labour members. He took back a white man, Ballinger, to assist him. But the decline of the ICU continued. The organisation split. Today the two sections are but a shadow of the early ICU, and Kadalie keeps a café in Port Elizabeth, where formerly the workers had been shot down while demonstrating for his release.

1938

5

British Barbarism in Jamaica:
Support the Negro Workers' Struggle!

[*Occasioned by the general strike and riots of 1937-8 in Jamaica,
this article appeared in the June 1938 issue of* Fight, *the newspaper
of the Revolutionary Socialist League, of which James was a leading member. It is interesting to note the development which takes
place between this article and "The Revolutionary Answer to the
Negro Problem" of ten years later (see no. 9), which similarly
touches on the connection of the black struggle to the socialist
movement.*]

> "I cannot believe that I was unsound in stating that the West
> Indian labourer does not even remotely resemble the English
> labourer."
>
> Leonard Lyle, President, Tate and Lyle Ltd
> (from a letter to *The Times*, 10 May 1938)

Tate & Lyle, as everyone who buys sugar should know, make a
fortune every year by selling to the British workers sugar grown
by Jamaican workers. They must keep these two divided at all
costs. Hence with that solemn shamelessness so characteristic of
British capitalism, Mr Lyle discovers that the West Indies labourer
does not remotely resemble the English labourer. The real trouble
is, of course, that he resembles the English labourer too much for
Mr Capitalist Lyle.

Jamaica is the largest of the British West Indian islands, and
has a population of almost a million, the majority negroes. The
negroes are descendants of slaves whom the British capitalists
agreed to free a hundred years ago because slave-labour in the
West Indies no longer paid. These negroes today have no language
but English, they have lost touch with Africa, their outlook is
Western, and in some islands over three-quarters of the population
is literate. But white capital has always dominated the islands and
continues to do so. The government is in the hands of the whites,
local and British. These give the coloured middle class good jobs
in the civil services to keep them quiet. The constitution of the
government gives a grudging concession here and there, but the
Colonial Office sees to it that power remains in the hands of the
Governor.

Sir Leonard Lyle will say it is because the West Indian labourer
does not resemble the British. But there is more in it than that,
much more.

In 1929 came the crisis and British capitalism was up to the nose. What was to be done? Not very much, but they could at least squeeze the colonies a little more. At Ottawa they decided to keep cheap Japanese goods out of the colonies and make these blacks, so different from the British worker, buy higher priced goods with lower wages. The islanders had no say in the matter, being of course under the benevolent protection of Britain. The result was widespread misery. Then came "recovery", i.e. unemployment became $1\frac{1}{2}$ million instead of $2\frac{1}{2}$. But profits went up. The West Indian labourer can read and write. He could see the profits going up, but he still had to live on his one or two shillings a day. Further, on some of the sugar estates the workers still lived in the hovels of fifty years back. The workers know about the social services in Britain, unemployment pay, small as it is, etc. But they are not allowed to have trade unions. They demanded better pay and better standards. The employers, like Leonard Lyle, however, thought that these men were impertinent. The result has been a series of riots in which the government has not hesitated to shoot, arrest leaders, imprison and deport agitators. But the situation is so bad and the workers so determined that the government and the capitalists see that they have to make some concessions, and gestures such as a few new houses, etc. They have allowed trades unions in Trinidad but they want them controlled by the government.

What the West Indian workers need is a radical change in the whole system of government. In 1897 a commission went to the West Indies and recommended that the big estates be broken up and peasant proprietors established. The secretary was a young man who in 1930 went back again on another commission, this time as chairman, Lord Olivier. He recommended again that the uneconomic estates should be broken up. But nothing has been done. The government is in the hands of the capitalists and planters and they are concerned with themselves and their profits. Trade unions? Manhood suffrage? A government elected by the people? Impossible! For, says Sir Leonard Lyle, the West Indian labourer is fundamentally different from the British worker.

A powerful movement is now well under way in all the islands. The British workers must support it. Once the West Indian workers have their democratic rights they are able and willing to struggle. The magnificent general strike in Trinidad proves that, as does the militancy of the Trinidad workers. Citrine and Transport House take no initiative in helping to organise them. The British workers must, in their unions, press for full democratic rights for the West Indian workers. Tate and Lyle are planning to open factories in Jamaica. They want to take advantage of labour which has not the right as yet to protect itself. Thus black is used against white and Leonard Lyle seeks to poison the mind of the British worker against

On 23 May, American sailors in the harbour of Kingston, the colonials.

Jamaica, refused to blackleg on the black dock workers and collected subscriptions for the strikers. That is true international solidarity. British workers will not be behindhand. Those who wish to send a resolution of protest to the Colonial Office, or of solidarity to the West Indians and a subscription, however small, can do so through the office of *Fight* or through the International African Service Bureau of 129 Westbourne Grove, an organisation devoted to the interests of the negro struggle.

1938

6

Down With Starvation Wages in South-East Missouri

[*James participated in the sharecroppers' strike in South-East Missouri in 1942, and the following pamphlet was published by Local 313 of the CIO-affiliated agricultural workers' union at Lilbourn, South Delmo Project. He has this to say about it:*

"This is a wonderful piece of work. I'll tell you why. I went down to Missouri and decided that the only thing that we could do, after I'd discussed with them, was to have a strike; the sharecroppers should have their own strike, and it was very successful in fact. But the pamphlet has an importance that must be noted. When the time came for us to have the strike, I called some of the leaders together and said, 'We have to publish something, for everybody to read about it.' They said yes. So I sat down with my pen and notebook and said, 'Well, what shall we say? So (I used to call myself Williams) they said, 'Well, Brother Williams, you know.' I said, 'I know nothing. This is your strike. You all are doing it, you have to go through it. I have helped you, but this pamphlet has to state what you have to say. Now, have you got something to say about what you think?' And I went through each of them, five or six of them; each said his piece, and I joined them together. Everybody said what he thought was important. I didn't write anything, none of them wrote it. . . . They said what they thought and I put it together."]

Black and White UNITE AND FIGHT!

WORKERS OF SOUTH-EAST MISSOURI

COTTON-CHOPPING IS BEGINNING. The landlords are going round offering $1.25 here. Then over there they offer $1.50. Then, where they think the workers are strong, they say they will pay $1.75 if other people will pay it. Workers, white and colored, have none of this. We want 30c an hour or we will not work.

BROTHERS AND SISTERS, for years we have starved at $1.00 a day. Then $1.25. We work from can to can't for $1.25. All of us know that we can't do that any longer. The Government is buying up all the cotton. The landlords are getting a good price. They are prosperous. Only we who produce the cotton are starving. The cost of living is higher than ever, but we still get the same pay.

THE GOVERNMENT SAID IT WOULD HELP the croppers through the A. A. A. The landlord made us into day laborers and stole the money we should have got. Now they give us a little crop of six acres. We can't live on it, but by that they hope to tie us down so that we can do day labor for them. They are fooling themselves if they think that they are fooling us. Long ago we used to make a little corn on the side. They stopped that. Little by little we are starving to death. We live in shacks where the rain comes in through a hundred holes and we have nothing to wear. Year after year it's the same thing, only worse. Now when at last we start to organize, they tell us to sacrifice for the war. We have nothing to sacrifice with.

WE CAN'T GO ON LIKE THIS. We have to better our position. We have had nothing to do since picking finished in December. After the chopping is finished in June, we will have nothing to do until September. For 8 months of the year we starve. Now that a little work is coming we must get a decent pay. Otherwise we are not men and women, we are just animals. We are worse than animals. The landlords feed the animals when they are not working. They don't feed us. We have to change these conditions and we can only change them by struggle.

YOU REMEMBER THE GREAT DEMONSTRATION in 1939. In 1940 Governor Stark heard that we wanted to make another one. He offered us 10,000 houses. But it was only to fool the workers. We only get 800, but we got SOMETHING because we struggled.

TO GET A DECENT WAGE we must struggle again. Now is the time. The cotton must be chopped or it will spoil. We don't want the cotton to spoil, but we want to live. The cotton is carefully cultivated. The animals are tended. The landlords are carefully fed and housed. They see to that. All of this comes from the cotton. But we who plough the land and plant the cotton and chop the cotton and pick the cotton — we are treated worse than stray dogs.

NO MORE OF THAT. That is going to stop now. We want a decent wage. If we get it, we will work. If we don't get it we will not work.

A child can understand our demands.

DEMANDS

1. *30c an hour for day of 10 hours*
2. *Tractor drivers to get 45c an hour*
3. *Time and a half for overtime*

Look at those demands. Is it a crime to ask for them? 30c is lower than even what the W. P. A. pays, and the W. P. A. is only relief. 10 hours a day is long enough for any man to work at hard labor in the Missouri sun. Nobody is doing us a favor by giving us work. The landlords will work us 24 hours a day if they get the chance. We must have a limit fixed. After that we must get more. The tractor drivers are doing skilled labor sitting on the tractor all day, sometimes at night. They must be well paid. That is what we must die for. We may have to die for democracy in Java or in Iceland. We can die for 30c an hour here first.

HOW TO STRUGGLE

To win these demands is simple. You must join the union. The old locals must be revived. New locals must be formed. If even you haven't a charter, call a meeting, write for a charter, saying you will pay afterwards, and begin to function like a local. All you have to do is to get in contact with Local No. 313, Lilbourn, South Delmo Project. The U. C. A. P. A. W. A. gave us full authority to fight and if need be strike to raise our wages. Bring everybody from your district in.

Don't work unless the landlord pays the 30c an hour. Just listen to the instructions which your leaders will work out together and bring back to you. Above all, Solidarity.

White and colored together like one race, the race of labor. United we stand. Divided we fall.

Every man pledges himself not to lift a stroke until he and all the others with him get 30c an hour. If the landlord offers 29½c don't take it. If he offers 30c an hour to 99 workers and leaves out one, don't take it. That will divide us and if we are divided we are lost. If you have started to work, stop.

Above all, no fighting, no disorder. The landlords will try to start race riots. They will provoke us. They will spread lies and rumors about Jap agents and Reds. Pay no attention. Listen to your leaders and the instructions of your committee. We are law-abiding citizens exercising our rights. It is better we die than live as we have been living.

SOLIDARITY, LABORERS OF SOUTH-EAST MISSOURI. WHITE AND COLORED TOGETHER. ONE FOR ALL AND ALL FOR ONE.

TO THE WHITE WORKERS ESPECIALLY

Brothers, you are workers just like we are. The landlords tell you not to join us because we are Black. What we want is to unite with you in the union. Don't you want 30c an hour just like us? You want it as much as we want it. If we only join together and fight the landlords together, they will have to pay. Their only hope is to keep us apart. We must join together. We Must. If we don't join we will continue to be as we are. Form your local. Get together a little group of workers. Then go to any colored worker you know and ask him what his group is doing. We are coming to you but do not wait on us. You come to us too. Let us meet half way. Forget the old prejudice. We have suffered more from it than you and we are willing to forget it. You must forget it too. For years you have listened to the politicians and the preachers of race prejudice. What have you got for it? Nothing but starvation, just like us. Join the union with us. Then we will tell the landlord that he will pay us all 30c an hour or he will chop his cotton himself. If he wouldn't pay then we won't work, white and colored together. All the troubles we have had in the past we must forget. This is no time to remember them. There was a lynching in Sikeston the other day and the Negroes are bitter about it, but that lynching was a landlords' trick to divide us. All our brothers in Sikeston are ready to join with you in the most important thing before you and before us — the fight for 30c an hour.

Look at the South, brother white worker. It is the most miserable part of America. Why? Because of the division between us. Are you going to sit down and let this go on forever? We know that some of you are thinking differently. But you must not only think. You must act. Be quick. Join the union. Fight with us and a new day will begin for the working people of Missouri.

LIES ABOUT JAP AGENTS

The landlords and the newspapers, and their secret and open supporters, call the union men Jap agents. Simply because we demand 30 cents an hour. So a man is a Jap agent when he says he will not work for $1.25 a day. If that is so, every landlord, every worker in the government, every county prosecutor is a Jap agent. For not one of them would work for $1.25 a day. We are not Jap agents. We are American citizens. Our labor built this country and we don't want any Hitler, or Mussolini or any Japanese ruling us. We say again that we are not Jap agents but loyal American citizens. But a man who has to live on 12 cents an hour only is a citizen in name. In reality he is a slave. Are we traitors to our country because when we work for six weeks out of 36 we say we should make at least 18 dollars a week? Cursed is the man who calls a worker a Jap agent because he demands 30 cents an hour. He is a slanderer. He is the enemy of democracy, not the worker. He is the traitor, he is the fifth columnist and he is the sixth columnist too, because he is spreading lying rumors, to discredit honest workers.

TO THE MERCHANTS

We say to the merchants: Why don't you support us? Every penny we get we spend with you. We cannot save anything. If we get 30 cents an hour it means we are able to buy a little more lard, a little more bread, a piece of meat once a week while the money lasts. After that we'll starve again. But it all goes to the merchant, to raise his income. So we look to the merchant, especially the little merchant, to support us, and stand by us if we are compelled to strike. If during the strike we ask for a little credit, then the merchant must give it.

TO THE OFFICIALS OF THE F. S. A.

We look to the officials of the F. S. A. for support. You and the home economists and the county demonstrators are always coming around to us telling us to eat liver and to eat eggs, for Vitamin A and Vitamin B. You tell us to give the children cod liver oil and milk. We can get eggs only if we learn to lay them and we can give the children milk only if we turn into cows. We are willing to give the children all you say. You see them once a month when you come around. We see them every day growing up hungry and starving and cold without clothes to wear. 30 cents an hour will not be much but it will be a beginning. We shall look to see if you are with us in this struggle. We want to see if you really want us to have eggs and liver and Vitamin A and Vitamin B. Don't you come telling us to think of our responsibilities to American labor and the duty to the Nation. We know our responsibility to American labor and the duty to the Nation. We know our responsibility to American labor. It is to get 30 cents an hour. Go and tell the landlords about the duty to the Nation. We are part of the Nation. If you want us to get vitamins, come out in support of our demand for 30 cents an hour. Say that we need it and must have it and that the landlords must pay. Otherwise we don't want to hear any more of your Vitamin A and Vitamin B.

TO LABOR ALL OVER THE COUNTRY

But it is to labor all over the country we appeal, to our brother workers. You have struggled for what you have, your 60 or your 80 cents an hour and time and a half for overtime. You get it every day in the year, at least while the war lasts. You have the right of collective bargaining. We have nothing, we are trying to get something. We appeal to you for support. We appeal to you to pass resolutions, to send telegrams to John L. Lewis and William Green and Phillip Murray. Ask them to help us put an end to this criminal state of affairs where workers work for 12c an hour, where landlords come in and break up our meetings. The police help them to do it as they did at Carruthersville. The workers in coal, in steel, in shoe factories, the garment workers, the warehouse workers, all of the truck drivers — remember us. Take up the battle for us. If we are compelled to come out on strike, send us food and money and raise your voices for us. We followed all the big battles you fought. We were always with you. We are proud to be in the ranks of organized labor. Help us now to win a simple living wage for six weeks out of 36. We shall be ready to support you when the time comes. We are labor men fighting for labor's rights. And who must help us but labor?

THE PREACHERS

All the preachers must get their flock together and preach to them about the union and solidarity in the struggle. If a preacher is not with us he is against us. That is the Voice of Scripture. Also the Laborer is worthy of his hire. That is Scripture also. We are worthy of 30c an hour. God helps those who help themselves. That is Scripture too. Solidarity in the Union, that is the way to get the Kingdom of Heaven upon Earth.

COME TO THE MASS MEETING

DEMANDS

1. *30c an hour for 10 hours*
2. *Tractor Drivers to get 54c an hour*
3. *Time and a half for overtime*

1942

7

Laski, St Paul and Stalin

[*Harold Laski's* Faith, Reason and Civilisation *was published in 1944. James's article is not simply a review, but an opportunity for him to develop his discussion of contemporary politics against the background of broader historical and cultural issues to which he later turned increasing attention. The article appeared under the pseudonym of "J. R. Johnson" in the June 1944 issue of* The New International, *New York.*]

The title of Laski's new book, *Faith, Reason and Civilisation*, is very accurate. He seeks by reason ("historical analysis") to give civilisation (capitalism in decline) a new faith (stalinism).

Yet this book is strange and new. Laski, ardent supporter of the imperialist war, begins by a strong tribute to the heroic deeds of European youth in the war against Hitler. But as he sees victory aproaching he fears that all this sacrifice and effort may have been in vain. Laski says, as he has so often said before, that capitalism must be superseded. But Churchill, the great hero of Britain in the war, is a hopeless reactionary who admired Mussolini as long as Mussolini did not attack Britain. Everywhere the outlook for the capitalist democracies is, on the whole, gloomy. We need a new faith, new values. Then the reader, with no more preparation, is hurled 2,000 years back into the world of early Christianity.

"Political convulsion seems to combine with intellectual decay to wreck the foundations of the Roman civilisation." But the great writers of the Bible, "Amos or the Second Isaiah . . . Saint Paul", by "the magic of their alchemy could not only promise regeneration to an Empire in decline; by the age of Constantine they had come to dominate the whole outlook of the Western world". It is the magic of Laski's alchemy which makes Amos and Isaiah promise regeneration to the Roman Empire. Though it is true that if they and Paul had promised any such thing they could have promised it only by magic. Let us, however, follow what Laski actually tries to do. He has by now reached Chapter IV, significantly entitled "Ideas as Acts". The argument is now in full blast. We cannot quote indefinitely. Page 27 should be read and re-read. Briefly, "The victory of Christianity over paganism meant a revitalisation of the human mind". And Laski immediately poses the question: "I do not think anyone can examine with care our contemporary situation without being constantly reminded that we again require some faith that will revitalise the human mind. Almost as clearly as in the declining days of the Roman Empire, our scheme of values seems to have broken down."

It is impossible to make head or tail of this historically. The Roman Empire really began to decline some two centuries at the very least after Amos, Isaiah and Paul. After Constantine adopted Christianity as the official religion, the Roman Empire fell into greater difficulties than ever. Laski, however, goes on to give us two chapters, one on the recovery, and the other on the substance of faith. Faith. Faith. Values. Values. He then proceeds to discuss "The Soviet Idea and Its Perspectives" and "The Soviet Idea and Victory". By now we are at Page 63. Then follows the longest chapter in the book, fifty-seven pages on "The Source of New Values". This is what really concerns Laski. His next chapter, on Epicurus and Lucretius, is proof of his interests in this book. It is only then that he takes up the modern theme, Bolshevism and capitalism, and moves rapidly to a conclusion. Laski does not deign to argue about stalinist Russia. He takes its desirability for granted. Like the Dean of Canterbury but with less excuse he falls back always on "Verily, verily, I say unto you . . .", "No one can help feeling . . .", "No one can deny . . .", and so on, whenever he wishes to make a point about Russia in particular. As the scheme of his book shows, he is concerned primarily with early Christianity and the search for values. We have written before and will write again of the "labour faker" politics of Laski. What we propose to do here is to deal with him on the ground he has chosen. He claims to be exhibiting "in a general way the marxist approach to the issues with which [he] deals". The only way to expose satisfactorily this claim is to show what we consider the marxist way of dealing with these issues. Thus we shall expose the falseness of his historical method, which is in direct co-relation with the falseness of his political conclusions and is either the cause or the effect of them.

It is today common knowledge that the state cult of religion in the classical world was aimed deliberately at keeping the masses in subjection. In two important periods, in Greece during the time of Epicurus and in the Rome of Lucretius, a philosophical movement fiercely attacked the official state mysticism. On each occasion the movement gained wide support among intellectuals, though the extent to which it gained really popular support is disputed. It is characteristic of Laski's historical analysis that he reports the desertion of the movement by the intellectuals because they feared the revolt of the masses, and then immediately loses himself in moral denunciations of them for doing so. Their desertion, according to him, resulted in the victory of "superstition", which dominated society and defeated "reason".

This, it is presumed, is marxism. In reality this is no more than petty-bourgeois radicalism. On a question so crucial to his whole argument, Laski does not have a single word to say about the social relations as they developed at the given stage of the process of production. This is his fundamental error and the error of most of his kind. The intellectuals who attacked the state religions of Greece and Rome were not intellectuals in general whose supineness we must note and beware of. They were the fruit of a rising "bourgeoisie", and as such were the protagonists of a materialist philosophy directed against the mysticism of a landowning aristocracy. One suggestive investigator claims that this "bourgeoisie" was an investing "bourgeoisie". In a commercial society, the relation between debtor and creditor, producer and consumer, becomes an abstract relation. The investor therefore sees himself as an isolated individual, in opposition to the landowner of the Gens who sees himself as part of an organic society. As carefully as he calculates his investments he calculates his pleasures, hence the hedonism of the Epicureans. In physics he sees nature as a collection of atoms united together in an ordered universe, etc. But this incipient capitalism which at various periods in the classical world was able to challenge landed property never became economically strong enough to supersede it. Marx states that the history of Rome was the history of landed property. No less and no more. No rival class emerged. The final breakdown of that economic order threw the whole society into chaos. Intellectuals, faithful or unfaithful, could not have saved it.

Yet Laski writes sentence after sentence like this: "The Rome that Sallust depicts for us had already begun to lose that inner integrity. . . ." Inner integrity indeed! Maybe that inner integrity was saved by the magic alchemy of Amos and Isaiah. But lost in the pursuit and recovery of inner integrity and faith and values, Laski shows little conception of Christianity in its relation to social forces. Hear him again: "In the result it [Christianity] had relatively little influence on the realm of social constitution because. . . ." Because what? Because "as it was shaped by Paul and his successors it emphasised this life only as the vestibule to eternity, and put the chief importance of its dreams on the next world rather than upon this." Why did they do this? And if they did this, why did Christianity become ultimately such a powerful force? There is no serious treatment of this in these pages, devoted as we have seen to drawing historical inspiration and contemporary enlightenment from the study of this period. We must develop this subject ourselves briefly. The values of Christianity are as intimately related to the values of the modern world as embryo is to mature man. The true historical connection will lead us straight to the heart of the modern problem and the fallacy of stalinism as a source of values for a decaying society.

The rise of early Christianity took place in historical connection with the decline of republican Rome. Ancient Rome was in unending chaos and it was only during the first century AD that the Augustan era opened up a new period of stabilisation under the Caesars. The decline of the public authority broke the traditional hold upon the mind of the masses. Paul might write as he pleased. The masses for their part believed that the end of the world was at hand. They confidently expected the second coming of Christ. That was their slogan for the building of a new society.

Few things are more historically dramatic, moving and significant, than this outcome of the recognition of human personality on a mass scale. But even along with that expectation of Christ's coming the early Church tried "to heal the sick, to feed the hungry, to succour the diseased, to rescue the fallen, to visit the prisoners, to forgive the erring, to teach the ignorant. . . ." This tremendous mass movement itself attempted to form a new society on earth. It failed as it was found to fail, but its greatness lay in the fact that it unequivocally established that all human beings were equal in the sight of God at least. In classical society the slave was a thing. The mere presentation of the doctrine of Christianity was revolutionary. It revitalised ancient thought. Good. But let us not forget what these early Christians actually tried to do. The revitalisation of the human mind was the second best and the result of the attempt to revitalise the human body.

When the Roman Empire which had unified European civilisation finally disintegrated into the isolated manorial units, Christianity, i.e. the Church, succeeded to the power of the Emperors. To confine the argument to the West, the Church it was which *organised production* in monastic centres. Priests and monks owned land and on the large domains *took the lead in the organisation of agriculture.* Possessing such tradition of learning as remained, the Church became the most powerful economic, social, and political force in the early medieval world. The secular feudal lords worked hand in hand with the Church. In time, however, urban civilisation revived in a commercial form. Once more, on this basis, a materialist philosophy, rationalism, became a force. But this time the intellectuals and rebel churchmen had a firmer social basis and Christianity had to make concessions. St Thomas Aquinas achieved a rationalisation of theology with philosophy. Catholicism proclaimed anew the unity of European civilisation. But whereas the Roman Empire had unified Europe but had divided the world into civilised and barbarians, the medieval Church admitted the equality of all nations. Whereas the Roman unity had been based on slavery, the medieval serf had not only a religious but a legal presonality. He could have a wife and family and own movables. And if he could not gain equality on earth, at least it could be his in heaven and meanwhile God had his representative on earth, the Catholic Church. What had been in Paul's day the leader of a popular mass movement was now the ruler of the civilised world. Today, as for centuries past, the church, having no economic power, can only attach itself to reaction.

Yet Laski with his concern about values and faith, spends page after page discussing, in the twentieth century, the value of Catholicism as a source of new values. "So that when men like Mr Dawson plead so persuasively for the return of the unity of Christian civilisation, especially for its return under the aegis of the Pope, the outsider is, I think, bound to ask upon what basis, especially in the realm of mind and morals, the return is to be effected. . . ." How delicate a negative! Laski understands nothing of Christianity, neither the early flowering nor the late maturity nor its futility today. The first eruption did not owe its power to "mind and morals". The Church in its most powerful days did not owe its power to "mind and morals". And before seriously considering the Pope as a world-leader today, "especially in the realm of mind and morals", Laski should reflect on the historical method of Stalin whose state is to be one source of the new values. It is reported that at one session of the Teheran Conference Roosevelt and Churchill discoursed at length on the role of the Vatican in post-war Europe. Stalin so pointedly refrained from taking part that these two co-thinkers of Laski on the importance of the Pope asked Stalin what was his opinion. Whereupon Stalin asked, "How many divisions has the Pope?" The discussion ceased.

Yet as we have stated there is a historical (and logical) connection between Christianity and the modern world. Only the truth is exactly the opposite of what Laski, with his perpetual petty-bourgeois concern over abstract values, thinks it is. Modern socialism is the concretisation of the desires and demands of Christianity both in its primitive and in its advanced stages. What the masses for centuries had to transfer to heaven is now and increasingly the aim of their daily lives. This must be grasped in its entirety. The early Church did make an effort to create the kingdom of heaven upon earth by helping the poor and the afflicted. The medieval Church preached the equality of nations and the unity of European civilisation under one visible ruler, the Catholic Church.

So far then medieval thought represented a social ideal infinitely superior to the best classical thought. Still it was only an ideal. Its only hope of embodiment was transferred to a celestial sphere. But the outstanding feature of the contemporary world is that the *principles* for which Christianity stood in its best days are now regarded as matters of life and death by the average worker. This is no accident at all though we can only state the facts here. European civilisation must become a unity? Hundreds of millions of European workers know that this must be achieved or the continent will perish. Equality of nations? That, too, the great masses of Europe passionately desire, not as an ideal but to be able to live in peace. A central government to represent the interests of all? As late as 1935, Lord Cecil could get eleven million votes in a plebiscite in Britain supporting the idea of a League of Nations. And when workers say a League of Nations and collective security they mean it. And that early attempt to succour the poor, to the afflicted, to teach the ignorant? The great mass of the workers in European countries conceive of Labour Parties as doing just that, within the conditions of the modern world.

The whole history of civilisation since Christianity consists in the concretisation of the values proclaimed so abstractly (and in time deceitfully) by Christianity. Once the human personality had arrived at the stage of theoretical equality, the further progress of civilisation is to be judged by the degree to which this equality is realised. Furthermore, every step toward greater equality has meant a deepening of the very concept of human personality. Commercial capitalism brought the Renaissance and the Humanists. The birth of industrial capitalism brought the Reformation with its principle of individual responsibility. The growing maturity of industrial capitalism brought the concept of political freedom — the Rights of Man. *But with the deepening profundity of thought develop the spontaneous claims of the masses of the people.* After the French revolution European society produced the highest peaks of bourgeois thinking. Ricardo, Hegel, Shelley, Beethoven, Saint-Simon, Goethe, these men and their generation laid the theoretical foundations of modern society. But two decades afterwards the workers in the streets of Paris demanded for the first time "the social republic". We do not idealise the workers. Engels says quite bluntly that what this social republic was to be they did not know. But the very bourgeois society which had produced its most gifted body of thinkers and artists had also given birth to a proletariat which instinctively demanded the application to itself of every value which the philosophers and the various classes they represented had demanded through the ages.

He who would exhibit the marxist method must grasp the full significance of that early uprising of the masses when Christianity proclaimed its message. We must watch not only the primitiveness and simplicity of its aims but their comprehensive scope. Then, by slow degrees, through the centuries, we see one part of the aim becoming concrete for one section of the population, and then another part for another section. Ideas arise from concrete conditions to become partially embodied in social classes and give rise to further interrelations between the spiral of real and ideal, content and form. This is the dialectic to which Marx gave a firm materialist basis in the developing process of production. As society develops, the possibilities for the individual development of man become greater and greater, but the conflict of classes becomes sharper and sharper. We stand today at an extreme stage of these interrelated phenomena of social development. When a modern worker demands the right of free speech, the right of free press, of free assembly, continuous employment, social insurance, the best medical attention, the best education, he demands in reality the "social republic". Spinoza and Kant would stand aghast at what the average worker takes for granted today. But he does not demand them as an individual or in the primitive manner the early Christian did. In America, for instance, there are some thirteen million workers organised for nothing else but the preservation and extension of these values. These are the values of modern civilisation. They are embodied in the very web and texture of the lives of the masses of the people. Never were such precious values so resolutely held as necessary to complete living by so substantial and powerful a section of society. Socialism means simply the complete expansion and fulfilment of these values in the life of the individual. This can only be attained by the most merciless struggle of the whole class against its capitalist masters. The realisation of this necessity is the final prelude to full self-consciousness. This is the basis of all values in contemporary society. All talk of values which does not see this is not only pernicious. It is dangerous. No man who understood this could jump across the centuries and seek a historical parallel for a modern faith in Amos and Paul. The abstract faith of those days is the concrete truth of today choked and stifled by capitalism. And no man who understood modern values would have to go looking anywhere for them. For those with eyes to see they are as big as mountains. Least of all would he go looking and finding them in stalinist Russia, where the ruling class is the mortal enemy of the working class. *If this is not so, why then the totalitarian state in Russia?* To see Laski wriggling in and around this dilemma is full of values as a lesson in faith. Tennyson, who looked into the future as far as human eye could see and saw the parliament of man, the federation of the world, would be in difficulties to recognise stalinist totalitarianism as its first instalment. But Laski's "faith" he knew and described perfectly in the famous line: "And faith unfaithful kept him falsely true."

It is time to place before these intellectuals, perpetually babbling about values, some of the elementary facts of modern life. Name any value you like. Artistic integrity? But it cannot exist in the totalitarian state. So powerful is the working class in a modern society, so widespread and rapid the means of transport and communication that once the working class is chained the totalitarian rulers dare not allow any innovation in any field. All effort must serve their domination or is *ipso facto* dangerous. The artist cannot live in an ivory tower in the totalitarian state. He cannot abstain. He must emerge from the ranks and shout his *Heil* or write his *Ode to Stalin* in manner more significant than the rest in accordance with his greater gifts.

The long overdue emancipation of women? But the totalitarian state passes the most reactionary laws and deprives woman of the gains she has made during over half a century. Witness the laws in stalinist Russia. The personal relationships of society? Where there is not free speech in public there cannot be free speech in private. There is no need to continue with the list. The values of democracy as defended by the working class are the values on which rest all other values, social, personal, artistic, critical, what you will. That is the culmination of the social development of two thousand years of civilisation. If the liberties of the working class are destroyed, the whole heritage of civilisation goes with them.

In America, Richard Wright and Martha Graham, Eugene O'Neill and John Dewey, James Farrell and Frank Capra, Wendell Willkie and Henry A. Wallace carry on their various activities by grace of the AFL and the CIO. Some of our politicos, literati, artists and others may not know this. The workers may not be aware of it either. It is true nevertheless, the great truth of our time. Furthermore, only the working class is organically a defender of democratic values. The middle class, or certain sections of it, under the whip of the social crisis, may throw over democracy and seek salvation from some fantastic doctrine. The farmers may follow their example. But organised labour occupies such a place in the social structure of an advanced community that *the greater the crisis, the more it must in its own self-defence defend its democratic rights,* and by so doing preserve all that is still valuable in the heritage of Western civilisation. Where these are at stake, as they are today, isn't it a crime to perpetuate this would-be philosophical prattle about values?

We can now draw the historical argument to a conclusion. Laski complains that, although we are on the eve of great changes in society, the period between 1914 and 1939 saw no great theoretical works heralding the new age, as had appeared in previous periods of social preparation. What blindness is this? It is of the same type which misses so completely the significance of the social revolution attempted by early Christianity and attributes a ridiculous significance to Amos and Isaiah. First of all, what has Laski himself been living on theoretically all these years but on parts of Lenin's *Imperialism,* to mention only one book? But secondly, he does not see that never before in history has social revolution been so openly and assiduously prepared for. He looks for books and does not see the Communist International in the days before Stalin began its emasculation. He looks for theories on law and government and does not see the unparalleled value for future society of the foundation of the *soviet* state by Lenin and Trotsky and its achievements, successes and failures until Stalin finally destroyed it by the constitution of 1936. The state resting on the soviets, the councils of the workers organised in the production process — this is what is new. How pitiable is this professor who has not a word of analysis of the new state form and the mountains of controversy it still evokes but complains that there are no books. Is greater proof needed of the bankruptcy of his historical method, alike in dealing with early Christianity, in discussing Papal leadership of modern society without a thought of the role of the Papacy in modern production, and now in bewailing the lack of great books during the last twenty-five years and using that as proof that the new society was not being prepared?

We denounce Laski's impudence in calling his vacuous theories an exhibition of the marxist method. We say that a marxist in discussing Christianity and the modern world should have at least indicated that the ideals of Christianity are embodied in the modern working-class movement.

We say finally that *for us, today,* the great inspiration of early Christianity is not the faith inspired by Amos, Isaiah and Paul. It is exactly the opposite. It is the fact that the masses, as soon as they felt themselves men, began straightaway to build the "social republic", or at least to expect it, and in our epoch we see their successors, organised labour, making mighty effort after mighty effort to destroy the hated old society and substitute the socialist order. What connection has Stalin's totalitarian state with all this except as its open enemy? "It is not yet clear that the kind of world envisaged after victory by Mr Churchill is the kind of world likely to appeal to Marshal Stalin. Such evidence as we have suggests that it is at least possible that they think on different lines." O delicate phrasemaker! You cannot even convincingly deceive yourself.

This is the fundamental political crime of Laski's book. He attempts to gild the totalitarian character of the stalinist state. He says: "If the Communist Party of the Soviet Union left the central principle of its faith to the chance decision of an electorate still in the phase where the denial of the socialist idea is the rule rather than the exception, that would be as remarkable as a willingness on the part of the Western democracies to see without repining the access of socialist parties to the state-power."

A generation after 1917 this is what Laski has the nerve to say of the electorate of Russia. He talks glibly of communism and the soviet idea. But that communism and the *soviet* idea represent a stage of democracy far beyond bourgeois democracy, to that he is totally impervious. He tells us that "the Soviet citizen enjoys what may perhaps be termed a democracy of the secondary order, the import of which we must not minimise". A democracy of a secondary order! Is this one of the new values? And what, pray, is a democracy of the secondary order? "He [the Soviet citizen] may not criticise Stalin. . . ." In other words, he may not criticise the economic, social or political policy of the state. Nay, more. When Stalin's sense of values decrees that Shostakovich's music is "modernistic" and needs to have "tunes", he cannot criticise that too. And when Molotov says that fascism is a question of taste, inasmuch as Molotov speaks for Stalin, the Soviet citizen cannot criticise that either. What is worse, he must immediately, at all meetings, public and private, heartily proclaim that fascism is a matter of taste. In return for this stultification, the Soviet citizen "can criticise his foreman or his manager; he can protest against the inefficiency of this factory or that farm or even department of state".

This is the democracy for which Laski so diligently seeks inspiration in early Christianity. Rickenbacker, a notorious reactionary, found Stalin's conception of the place of workers in stalinist society very satisfactory. And Eric Johnston, president of the United States Chamber of Commerce, told the Russian leaders that when he, as an American capitalist, looked at their guaranteed profit he felt "like a hero". The values that they found are more serious than Laski's. That the standard of living of the Russian masses is lower than it was before 1914 has no meaning for Laski.

What is worse is that Laski has the imprudence to use the term "élite" to describe the ruling class in his new society. This is no accident. It follows automatically from his attitude to the crimes committed by the Russian élite against the Russian people — "immense blunders and fantastic cruelties", to use his own words. He brazenly says: "I accept the ugliness of all these things and I do not even attempt to excuse them." And then this seeker after new values, having found them in this élite state, gives us a demonstration of the intellectual values with which he seeks new social values. "Few Roman Catholics would today defend the barbarities of the Inquisition; but they would deny that these barbarities disprove the validity of the Roman claim." It the Catholics can do it, why can't we? Once you abandon the democratic rights of the working class in contemporary society, all is lost, even logic and good sense.

Laski has two main points. He says that the structure of the Soviet economy allows the unlimited extension of consumer demand. That, we shall have to see. Secondly, he leans heavily on the Russian military victories which have without doubt been the outstanding military feature of the war. He forgets that modern Russia is the product of a revolution which wiped out the social sores of centuries and created a modern *people* in a modern *state*. No one in his senses denies that. And this modern state the workers and peasants decided to defend despite the crimes of the élite. What they really think of the élite we shall all have the opportunity of seeing in the coming period. We venture the opinion, however, that they will not think what Laski thinks.

Laski's book is characteristic of an increasing intellectual disintegration among intellectuals of all types. He may say, as he does in this one, that the intellectuals must take their stand with the masses. Any intellectual with Laski's ideas who takes his stand with the masses can only help to corrupt them. Daniel Bell in the May issue of *Politics* attacks Laski, but these two are of the same brand. Laski, running away from Churchill and proletarian power, embraces the stalinist "ethos" and bathes himself in the faith it gives. Bell detests the doctrine but agrees that it is religion. "The dividing line which modern society strove to maintain between religious and social facts has disappeared in Russia. . . . That is what gives it the unity and cohesion." From both of these the marxists have to separate themselves with an unrelenting hostility. The Russian proletariat of today is the product of the development of European civilisation. Nothing on earth can prevent its struggle for proletarian democracy. Bell confounds a modern proletariat with the masses of antiquity. It is Laski turned inside out.

It will be instructive to end with a glance at some of the most outstanding of those who, in recent years, whatever their differences, and we do not deny or minimise these differences, have one thing in common, rejection of the international socialist revolution as analysed by Lenin. Ortega y Gasset, a Spanish intellectual, wrote a book some years ago called *The Revolt of the Masses*.

Values concerned him. He was not looking for new ones. He wished to defend the old ones against the workers. They are now in the safe keeping of Franco. Julien Benda created a furore with his *The Treason of the Intellectuals*. They, these unfortunates, were not sufficiently concerned with spiritual values. Presumably these are now safe with Pétain and Laval. After a long lifetime spent in defending the sacred values of liberalism, Croce sought to put them into practice in the cabinet of Badoglio. Santayana, who wrote exquisitely on values for many years, now declares his sympathy for the values established and preserved as long as possible by Mussolini. Laski seeks and finds his spiritual home in Stalin's "democracy of a secondary type".

Sidney Hook, another expert shuffler of the value-cards, now concerns himself with the "hero" in history. Burnham goes back for inspiration to Machiavelli. At least he drew the line at Amos and Isaiah. And so they gyrate.

We, on the contrary, stand on the leninist ground that the present epoch is an epoch of imperialist war and proletarian revolution. We, under all circumstances, place foremost the defence of the working class as the defence of modern civilisation. Our task is to help in making the workers aware by precept and organisation of their great task of emancipation in a society which increasingly shoves the whole of humanity down the road to barbarism. Those are the values by which we live and we are the merciless enemy of those who, under whatever banner, seek to inject other values into the working-class movement.

1944

8

The British Vote for Socialism

[This article on the significance of the 1945 election results was one of several in which James, with his "Old World" background, familiarised his American comrades with European issues which in his opinion they were used to handling in the abstract; he also wrote on French and German politics of this period. The article appeared in the September 1945 issue of The New International, *under the pseudonym of "J. R. Johnson".]*

Few, if any, elections in modern times have had the significance and opened out perspectives on a scale comparable with the recent British election. Its evaluation can proceed along three main lines. The first is the meaning of it in relation to Britain itself. The second is its repercussions in Europe and the world. The third is its influence on the political development of the American working-class movement. These three can be separated only for purposes of convenience. If, for example, at the coming French elections in October, it were made clear that the British victory had stimulated the French electorate toward a repudiation of de Gaulle similar to the repudiation of Churchill, then the repercussion back on Britain would be tremendous. For the time being, however, we shall confine ourselves to the first — the significance of the election as a purely British phenomenon.

There is only one fundamental question which has to be decided. Is the election merely an unmistakable sign of a desire for "social progress", or a desire for social reconstruction of Britain, in a word, for socialism? The American bourgeoisie has been at pains in its press to explain that what the British workers in reality want is higher wages, greater social security, no unemployment, a vast housing programme, in general, improvement on the admittedly unsatisfactory conditions which prevailed before the war; be it understood also that the workers expect some reward also for the sacrifices endured during the war. Despite the warning notes uttered by some correspondents from abroad and a few commentators here, the emphasis has been upon the mild programme of nationalisation put forward by the Labour Party and upon the well known, alas, only too well known, sobriety and conservatism of the British labour leaders. American capitalism also, according to this theory, has played its own progressive part in this education of the British working class. American soldiers held forth to British workers on apartments with central heating and frigidaires and the high standard of living which had been granted to American labour by American capitalism. This stimulated the British working class to demand the same and therefore to vote Labour in overwhelming majority.

All these ideas are just so much whistling in the dark. As far as the great masses of the British people are concerned, their vote is a repudiation of British capitalist society in Britain and a mandate to the British Labour Party to institute socialism. The people who think or would like to think what the American bourgeoisie is teaching in its press are the British labour leaders. But we draw a sharp distinction between the masses of the British people as a whole and the labour and trade union bureaucracy, a distinction as sharp as that which Lenin in his time and Trotsky from the days of *Whither England?* to his death used to draw. The first purpose of this article is to make this clear, not by speculation into the psychology of the British working class, but by a review of the development of the British Labour Party and its relation to economic and social changes in Britain and in the world at large. It is sufficient to say that our approach is based on that conception of British development expressed consistently by Trotsky and nowhere so sharply as in his *History of the Russian Revolution*. There he writes: "Only a blind man could fail to see that Great Britain is headed for gigantic revolutionary earthquake shocks, in which the last fragments of her conservatism, her world domination, her present state machine, will go down without a trace. MacDonald is preparing these shocks no less successfully than did Nicholas II in his time, and no less blindly. So here, too, as we see, is no poor illustration of the problem of the role of the 'free' personality in history."

That was over a dozen years ago. Since then the British people have lived through tumultuous years. They are not blind men. Their vote is a declaration that they are not blind.

Marx and Engels knew the British working class very well. As far back as the Civil War in the United States, Marx, watching the reaction of the British people as a whole to this world-shaking event, paid a great tribute to what he called the "incontestable excellence" of the British working masses. This, he said, was the greatest strength of Britain. Over the years which followed, he and Engels agreed that, owing to the superior position of Britain on the world market, the English working class had become the most bourgeoisified working class in Europe. And this was likely to continue until Britain had lost its privileged position on the world market. In his preface to the English translation of *Capital*, published in 1886, Engels showed that for him a new stage had arrived in the development of the British proletariat. He said that the number of unemployed kept swelling from year to year and "we can almost calculate the moment when the unemployed, losing patience, will take their fate into their own hands".

What saved Britain and not only Britain but the advanced countries of Europe, was the development of imperialism. But imperialist super-profits could only keep a small portion of the working class enchained, and toward the end of the century a series of individual movements sprang up in Great Britain which in 1900 culminated in the formation of the British Labour Party. The formation of the British Labour Party coincided with the recognition by a substantial section of the British bourgeoisie that Britain was fast losing its domination of the world market. The statesman whose name is forever associated with this recognition was Joseph Chamberlain, father of Neville. At one time mayor of Birmingham and one of the most dynamic and far-seeing politicians of his day, Chamberlain claimed that Britain's policy of free trade was leading the country to catastrophe. Reversing the traditional policy of a century, he became a protectionist and when asked by the British Prime Minister what position he wanted in the Cabinet, he chose the theretofore unimportant post of Colonial Secretary. From 1900 to the present day, the history of Britain can be summarised as follows: consistent decline of the British economy upon the world market, increasing convulsions in Britain, uninterrupted growth of the Labour Party as a socialist party, preaching that the only salvation for Britain's difficulties was the "social ownership of the means of production, distribution and exchange". Who does not understand this cannot understand the British election. This is no question of a sudden clutching at a panacea by the British people, or a psychological change in the minds of the electorate or a violent revulsion against the war. As is characteristic of Britain, the idea of socialism is permeated with constitutional illusions. But the vote for socialism is the culmination of a process which can be easily traced.

The first stage is the Liberal-Labour government of Asquith. Between 1906 and 1914, Lloyd George carried out a series of measures aimed at increasing social security in Great Britain. This was done for the specific and avowed purpose of preventing the growth of socialism. The power of the House of Lords was broken by the Asquith-Lloyd George administration in the constitutional crisis of 1911. The attack on the Lords was supported not only by the workers but by petty-bourgeois liberal ideologists and sections of the bourgeoisie which saw in the continuance of the House of Lords, with its traditional powers, the surest way to encourage the growth and sharpen the attack of the socialists.

Just as in World War II, the National Government which ran World War I found it necessary to include Labour members in its personnel. In 1918, immediately after the victory, Lloyd George engineered an election in order to capitalise on his personal prestige. The Labour Party polled two million votes, a higher vote than it had ever had before. Lloyd George promised to make Britain "a fit country for heroes to live in". Before long every music hall in the country resounded to the witticism that post-war Britain was a country in which only heroes could live.

In the election of 1923 the British people gave to the Labour

Party the greatest number of seats among the three contending parties. The Liberal Party and the Conservatives together held a majority over the Labour Party which, however, formed a government with their consent. This government introduced not one single socialist measure. It had preached socialism for twenty-three years. In the campaign the Tories, then as now, had made it clear to the British people that as far as they, the property owners, were concerned, the Labour Party was a socialist party. Victory for the Labour Party, the Tories explained to the British electors, meant the substitution of a socialist society for a capitalist society in Britain. They called the labour leaders red revolutionaries, which, of course, the labour leaders vigorously denied. Their denial was not without some justification. The British people or the masses who support the Labour Party were and are not marxists.

But the debate in Britain among the working class and those classes closest to it has for years now not been as to whether socialism is workable or not; the debate has been as to whether it is to be achieved by constitutional or revolutionary means. On that question, the overwhelming majority of British opinion, deeply suffused as it is with democratic tradition and British empiricism, has more or less expressed itself as follows: we shall adopt the parliamentary procedure and if afterwards the Tories should attempt to prevent the carrying out of the will of the people, the Labour government would be in a position to use the machinery of government, the army and the police against the self-exposed enemies of democracy.

After a few short months of government in 1924 the Labour government was thrown out of power and was defeated in the election which followed. The reasons for its defeat were two-fold: it had shown itself conspicuously unable to make any radical change in the increasing dislocation of the British economy. It had thereby alienated those middle-class elements which had come tentatively towards it through disgust with the Tory Party. On the other hand, the Zinoviev letter, skilfully used by the Tories, created a stampede toward the Conservative Party as the bulwark of British stability against red revolution.

The five years which followed were years critical in the history of the development of political crystallisation in Britain. Churchill, as Chancellor of the Exchequer, faced with Britain's declining position on the world market, brought Britain back to the gold standard. What Britain needed was a reorganisation of its economy. This was beyond the Tory Party and Churchill's step fell heavily on the working class. One of its results was the general strike in 1926 and the growing hostility among the British people to the Tory government and the perpetual crisis of Britain. That is why, in 1929, after five years of the famous capitalist prosperity, the British people gave to the Labour Party a still greater number of seats than in 1924. The Labour Party had excused itself for its failure in 1923 on the score that it was unable to introduce any socialist measure because it did not have an absolute majority. Millions tried to give it that majority in 1929.

A few words are here in place as to the stratification of British voting. In 1929, the Labour government received eight million votes on its programme of socialism. Socialism by constitutional means to be sure, but socialism nevertheless. Britain was suffering from unemployment and the Labour programme as explained to the masses of the people attributed the unemployment to capitalist society and private ownership. The basis of the vote was the working class. By this time, almost to a man, those millions of the population engaged in direct production and transport were voting the Labour ticket. They would not think of voting anything else but Labour, and it is the foundation of their creed that capitalist society is the root and origin of all their social ills. They do not necessarily take this very seriously at all times. But in Sunday schools, in Labour classes, in Labour rallies, at regular Labour Party meetings, in their trade unions, at election time, the Labour Party has brought them up on the idea that capitalist private property must be superseded by socialist abolition of private property. Britain, however, is almost seventy percent proletarianised and many millions of this proletariat is in distributive and service trades. In 1921 this number was seven million, as compared to the ten million of the population engaged in direct productive industry. Many of these consider themselves workers, but of the seven millions, four millions were classified in 1921 under commerce, finance and personal service. Britain is a country with a numerous traditional aristocracy and a strong rentier class. A substantial number of the population lives, directly or indirectly, by attending to the needs of these parasites, thereby becoming themselves parasitic. In 1924, the salaried workers were nearly three million as opposed to fifteen million actual wage earners. This is a very high proportion. These people for years voted Liberal or stuck to their patrons, the Conservatives. Since 1918, however, with the increasing strength and confidence of the Labour Party this vote has been shifting towards the Labour Party. The significance of the 1929 vote was that more and more of them were looking towards labour.

The failure of the Labour Party in 1929 was even worse than in 1924. Unemployment went from one million in 1929 to nearly three million in 1931. Those who believe that it is the mildness of the programme of the British Labour Party which has attracted the British voter should ponder upon the following statement by the greatest British parliamentarian of the last forty years and one who has repeatedly showed his understanding of the British people and their political situation:

"Millions consequently threw in their lot with a new party. To them this party was the party of the last hope. It is now rapidly becoming the party of lost hope. Speakers and agents of all parties returning from the last by-election in a great industrial constituency had the same tale to tell. It was one of the gloom and despair which had fallen on this working-class district owing to the failure of the government they had helped at the last general election to put into power to bring any amelioration into their conditions and prospects. If Labour fails this time, confidence in parliamentary institutions will for a period disappear in myriads of loyal British homes and hearts."

The writer is David Lloyd George. This is testimony, if any were needed, of what the British people expected of the British Labour Party in 1929 and their reactions to its failure. As a climax to two years of failure came the disastrous split of 1931.

The circumstances of that split are not at all personal or accidental. In reality they mark a stage in the development of the bankruptcy of the Labour Party leaders. At the same time, the way in which the masses took the blow and recovered from it, testifies to the "uncontestable excellence" of the British working people.

In 1931, the world economic crisis and Churchill's restoration of Britain to the gold standard in 1924 on the basis of the declining British economy had superimposed a financial crisis upon the prevailing economic depression. It is argued that the crisis was a result of the manipulation of British financial magnates with assistance from Wall Street, a manipulation aimed at discrediting the Labour government. The mere fact, however, that such a development was possible, shows the critical situation to which the country had been reduced. Maliciously stimulated by the bourgeois press, a feeling of near panic spread over Britain. With their record of failure behind them, facing disaster, and conscious that they had no programme to solve capitalist chaos, the Labour leaders sought to save face by a display of their socialist programme. They fell back on the perpetual alibi — only socialism can save the country but we had no absolute majority. Stanley Baldwin, the Conservative Prime Minister, was quite aware of the temper of the country and the miserable record of his own Conservative Party between 1924 and 1929. He, therefore, prevailed upon Ramsay MacDonald, the Prime Minister of the Labour Government and Philip Snowden, the Chancellor of the Exchequer, to join with him in a national government. He also invited some of the leaders of the Liberal Party to join this government. The significance of this was not fully appreciated at the time, and in fact could not have been. The astute Englishman, astute in his petty party politics, was one of the first in Europe to recognise that pure and simple conservatism was bankrupt in Europe. He hid monopoly-capitalist politics behind the smokescreen of national unity, the practice which was carried to its highest pitch by Adolf Hitler afterwards and imitated in varying degrees by every government of Europe.

How would the country react to it? The *Manchester Guardian,* for instance, a great leader of liberal opinion in Britain, hesitated up to the last moment before it finally decided not to support the National Government. The real blow to the Labour Party, however, was given by Philip Snowden, one of its founders, and admittedly its intellectual leader. Snowden went on to the radio a few days before the critical election and let out a blast *against* the very socialist programme which he more than any other politician in England had helped to create. The country, said Snowden, was in serious crisis. It faced the possibilities of inflation and loss of the savings of the poor. At this time, said Snowden, the Labour Party comes forward with a programme of socialisation of the means of production, distribution, etc., as a solution to the crisis. This, he declared, was the straight road to catastrophe.

The British people were thunderstruck. The petty bourgeoisie streamed away from the Labour Party. Who, in the name of heaven, could vote for a party whose leaders had asked for power as the party of the last hope, and had now not only abandoned its organisation but had repudiated its programme? If this was not the time for socialism, when would be the time? But far-seeing conservative observers noted two ominous signs. The "national" election destroyed the Liberal Party as an effective political force. And, more important, the actual working-class vote stood steady as a rock. MacDonald and Snowden had demoralised the petty bourgeoisie. They took with them into the national caucus only leaders. Labour was unshaken and would henceforth be the only alternative to conservatism. The Labour Party returned to Parliament after the election with less than forty seats.

History moves according to certain laws. These laws are to be elucidated from the living specific concrete development. There the logical movement which they indicate is repeated in a higher spiral, modified or accentuated by the changing historical conditions. This is magnificently demonstrated by British policies between 1901 and 1945. As we look back at Britain between 1900 and 1931, the pattern is startlingly clear. The declining British economy gives rise to the political organisation of labour which gradually assumes a commanding position in national politics. But Britain is still wealthy enough to make concessions. The Liberal Party makes them up to 1914 but in no way severely halts the growth of labour's political organisation. World War I is a catastrophe for Britain's position on the world market. Between 1918 and 1931, the Liberal Party is gradually extinguished. More and more the Labour Party assumes the position of the alternative party with labour as its basis and attracting to it the restless petty bourgeoisie under the whip of bankrupt British capitalism. The masses of the people push political labour towards the power. Socialist in name only, the labour leaders are incapable of solving capitalist crisis by capitalist methods. In 1931 their bankruptcy takes organisational form. The most distinguished of them abandon the party and join the bourgeoisie. The petty bourgeoisie which has been coming more or less

steadily towards Labour abandons it in dismay and rallies behind
the Conservatives. Labour stood firm because it had to and some
of the Labour leaders (apart from the trade unionists) remained.
But a man like Herbert Morrison, for instance, moved heaven and
earth to be included in Baldwin's National Government. Only when
the door was slammed in his face did he turn back to labour and
"socialism". This was the movement of classes and their political
representatives. We shall now see the same essential pattern
repeated on a higher plane, but within the changing circumstances
of the developing world crisis.

The labour movement recovered from the 1931 crisis with
astonishing rapidity. But whereas hitherto the struggle between
capital and labour had been carried on almost exclusively on the
national field, it was now widened to extend to every tentacle of
the British Empire, i.e. to the four corners of the earth. Organised
labour could not work out a foreign policy of its own and although
it made heroic efforts to do so, found that its weakness here continually disrupted its renovated power on the home front. This
pattern is repeated to a climax in 1935 and once more again in 1940.
The victory over Germany in 1945 releases labour from this
dilemma and clears the way for a victory long delayed and for that
very reason all the more devastating.

It used to be a commonplace in Britain that elections are never
decided on foreign policy. From 1931, however, the depths of the
British crisis was shown precisely by the repeated crisis in foreign
policy and the impossibility of separating it from home policy. In
1931 came the crisis over the Japanese invasion of Manchuria. In
a League of Nations session that attracted the attention of the
whole world, Sir John Simon, then British Foreign Secretary, made
a speech giving the British point of view. At its conclusion
Matsuoka, the Japanese delegate, stated that Sir John Simon had
said in a few words what he had been trying for days to tell the
League. A roar of protest rose in Britain. The British Labour
Party, meeting in congress at Hastings in 1932, passed an almost
unanimous resolution that British labour would never support
British imperialism in another imperialistic war. On the day after
the conference, the British labour leaders outvied themselves in
explaining that the resolution did not mean what it said. Perhaps
the resolution and the labour leaders did not. As far as they understood the resolution, the British workers most certainly did as
would be abundantly proved before long. Even before the National
Government had been formed, the series of Round Table Conferences on India had begun, and in them much of the Indian
question was laid bare before the British people to their shame and
confusion. Gandhi was warmly welcomed in Lancashire of all
places.

The National Government decided on a protectionist policy at
last and this was trumpeted forth and sealed at the Ottawa Conference in 1932. It brought no relief and only precipitated a series

of colonial revolts, protesting at the rising prices for manufactured
goods and the lowered prices for raw materials which Ottawa
imposed on the colonial peoples. The risings received a hitherto
unexampled publicity in the British press. In 1933 came another
much trumpeted panacea — the World Economic Conference. It
collapsed dramatically within a few days of its opening session.
Meanwhile, the wrath of the British people at Tory helplessness
before the crisis grew. There was a sense of social crisis in the
atmosphere. Hitler's accession to power gave Sir Oswald Mosley his
chance. Lord Rothermere of the *Daily Mail* placed his paper, with
nearly two million circulation, at the disposal of Fascist Mosley,
and for months the *Daily Mail* was a Fascist organ. In the middle
of 1934, the June purge in Germany broke the alliance between
Mosley and the *Daily Mail*. It was this period of disillusionment
with British capitalism which preceded a wave of sympathy for
stalinist Russia and the skilfully propagandised "success" of the
Five Year Plan. The British worker remained invincibly opposed
to the British Communist Party, but the stalinist "planned
economy", as the antithesis of capitalism with its unemployment
and distressed areas, made great headway among the British
workers. Under cover of Russian popularity and Russian endorse-
ment of the League of Nations, the British Labour leaders, still
kept up a great show of hostility to imperialism, revoked the Hastings position, and adopted the doctrine of collective security. But
the miners, 700,000 strong, reaffirmed the original stand. Baldwin
took the opportunity to deliver a blast at the whole concept of
collective security. The November municipal elections of 1934
showed how far the Labour Party had recovered the confidence
of the country. Labour won sweeping victories and as far back
as 1934, constituencies which had been Tory for fifty years, went
Labour. Everything seemed set for a great victory at the coming
parliamentary elections. What smashed Labour's chances was
foreign policy — this time the Ethiopian crisis.

As war with Mussolini grew imminent the British workers reacted
strongly. Lord Robert Cecil, a League of Nations maniac, instituted
a private poll. *It gathered over eleven million votes for collective
security and over six million for an armed League of Nations*. Thus
the British workers expressed their distrust of British Tory foreign
policy. Baldwin was pursuing an anti-League policy. But British
indignation ultimately broke Sir Samuel Hoare who had replaced
Sir John Simon as Foreign Secretary and nearly broke Anthony
Eden who replaced him. The Labour Party leadership found itself
in an impossible dilemma. It had, in traditional Second International fashion, opposed all credits for the war budget. Yet in an
official resolution it shouted war at Mussolini *even before Baldwin
did so*. With remarkable skill and promptitude, Baldwin went on
the radio and endorsed the League of Nations and collective
security wholeheartedly. The election was a war election if ever
there was one. The Labour Party added well over a hundred seats

to its miserable thirty. But the British electorate, with the British and Italian fleets facing each other in the Mediterranean and listening to two major political parties saying much the same thing, gave Baldwin the support he asked for. People do not choose the eve of a war to start a social experiment. The decisive middle classes hesitated and chose Baldwin. It was openly stated in the Commons that Labour had lost the election by its apparently inept resolution, declaring war on Mussolini. It was not the Labour Party leadership which was inept but the short-sighted commentators. In essence the Labour leadership had done in the international crisis of 1935 precisely what it had done in the national crisis of 1931. It had betrayed its incapacity to produce a policy of its own and it had gone over to the side of the bourgeoisie.

The climax came with the Hoare-Laval pact which followed closely upon the election. It was a typical imperialist instrument for the division of Ethiopia and it was initiated by Anthony Eden. It fell like a skyful of cold water on the deceived and cheated British electorate. It was not for this they had voted. Labour had been impotent to produce an alternative and thus the masses had lost both at home and abroad. From that moment the National Government was distrusted in its foreign policy as much as it was hated for its home policy.

The years 1936 to 1940 were the years in which the British petty bourgeoisie came to the conclusions which the war crystallised and concentrated explosively. In that period there was not one single measure taken by the National Government to give anyone the belief that it could solve the economic decline of Britain which was so long patent to the British people. Roosevelt in the United States initiated a New Deal and Blum in France headed the short-lived experiment of the Popular Front British Toryism did nothing for there was nothing that it could do. In foreign policy, however, it demonstrated to the full its hostility to democracy and its readiness to collaborate with Hitler and Mussolini. The British people knew in their bones that the National Government had pursued its own narrow class interests in Europe, the Mediterranean and the Far East and thus precipitated the war of 1939. This is not wisdom after the event. The Labour leaders for three solid years inside and outside Parliament kept up a ceaseless agitation against Chamberlain on just those grounds. The lesson, easy enough to read in life, was dinned home by these politicians from the safe refuge of opposition. Thus both on home policy and foreign policy the bankruptcy and treachery of the British ruling class was revealed. "The Cliveden Set" was in reality not a *set* but *the capitalist class* of Britain, which almost in its entirety supported Chamberlain until the breakdown of his policy opened the abyss before their feet. Once more as the election due in 1940 approached the British working class and its allies were baffled and torn by the approach of war. This time no election took place at all. But the internal tension was far greater than in 1935. The British workers and the population as a whole were deeply hostile to the war and far more distrustful of Chamberlain in the crisis of 1939 than they had been of Baldwin in 1935. But the switch from Chamberlain to Churchill and the terror inspired by the early German victories enabled the Labour leaders to repeat their usual performance — join up with the bourgeoisie.

There is no need to recapitulate the social consequences of the war. The fatal error would be to see it as anything else but a continuation and concentration of the tendencies which we have traced since 1918. The war has made final that recognition of Britain's decline which has steadily grown among the British people since 1918. It has made final that recognition of the hopelessness of capitalism which has steadily grown among the British people since 1918. It has made final that recognition of the ineradicable treachery of the British ruling class which has steadily grown among the British people since 1931. Britain can no longer go on in the old way. Capitalism is bankrupt. The Labour Party claims that it is a socialist party, the party of a new society. The petty bourgeoisie and the rural constituencies have made up their minds, or rather have had their minds made up for them. The Labour Party claimed that it could not act in 1923 because it did not have an absolute majority. Again in 1929 it did not have an absolute majority. In 1934 it was getting ready to do better than in 1929 but the war scare of 1935 frightened these fluctuating classes away. The war in 1940 and the acceptance of the coalition by official Labour robbed them of the opportunity of expressing themselves. Now in the first chance they have got, in their quiet, parliamentary, unspectacular, sober, but infinitely determined British way, they have spoken their verdict. They have voted for a socialist society. In their eyes the essence of the change is the nationalisation of the means of production, destruction of the power of the capitalists and the landlords, an economy planned for the use of the people and not taking its anarchic way for the profit of the few.

It is impossible here even to examine the outlines of the dreadful economic and international political situation in which Britain finds itself today. It was necessary first of all to clear out of the way the motivated illusions which the American bourgeoisie has been trying to instill into the American workers. Some of these scoundrels have even tried to attribute Churchill's defeat to his stupid political campaign. Churchill's campaign was in fact the most striking demonstration of the helplessness of the British bourgeoisie. He had no programme because he could have none. It would be interesting to see one written by his critics. Churchill said that socialism was the issue. He knows Britain too well to have thought that after 1924 and 1929 the issue of socialism could be camouflaged. Neither could Churchill attack the idea of a planned economy *per se*. His whole war administration would have been a refutation of the argument that private enterprise was the only feasible method of reconstructing the country. What he did do was strictly in character with our times. He took the position that socialism meant a British Gestapo. In other words, *he could only agitate against Attlee's "socialist" economic proposals by building a bogey of their political consequences. Exactly the same type of argument is being used in Europe and in the United States against socialism.* It is a long, long way from 1918, when the very idea of socialism as a type of economy was denounced by the bourgeoisie as ridiculous and utopian. But it is precisely here also that the fatal weakness of the Labour leaders is already revealed. *Their* campaign was the quintessence of ineptitude. *They* had a programme. They could have put it forward like the confident builders of a new society. Instead, every statement, modest as it was, had a qualification. The same petty bourgeoisie whom they were trying not to "alienate", the farmers, reputedly so conservative, were the very ones whom the election shows were only waiting for the chance to give Labour an unmistakable mandate. And what is Attlee's programme, as announced in the King's speech? Labour will nationalise the coal industry. This measure, if you please, was recommended by an all-party government commission *over twenty years ago.* They will also nationalise the Bank of England, which already functions as a semi-public body. They will repeal the Trades Disputes Act, i.e. they will repeal what is a stiff version of the American Hatch Act. The election programme promised to "nationalise" electric and gas utilities. But now that they are in power they propose only to "co-ordinate" them. They are the same people of 1924 and 1929. In his first speech to the Commons, Attlee told the people: "Before the war there was much that was in our view wrong in the economic and social conditions in this country." So that is it. In "our view" much "was wrong". Also, "We must set ourselves resolutely to the task of increasing our exports." The reorganisation of the economy, as an indispensable instrument — the mobilisation of the people who supported him, this cannot even enter the vision of this petty clerk of the bourgeoisie. Today the Labour leaders can do what they want with Britain. If they were to tell the people what is required, call upon them to sacrifice, yes, to sacrifice themselves to build a new Britain as they sacrificed themselves to save the old, the British people would perform prodigies of reconstruction which would put their great war effort to shame. The bourgeoisie is today powerless. The army, a non-professional army, overwhelmingly supported Labour and if, in response to a genuine socialisation, any reactionary elements showed opposition, Attlee can be certain of the support of the overwhelming majority of the workers and soldiers. But no! He will "resolutely" increase exports. Circumstances may lead these opportunists to sporadic adventures, but isn't it clear that they are, in essence, as helpless before the creaking structure of British capitalism as the Tory leaders have shown themselves to be during the last quarter of a century? All questions of policy are subordinate to the fact that only a social revolution can save Britain from catastrophe and the Labour leaders are not revolutionary. If in Trotsky's opinion MacDonald prepared the catastrophes which awaited the country, on the high plane to which he had been pushed, Attlee will prepare them still more and still faster. Today history is in no waiting mood.

Is the British working class revolutionary? No serious marxist can ask that question. Their historical development has not ceased with the election. The bankrupt British economy, the helplessness of the bourgeoisie have led the workers step by step to a situation where they have won over the middle classes and placed the Labour leaders in a situation where they have no bourgeois political party to run to, where they cannot blame anything upon the absence of a majority. The election is the climax of one period and *therefore* the beginning of a new. If Attlee and his colleagues meant business the first thing they would do would be to mobilise the creative energies and aspirations of the British people as a bulwark for a revolutionary programme. But that they will not do. The revolutionary manifestations of the British workers and their allies will therefore come from some other sources — the whip of the counter-revolution, seeking to gain outside of Parliament the power that it has lost inside. The response of the British people will be tremendous. Let no one have any fear of that. Or disillusionment with the Labour government will open up a new period of clarification and a struggle for new ways and means to achieve the goals they have pursued since 1918. On our British comrades of the Fourth International, who have acquitted themselves so manfully during the war, falls the heavy burden and the proud privilege of being the spearhead of the revolutionary reorientation. To look back and learn the lessons of the past years, which reached their climax in the election, can be the source of an inexhaustible confidence and energy in teaching the British workers and learning from them the revolutionary demands of the new period.

1945

9

The Revolutionary Answer to the Negro Problem in the USA

[*This essay was first published in New York in 1948 under the pseudonym of "J. Meyer", in a volume entitled* Documents on the Negro Struggle. *Actually the text of a conference report to the Socialist Workers' Party, this is, according to James himself, "a clear political programme which summarised the political attitudes and ideas which I had placed before Trotsky in 1938" concerning the need for blacks to organise themselves autonomously without being subordinate to the leaderships of the trade unions or marxist parties.*]

The decay of capitalism on a world scale, the rise of the CIO in the United States, and the struggle of the Negro people, have precipitated a tremendous battle for the minds of the Negro people and for the minds of the population in the US as a whole over the Negro question. During the last few years certain sections of the bourgeoisie, recognising the importance of this question, have made a powerful theoretical demonstration of their position, which has appeared in *The American Dilemma* by Gunnar Myrdal, a publication that took a quarter of a million dollars to produce. Certain sections of the sentimental petty bourgeoisie have produced their spokesmen, one of whom is Lillian Smith. That has produced some very strange fruit, which however has resulted in a book which has sold some half a million copies over the last year or two. The Negro petty bourgeoisie, radical and concerned with communism, has also made its bid in the person of Richard Wright, whose books have sold over a million copies. When books on such a controversial question as the Negro question reach the stage of selling half a million copies it means that they have left the sphere of literature and have now reached the sphere of politics.

We can compare what we have to say that is new by comparing it to previous positions on the Negro question in the socialist movement. The proletariat, as we know, must lead the struggles of all the oppressed and all those who are persecuted by capitalism. But this has been interpreted in the past — and by some very good socialists too — in the following sense: the independent struggles of the Negro people have not got much more than an episodic value, and as a matter of fact, can constitute a great danger not only to the Negroes themselves, but to the organised labour movement. The real leadership of the Negro struggle must rest in the hands of organised labour and of the marxist party. Without that the Negro struggle is not only weak, but is likely to cause difficulties for the Negroes and dangers to organised labour. This, as I say, is the position held by many socialists in the past. Some great socialists in the United States have been associated with this attitude.

We, on the other hand, say something entirely different.

We say, number one, that the Negro struggle, the independent Negro struggle, has a vitality and a validity of its own; that it has deep historic roots in the past of America and in present struggles; it has an organic political perspective, along which it is travelling, to one degree or another, and everything shows that at the present time it is travelling with great speed and vigour.

We say, number two, that this independent Negro movement is able to intervene with terrific force upon the general social and political life of the nation, despite the fact that it is waged under the banner of democratic rights, and is not led necessarily either by the organised labour movement or the marxist party.

We say, number three, and this is the most important, that it is able to exercise a powerful influence upon the revolutionary proletariat, that it has got a great contribution to make to the development of the proletariat in the United States, and that it is in itself a constituent part of the struggle for socialism.

In this way we challenge directly any attempt to subordinate or to push to the rear the social and political significance of the independent Negro struggle for democratic rights. That is our position. It was the position of Lenin thirty years ago. It was the position of Trotsky which he fought for during many years. It has been concretised by the general class struggle in the United States, and the tremendous struggles of the Negro people. It has been sharpened and refined by political controversy in our movement, and best of all, it has had the benefit of three or four years of practical application in the Negro struggle and in the class struggle by the Socialist Workers' Party during the past few years.

Now if this position has reached the stage where we can put it forward in the shape that we propose, that means that to understand it should be by now simpler than before; and by merely observing the Negro question, the Negro people, rather, the struggles they have carried on, their ideas, we are able to see the roots of this position in a way that was difficult to see ten or even fifteen years ago. The Negro people, we say, on the basis of their own experiences, approach the conclusions of marxism. And I will have briefly to illustrate this as has been shown in the Resolution.

First of all, on the question of imperialist war. The Negro people do not believe that the last two wars and the one that may overtake us, are a result of the need to struggle for democracy, for freedom of the persecuted peoples by the American bourgeoisie. They cannot believe that.

On the question of the state, what Negro, particularly below the Mason-Dixon line, believes that the bourgeois state is a state above all classes, serving the needs of all the people? They may not formulate their belief in marxist terms, but their experience drives them to reject this shibboleth of bourgeois democracy.

On the question of what is called the democratic process, the Negroes do not believe that grievances, difficulties of sections of the population, are solved by discussions, by voting, by telegrams to Congress, by what is known as the "American way".

Finally, on the question of political action. The American bourgeoisie preaches that Providence in its divine wisdom has decreed that there should be two political parties in the United States, not one, not three, not four, just two: and also in its kindness, Providence has shown that these two parties should be one, the Democratic Party and the other, the Republican, to last from now until the end of time.

That is being challenged by increasing numbers of people in the United States. But the Negroes more than ever have shown — and any knowledge of their press and their activities tells us that they are willing to make the break completely with that conception.

As Bolsheviks we are jealous, not only theoretically but practically, of the primary role of the organised labour movement in all fundamental struggles against capitalism. That is why for many years in the past this position on the Negro question has had some difficulty in finding itself thoroughly accepted, particularly in the revolutionary movement, because there is this difficulty — what is the relation between this movement and the primary role of the proletariat — particularly because so many Negroes, and most disciplined, hardened, trained, highly developed sections of the Negroes, are today in the organised labour movement.

First the Negro struggles in the South are not merely a question of struggles of Negroes, important as those are. It is a question of the reorganisation of the whole agricultural system in the United States, and therefore a matter for the proletarian revolution and the reorganisation of society on socialist foundations.

Secondly, we say in the South that although the embryonic unity of whites and Negroes in the labour movement may seem small and there are difficulties in the unions, yet such is the decay of Southern society and such the fundamental significance of the proletariat, particularly when organised in labour unions, that this small movement is bound to play the decisive part in the revolutionary struggles that are inevitable.

Thirdly, there are one and a quarter million Negroes, at least, in the organised labour movement.

On these fundamental positions we do not move one inch. Not only do we not move, we strengthen them. But there still remains the question: what is the relationship of the independent Negro mass movement to the organised labour movement? And here we come immediately to what has been and will be a very puzzling feature unless we have our basic position clear.

Those who believed that the Negro question is in reality, purely and simply, or to a decisive extent, merely a class question, pointed with glee to the tremendous growth of the Negro personnel in the organised labour movement. It grew in a few years from three hundred thousand to one million; it is now one and a half million. But to their surprise, instead of this lessening and weakening the struggle of the independent Negro movement, *the more the Negroes went into the labour movement, the more capitalism incorporated them into industry, the more they were accepted in the union movement. It is during that period, since 1940, that the independent mass movement has broken out with a force greater than it has ever shown before.*

That is the problem that we have to face, that we have to grasp. We cannot move forward and we cannot explain ourselves unless we have it clearly. And I know there is difficulty with it. I intend to spend some time on it, because if that is settled, all is settled. The other difficulties are incidental. If, however, this one is not clear, then we shall continually be facing difficulties which we shall doubtless solve in time.

Now Lenin has handled this problem and in the Resolution we have quoted him. He says that the dialectic of history is such that small independent nations, small nationalities, which are powerless — get the word, please — *powerless*, in the struggle against imperialism, *nevertheless* can act as one of the ferments, one of the bacilli, which can bring on to the scene the real power against imperialism — the socialist proletariat.

Let me repeat it please. Small groups, nations, nationalities, themselves powerless against imperialism, nevertheless can act as one of the ferments, one of the bacilli which will bring on to the scene the real fundamental force against capitalism — the socialist proletariat.

In other words, as so often happens from the marxist point of view, from the point of view of the dialectic, this question of the *leadership* is very complicated.

What Lenin is saying is that although the fundamental force is the proletariat, although these groups are powerless, although the proletariat has got to lead them, it does not by any means follow that they cannot do anything until the proletariat actually comes forward to lead them. *He says exactly the opposite is the case.*

They, by their agitation, resistance and the political developments that they can initiate, can be the means whereby the proletariat is brought on to the scene.

Not always, and every time, not the sole means, but one of the means. That is what we have to get clear.

Now it is very well to see it from the point of view of marxism which developed these ideas upon the basis of European and Oriental experiences. Lenin and Trotsky applied this principle to the Negro question in the United States. What *we* have to do is to make it concrete, and one of the best means of doing so is to dig into the history of the Negro people in the United States, and to see the relationship that has developed between them and revolutionary elements in past revolutionary struggles.

For us the centre must be the Civil War in the United States and I intend briefly now to make some sharp conclusions and see if they can help us arrive at a clearer perspective. Not for historical knowledge, but to watch the movement as it develops before us, helping us to arrive at a clearer perspective as to this difficult relationship between the independent Negro movement and the revolutionary proletariat. The Civil War was a conflict between the revolutionary bourgeoisie and the Southern plantocracy. That we know. That conflict was inevitable.

But for twenty to twenty-five years before the Civil War actually broke out, the masses of the Negroes in the South, through the underground railroad, through revolts, as Aptheker has told us, and by the tremendous support and impetus that they gave to the revolutionary elements among the Abolitionists, absolutely prevented the reactionary bourgeoisie — (revolutionary later) — absolutely prevented the bourgeoisie and the plantocracy from coming to terms as they wanted to do.

In 1850 these two made a great attempt at a compromise. What broke that compromise? It was the Fugitive Slave Act. They could prevent everything else for the time being, but they could not prevent the slaves from coming, and the revolutionaries in the North from assisting them. So that we find that here in the history of the United States such is the situation of the masses of the Negro people and their readiness to revolt at the slightest opportunity, that as far back as the Civil War, in relation to the American bourgeoisie, they formed a force which *initiated* and *stimulated* and *acted as a ferment*.

That is point number one.

Point number two. The Civil War takes its course as it is bound to do. Many Negroes and their leaders make an attempt to get incorporated into the Republican Party and to get their cause embraced by the bourgeoisie. And what happens? The bourgeoisie refuses. It doesn't want to have Negroes emancipated.

Point number three. As the struggle develops, such is the situation of the Negroes in the United States, that the emancipation of the slaves becomes *an absolute necessity*, politically, organisationally and from a military point of view.

The Negroes are incorporated into the battle against the South. Not only are they incorporated here, but later they are incorporated also into the military government which smashes down the remnants of resistance in the Southern states.

But, when this is done, the Negroes are deserted by the bourgeoisie, *and there falls upon them a very terrible repression*.

That is the course of development in the central episode of American history.

Now if it is so in the Civil War, we have the right to look to see what happened in the War of Independence. It is likely — it is not always certain — but it is *likely* that we shall see there some *anticipations* of the logical development which appeared in the Civil War. They are there.

The Negroes begin by demanding their rights. They say if you are asking that the British free you, then we should have our rights and, furthermore, slavery should be abolished. The American bourgeoisie didn't react very well to that. The Negroes insisted — those Negroes who were in the North — insisted that they should be allowed to join the Army of Independence. They were refused.

But later Washington found that it was imperative to have them, and four thousand of them fought among the thirty thousand soldiers of Washington. They gained certain rights after independence was achieved. Then sections of the bourgeoisie who were with them deserted them. And the Negro movement collapsed.

We see exactly the same thing but more intensified in the Populist movement. There was a powerful movement of one and one quarter of a million Negroes in the South (The Southern Tenant Farmers' Association). They joined the Populist movement and were in the extreme left wing of this movement, when Populism was discussing whether it should go on with the Democratic Party or make the campaign as a third party. The Negroes voted for the third party and for all the most radical planks in the platform.

They fought with the Populist movement. But when Populism was defeated, there fell upon the Negroes between 1896 and about 1910 the desperate, legalised repression and persecution of the Southern states.

Some of us think it is fairly clear that the Garvey movement came and looked to Africa because there was no proletarian movement in the United States to give it a lead, to do for this great eruption of the Negroes what the Civil War and the Populist movement had done for the insurgent Negroes of those days.

And now what can we see today? Today the Negroes in the United States are organised as never before. There are more than half a million in the NAACP, and in addition to that, there are all sorts of Negro groups and organisations — the churches in particular — *every single one of which is dominated by the idea that each organisation must in some manner or another contribute to the emancipation of the Negroes from capitalist humiliation and from capitalist oppression.* So that the independent Negro movement that we see today and which we see growing before our eyes is nothing strange. It is nothing new. *It is something that has always appeared in the American movement at the first sign of social crisis.*

It represents a climax to the Negro movements that we have seen in the past. From what we have seen in the past, we would expect it to have its head turned towards the labour movement. And not only from a historical point of view but today concrete experience tells us that the masses of the Negro people today look upon the CIO with a respect and consideration that they give to no other social or political force in the country. To anyone who knows the Negro people, who reads their press — and I am not speaking here specially of the Negro workers — if you watch the Negro petty bourgeoisie — reactionary, reformist types as some of them are, in all their propaganda, in all their agitation — whenever they are in any difficulties, you can see them leaning toward the labour movement. As for the masses of Negroes, they are increasingly pro-labour every day. So that it is not only marxist ideas; it is not only a question of bolshevik-marxist analysis. It is not only a question of the history of Negroes in the US.

The actual concrete facts before us show us, and anyone who wants to see, this important conclusion, that the Negro movement logically and historically and concretely is headed for the proletariat. That is the road it has always taken in the past, the road to the revolutionary forces. Today the proletariat is that force. And if these ideas that we have traced in American revolutionary crises have shown some power in the past, such is the state of the class struggle today, such the antagonisms between bourgeoisie and proletariat, such, too, the impetus of the Negro *movement toward the revolutionary forces*, which we have traced in the past, is *stronger today than ever before*. So that we can look upon this Negro movement not only for what it has been and what it has been able to do — we are able to know as marxists by our own theory and our examination of American history that it is headed for the proletarian movement, that it must go there. There is nowhere else for it to go.

And further we can see that if it doesn't go there, the difficulties that the Negroes have suffered in the past when they were deserted by the revolutionary forces, those will be ten, one hundred, ten thousand times as great as in the past. The independent Negro movement, which is boiling and moving, must find its way to the proletariat. If the proletariat is not able to support it, the repression of past times when the revolutionary forces failed the Negroes will be infinitely, I repeat, infinitely, more terrible today.

Therefore our consideration of the independent Negro movement does not lessen the significance of the proletarian — the essentially proletarian — leadership. Not at all. It includes it. We are able to see that the mere existence of the CIO, its mere existence, despite the fakery of the labour leadership on the Negro question, as on all other questions, is a protection and a stimulus to the Negroes.

We are able to see and I will show in a minute that the Negroes are able by their activity to draw the revolutionary elements and more powerful elements in the proletariat to their side. We are coming to that. But we have to draw and emphasise again and again this important conclusion. If — and we have to take these theoretical questions into consideration — if the proletariat is defeated, if the CIO is destroyed, then there will fall upon the Negro people in the US, such a repression, such persecution, comparable to nothing that they have seen in the past. We have seen in Germany and elsewhere the barbarism that capitalism is capable of in its death agony. The Negro people in the US offer a similar opportunity to the American bourgeoisie. The American bourgeoisie have shown their understanding of the opportunity the Negro question gives them to disrupt and to attempt to corrupt and destroy the labour movement.

But the development of capitalism itself has not only given the independent Negro movement this fundamental and sharp relation with the proletariat. It has created Negro proletarians and placed them as proletarians in what were once the most oppressed and exploited masses. But in auto, steel, and coal, for example, these proletarians have now become the vanguard of the workers' struggle and have brought a substantial number of Negroes to a position of primacy in the struggle against capitalism. The backwardness and humiliation of the Negroes that shoved them into these industries is the very thing which today is bringing them forward, and they are in the very vanguard of the proletarian movement from the very nature of the proletarian struggle itself. Now, how does this complicated interrelationship, the "leninist" interrelationship express itself? Henry Ford could write a very good thesis on that if he were so inclined.

The Negroes in the Ford plant were incorporated by Ford: first of all he wanted them for the hard, rough work. I am also informed by the comrades from Detroit he was very anxious to play a paternalistic role with the Negro petty bourgeoisie. He wanted to show them that he was not the person that these people said he was — look! he was giving Negroes opportunities in his plant.

Number three, he was able thus to create divisions between whites and Negroes that allowed him to pursue his anti-union, reactionary way.

What has happened within the last few years that is changed? The mass of the Negroes in the River Rouge plant, I am told, are one of the most powerful sections of the Detroit proletariat. They are leaders in the proletarian struggle, not the stooges Ford intended them to be.

Not only that, they act as leaders not only in the labour movement as a whole but in the Negro community. It is what they say that is decisive there. Which is very sad for Henry. And the Negro petty bourgeois have *followed the proletariat*. They are now going along with the labour movement: they have left Ford too. It is said that he has recognised it at last and that he is not going to employ any more Negroes. He thinks he will do better with women. But they will disappoint him too. . . .

Let us not forget that in the Negro people, there sleep and are now awakening passions of a violence exceeding, perhaps, as far as these things can be compared, anything among the tremendous forces that capitalism has created. Anyone who knows them, who knows their history, is able to talk to them intimately, watches them at their own theatres, watches them at their dances, watches them in their churches, reads their press with a discerning eye, must recognise that although their social force may not be able to compare with the social force of a corresponding number of organised workers, the hatred of bourgeois society and the readiness to destroy it when the opportunity should present itself, rests among them to a degree greater than in any other section of the population in the United States.

1948

10

The Class Struggle

[State Capitalism and World Revolution, *from which this essay is taken, was first published in 1950. It represents the culminating point of James's efforts during the 1940s to develop a critique of trotskyism and, in E. P. Thompson's words, to "tease out the muddle of ideology" which existed in the marxist movement during the 1940s. Although a product of James's American sojourn, its influence on the European left has been far-reaching.*]

The stalinist theory is, despite zigzags, logical and consistent. Like every theory of all exploiters it is the theory of the rulers, the result of their struggle with the direct producers whom they exploit, and of competition with other rulers. The theory justifies stalinist exploitation of the Russian workers. It can be used as a weapon against the traditional bourgeoisie in the struggle for the domination of the world working-class movement without impairing the position of the rulers inside Russia. It fortifies this position in the minds of the public which·is interested in these questions and the members and fellow-travellers of the stalinist parties.

The theory itself is an adaptation of the pre-marxian petty-bourgeois ideology from Kant to Sismondi and Proudhon to the specific conditions of state-capitalism. That we shall go into later. But then as now its purpose can be summed up in a phrase — the radical reorganisation of society with the proletariat as object and not as subject, i.e. with no essential change in the mode of labour. The crisis of world capitalism, a hundred years of marxism, thirty years of leninism, impose upon this theory, as a primary task, the need to destroy and to obscure the theory of class struggle in the process of production itself, the very basis of marxism and of the proletarian revolution.

The stalinists did not arbitrarily "choose" this theory. Politics on the basis of the analysis of property is of necessity the struggle over correct policy and the correction of "evil". Social division, if not rooted in *classes*, automatically becomes a selection of personnel. The criterion not being a criterion of class becomes automatically a criterion according to competence, ability, loyalty, devotion, etc. This personnel, comprising many millions, the stalinists have enshrined in the 1936 constitution under the name of "our socialist intelligentsia". The most competent, the most able, most loyal, most devoted, the elite become the party. The instrument of the party is the state. The corollary to disguising the rulers of production as "our socialist intelligentsia" is the stalinist denunciation of bureaucracy as inefficiency, red tape, rudeness to workers, laziness, etc. — purely subjective characterisations.

The first task of the revolutionary International is clarification of this term, bureaucracy. The stalinists take advantage of the fact that Marx often used the term, bureaucracy, in relation to the mass of state functionaries. But with the analysis of state-capitalism by Engels, the word bureaucracy began to take on a wider connotation. Where Engels says, "Taking over of the great institutions for production and communication, first by joint-stock companies, later on by trusts, then by the state," he adds: "The bourgeoisie demonstrated to be a superfluous class. All its social functions are now performed by salaried employees" (*Socialism, Utopian and Scientific*). These are bureaucrats.

The moment Lenin saw the Soviet, the new form of social organisation created by the masses, he began to extend the concept, bureaucracy, to include not only officials of government but the officials of industry, all who were opposed to the proletariat as masters. This appears all through *State and Revolution* and, in its most finished form, in the following:

> "We cannot do without officials *under capitalism, under the rule of the bourgeoisie*. The proletariat is oppressed, the masses of the toilers are enslaved by capitalism. Under capitalism democracy is restricted, cramped, curtailed, mutilated by all the conditions of wage-slavery, the poverty and the misery of the masses. This is why and the only reason why the officials of our political and industrial organisations are corrupted — or more precisely, tend to be corrupted — by the conditions of capitalism, why they betray a tendency to become transformed into bureaucrats, i.e. into privileged persons divorced from the masses and *superior to* the masses.
>
> This is the *essence* of bureaucracy, and until the capitalists have been expropriated and the bourgeoisie overthrown, *even* proletarian officials will inevitably be 'bureaucratised' to some extent."

Lenin's whole strategic programme between July and October is based upon the substitution of the power of the armed masses for the power of the bureaucrat, the master, the official in industry and in politics. Hence his reiterated statement that if you nationalise and even confiscate, it means nothing without workers' power. Just as he had extended the analysis of capitalism, to state-capitalism and plan, Lenin was developing the theory of class struggle in relation to the development of capitalism itself. This strengthened the basic concepts of marxism.

Marx says:

> "The authority assumed by the capitalist by his personification of capital in the direct process of production, the social function performed by him in his capacity as a manager and ruler of production, is essentially different from the authority exercised

upon the basis of production by means of slaves, serfs, etc.

Upon the basis of capitalist production, the social character of their production impresses itself upon the mass of direct producers as a strictly regulating authority and as a social mechanism of the labour process graduated into a complete hierarchy. This authority is vested in its bearers only as a personification of the requirements of labour standing above the labourer" (*Capital*, Vol. III).

This is capitalist production, this hierarchy. The special functions are performed "within the conditions of production themselves by special agents in opposition to the direct producers". These functionaries, acting against the proletariat in production, are the enemy. If this is not understood, workers' control of production is an empty phrase.

With the development of capitalism into state-capitalism, as far back as 1917, Lenin, in strict theory, denounced mere confiscation in order to concentrate his whole fire upon the hierarchy in the process of production itself, and to counterpose to this, workers' power. It thus becomes ever more clear why the stalinists in their theory will have nothing whatever to do with state-capitalism and rebuke and stamp out any suggestions of it so sharply. The distinction that Lenin always kept clear has now developed with the development of capitalism over the last thirty years. It has now grown until it becomes the dividing line between the workers and the whole bureaucratic organisation of accumulated labour, science and knowledge, acting against the working class in the immediate process of production and everywhere else. This is the sense in which the term bureaucracy must be used in Russia.

It is upon this leninist *analysis* that the theory of state-capitalism rests and inseparable from this theory, the concept of the *transition* from social labour as compulsion, as barracks discipline of capital, to social labour as the voluntary association, the voluntary labour discipline of the labourers themselves. Lenin, in "The Great Beginning", theoretically and practically wrote an analysis of labour in Russia which the development of society *on a world scale* during the last thirty years now raises to the highest position among all his work on Russia. This must be the foundation of a marxist approach to the problems of economics and politics under socialism. In that article Lenin did two things:

(a) established with all the emphasis at his command that the essential character of the dictatorship of the proletariat was "not violence and not mainly violence against the exploiters". It was the unity and discipline of the proletariat trained by capitalism, its ability to produce "a higher social organisation of labour";

(b) analysed the communist days of labour given to the Soviet state and sought to distinguish the specific social and psychological characteristics of a new form of labour, and the relation of that to the productivity of labour.

With all its mighty creations of a Soviet state and Red Army, and the revolution in the superstructure, it is here that the Russian socialist revolution could not be completed. The "historical creative initiative" in production, the "subtle and intricate" relations of a new labour process—these never developed for historical reasons. But there has been a vast development of capitalism and of the understanding of capitalism all over the world since the early days of the Russian revolution. The British Chancellor of the Exchequer, the stalinist bureaucracy, the whole capitalist class in the US (and in the US more than anywhere else) — all declare that the problem of production to-day is the productivity of labour and the need to harness the human interest, i.e. the energy and ability of the worker. Many of them are aware that it is the labour process itself which is in question.

What they see partially, contemporary marxism must see fully and thereby restore the very foundations of marxism as a social science.

It is in the concrete analysis of labour inside Russia and outside Russia that the Fourth International can find the basis of the profoundest difference between the Third International and the Fourth International. The whole tendency of the stalinist theory is to build up theoretical barriers between the Russian economy and the economy of the rest of the world. The task of the revolutionary movement, beginning in theory and as we shall see, reaching to all aspects of political strategy, is to break down this separation. The development of Russia is to be explained by the development of world capitalism and specifically, capitalist production in its most advanced stage, in the United States. Necessary for the strategic task of clarifying its own theory and for building an irreconcilable opposition to stalinism, it is not accidental that this method also is the open road for the revolutionary party to the socialism inherent in the minds and hearts, not only of the politically advanced but the most backward industrial workers in the United States.

It is for this reason that the analysis of the labour process in the United States must concern us first and only afterwards the labour process in stalinist Russia.

Roughly, we may attribute the decisive change in the American economy to the last part of the nineteenth century and the first part of the twentieth century, taking 1914 as a convenient dividing line. After World War I the Taylor system, experimental before the war, becomes a social system, the factory laid out for continuous flow of production, and advanced planning for production, operating and control. At the same time there is the organisation of professional societies, management courses in college curricula and responsible management consultants. Between 1924 and 1928 there is rationalisation of production and retooling (Ford)*. Along

---

*A similar process in Germany led straight to Hitler.

with it are the tendencies to the scientific organisation of production, to closer co-ordination between employers, fusion with each other against the working class, the intervention of the state as mediator and then as arbiter.

For the proletariat there is the constantly growing sub-division of labour, decrease in the need of skills, and determination of the sequence of operations and speed by the machine. The crisis of 1929 accelerated all these processes. The characteristic, most advanced form of American production becomes Ford. Here production consists of a mass of hounded, sweated labour (in which, in Marx's phrase, the very life of society was threatened); and opposed to it as a class, a management staff which can carry out this production only by means of a hired army (Bennett) of gangsters, thugs, supervisors who run production by terror, in the plant, in the lives of the workers outside production, and in the political control of Detroit. Ford's régime before unionisation is the prototype of production relations in fascist Germany and stalinist Russia.

But — and without this, *all* marxism is lost — inextricably intertwined with the totalitarian *tendency* is the response of the working class. A whole new layer of workers, the result of the economic development, burst into revolt in the CIO. The CIO in its inception aimed at a revolution in production. The workers would examine what they were told to do and then decide whether it was satisfactory to them or not. This rejection of the basis of capitalist economy is the preliminary basis of a socialist economy. The next positive step is the total management of industry by the proletariat. Where the Transitional Programme says that the "CIO is the most indisputable expression of the instinctive striving of the American workers to raise themselves to the level of the tasks imposed upon them by history", it is absolutely correct. The task imposed upon them by history is socialism and the outburst, in aim and method, was the first instinctive preparation of the social revolution.

Because it was not and could not be carried through to a conclusion, the inevitable counterpart was the creation of a labour bureaucracy. The history of production since is the corruption of the bureaucracy and its transformation into an instrument of capitalist production, the restoration to the bourgeoisie of what it had lost in 1936, the right to control production standards. Without this mediating role of the bureaucracy, production in the United States would be violently and continuously disrupted until one class was undisputed master.

The whole system is in mortal crisis from the reaction of the workers. Ford, whose father fought the union so uncompromisingly as late as 1941, now openly recognises that as far as capitalism is concerned, improvements in technology, i.e. the further mechanisation of labour, offers no road out for the increase of productivity which rests entirely with the working class. At the same time, the workers in relation to capitalism resist any increase in productivity. The resistance to speed-up does not necessarily mean as most think that workers are required to work beyond normal physical capacity. It is resistance by the workers to any increased productivity, i.e. any increase of productivity by capitalist methods. Thus, both sides, capital and labour, are animated by the fact that for each, in its own way, the system has reached its limit.

The real aim of the great strikes in 1946 and since is the attempt to begin on a higher stage what was initiated in 1936. But the attempt is crippled and deflected by the bureaucracy, with the result that rationalisation of production, speed-up, intensification of exploitation are the order of the day in industry.

The bureaucracy inevitably must substitute the struggle over consumption, higher wages, pensions, education, etc., for a struggle in production. This is the basis of the welfare state, the attempt to appease the workers with the fruits of labour when they seek satisfaction in the work itself. The bureaucracy must raise a new social programme in the realm of consumption because it cannot attack capitalism at the point of production without destroying capitalism itself.

The series of pension plans which have now culminated in the five-year contract with General Motors is a very sharp climax of the whole struggle. This particular type of increase in consumption subordinates the workers to production in a special manner after they have reached a certain age. It confines them to being an industrial reserve army, not merely at the disposal of capital in general but within the confining limits of the specific capitalist factory which employs them. The effect, therefore, is to reinforce control both of employers and bureaucracy over production.

But along with this intensification of capitalist production and this binding of the worker for five years *must* go inevitably the increase of revolt, wildcat strikes, a desperate attempt of the working class to gain for itself conditions of labour that are denied to it both by the employers and the labour bureaucracy. While the bureaucracy provides the leadership for struggles over consumption, it is from the workers on the line that emerges the initiative for struggles over speed-up. That is precisely why the bureaucracy, after vainly trying to stop wildcat strikes by prohibiting them in the contract, has now taken upon itself the task of repressing by force this interruption of production. It expels from the unions workers who indulge in these illegal stoppages, i.e. who protest against the present stage of capitalist production itself. The flying squads, originated by the union for struggle against the bourgeoisie, are now converted by the bureaucracy into a weapon of struggle against the proletariat, and all this in the name of a higher standard of living, greater consumption by the workers, but in reality to ensure capitalist production.

The increase of coercion and terror by the bureaucracy increases the tendency of the workers to violent explosion. This tendency, taken to its logical conclusion, as the workers will have to take it, means the reorganisation of the whole system of production itself — socialism. Either this or the complete destruction of the union movement as the instrument of proletarian emancipation and its complete transformation into the only possible instrument of capital against the proletariat at this stage of production.

This is the fundamental function of the bureaucracy *in Russia*. Already the tentative philosophy of bureaucracy in the United States, its political economy of regulation of wages and prices, nationalisation and even planning, its ruthless political methods, show the organic similarity of the American labour bureaucracy and the stalinists. The struggle in the United States reveals concretely what is involved in the stalinist falsification of the marxist theory of accumulation, etc., and the totalitarian violence against the proletariat which this falsification protects.

In the recent coal strikes, despite the wage and welfare gains of the miners, the heads of the operators declared that control of production had been restored to them by the two-year contract. C. E. Wilson, president of General Motors, hailed the five-year settlement as allowing the company "to run our own plants", and as "the union's complete acceptance of technological progress". Reuther hailed the General Motors settlement as a "tremendous step forward" in "stabilising labour relations at GM". An editor of *Fortune* magazine hailed the contract as the harbinger of "new and more meaningful associative principles" with the corporation as "the centre of a new kind of community".

The stalinist bureaucracy is the American bureaucracy carried to its ultimate and logical conclusion, both of them products of capitalist production in the epoch of state-capitalism. To reply to this that the bureaucracy can never arrive at maturity without a proletarian revolution is the complete degradation of marxist theory. Not a single marxist of all the great marxists who analysed state-capitalism, not one ever believed capitalism would reach the specific stage of complete centralisation. It was because of the necessity to examine all its tendencies in order to be able to mobilise theoretical and practical opposition in the proletariat that they followed the dialectical method and *took these tendencies to their conclusions as an indispensable theoretical step.* In the present stage of our theory it is the scrupulous analysis of production in the United States as the most advanced stage of world capitalism that forms the indispensable prelude to the analysis of the labour process of Russia.

The Russian revolution of October 1917 abolished feudalism with a thoroughness never before achieved. The stage was therefore set for a tremendous economic expansion. Lenin sought to mobilise the proletariat to protect itself from being overwhelmed by this economic expansion. The isolated proletariat of backward Russia was unable to do this. The subsequent history of the labour process of Russia is the telescopic re-enactment of the stages of the process of production of the United States; and, added to this, the special degradation imposed upon it by the totalitarian control of the bureaucracy and the plan.

The Russian revolution in 1917 substituted for the authority of the capitalist in the factory the *workers' control of production.* Immediately there appeared *both* the concrete development of self-initiative in the factory *and* the simplification of the state apparatus outside. There was workers' control, with some capitalists as owners, but *mere* owners. Production conferences, not of bureaucrats but of workers, decided what and how to produce. What capitalists there remained seemed to vanish into thin air once their economic power was broken, and workers' control was supplemented the following year by nationalisation of the means of production. The red thread that runs through these first years of workers' rule, workers' control, seems to suffer a setback under war communism in general and with order 1042* in particular. It takes less than a year for the workers to force a change, and the all-important trade union debate of 1920 follows. Lenin fights successfully both Trotsky, the administrator, and Shlyapnikov, the syndico-anarchist, and strives to steer a course in consonance with the Declaration of the Rights of the Toilers, that only the masses "from below" can manage the economy, and that the trade unions are the transmission belts to the state wherein "every cook can be an administrator".

In the transition period between 1924 and 1928 when the First Five-Year Plan is initiated, the production conferences undergo a bureaucratisation, and with it the form of labour. There begins the alienation of mass activity to conform to specified quantities of *abstract labour* demanded by the plan "to catch up with capitalism". The results are:

(a) In 1929 ("the year of decision and transformation") there crystallises in direct opposition to management by the masses "from below" the *conference of the planners,* the engineers, economists, administrators; in a word, the specialists.

(b) Stalin's famous talk of 1931 "put an end to depersonalisation". His "six conditions" of labour contrasted the masses to the "personalised" individual who would outdo the *norms of the average.* Competition is not on the basis of creativity and Subbotniks,† but on the basis of the *outstanding* individual (read: bureaucrat) who will devise norms and have others surpass them.

(c) 1935 sees Stakhanovism and the definitive formation of an

---

*This was the order issued in the attempt to get the completely disorganised railroad system to function. The railroads were placed under almost military rule, subordinating the ordinary trade union democracy to "Chief Political Departments" which were established in the railway and water transport workers' unions. As soon as the critical situation had been solved, the transport workers demanded the abolition of the "Chief Political Departments" and the immediate restoration of full trade-union democracy.
†*Subbotniks* were the workers who on their own initiative volunteered to work five hours overtime on Saturdays without pay in order to help the economy of the workers' state. From the word *Subbota,* meaning Saturday.

aristocracy of labour. Stakhanovism is the pure model of the manner in which foremen, overseers and leadermen are chosen in the factories the world over. These individuals, exceptional to their class, voluntarily devote an intensity of their labour to capital for a brief period, thus setting the norm, which they personify, to dominate the labour of the mass for an indefinite period.

With the Stakhanovites, the bureaucratic administrators acquire a social base, and alongside, there grows the instability and crisis in the economy. It is the counter-revolution of state-capital.

(d) Beginning with 1939 the mode of labour changes again. In his report on the Third Five-Year Plan, Molotov stressed the fact that it was insufficient to be concerned merely with the mass of goods produced. The crucial point for "outstripping capitalism" was *not the mass* but the *rate* at which that mass was produced. It was necessary that per capita production be increased, that is to say, that each worker's productivity be so increased that fewer workers would be needed to obtain an ever greater mass of goods. Intensity of labour becomes the norm.

During the war that norm turned out to be the most vicious of all forms of exploitation. The stalinists sanctified it by the name of "socialist emulation". "Socialist emulation" meant, firstly, that the pay incentive that was the due of a Stakhanovite was no longer the reward of the workers as individuals, once they *as a mass* produced according to the new raised norm. In other words, the take-home pay was the same despite the speed-up on a plant-wide basis. Secondly, and above all, competition was no longer limited to individual workers competing on a piecework basis, nor even to groups of workers on a plant-wide basis, but was extended to cover *factory against factory*.

Labour reserves are established to assure the perpetuation of skills and a sufficient labour supply. Youths are trained from the start *to labour as ordered*. The climax comes in 1943 with the "discovery" of the conveyor belt system. This is the year also of the stalinist admission that the law of value functions in Russia.

We thus have:

1918: The Declaration of the Rights of Toilers—*every* cook an administrator.

1928: *Abstract* mass labour — "lots" of it "to catch up with capitalism".

1931: Differentiation within labour — "personalised" individual; the pieceworker the hero.

1935: Stakhanovism, *individual competition* to surpass the norm.

1936-37: Stalinist constitution; Stakhanovites and the intelligentsia *singled out* as those "whom we respect".

1939-41: *Systematisation* of piecework; factory competing against factory.

1943: "The year of the conversion to the conveyor belt system."

Whereas in 1936 we had the singling out of a ruling class, a "simple" division between mental and physical work, we now have the *stratification* of mental and physical labour. Leontiev's *Political Economy in the Soviet Union* lays stress not merely on the intelligentsia against the mass, but on specific skills and differentials, lower, higher, middle, in-between and highest.

If we take production since the Plan, not in the detail we have just given, but only the major changes, we can say that 1937 closes one period. It is the period of "catching up with and outdistancing capitalism" which means *mass* production and relatively simple planning. But competition on a *world* scale and the approaching Second World War is the severest type of capitalist competition for world mastery. This opens up the new period of per capita production as against mere "catching up". Planning must now include productivity of labour. Such planning knows and can know only machines and *intensity* of exploitation. Furthermore, it includes what the Russians call *rentabel'nost'*, that is to say, profitability. The era of the state helping the factory whose production is especially needed is over. The factory itself must prove its worthiness by showing a profit and a profit big enough to pay for *"ever-expanded"* production. And that can be done only by ever-expanded production of abstract labour in mass *and in rate*.

Nowhere in the world is labour so degraded as in Russia to-day. We are here many stages beyond the degradation which Marx described in the General Law of Accumulation. For not merely is the Russian labourer reduced to an appendage to a machine and a mere cog in the accumulation of capital. Marx said that the reserve army kept the working labourer riveted to his martyrdom. In Russia, because of the power to plan, the industrial reserve army is planned. Some 15 million labourers are planned in direct forced labour camps. They are organised by the MVD (GPU) for production. The disciplinary laws which began with reduction in wages for coming 15 minutes late have as their final stage, for lack of discipline, "corrective labour", i.e. the concentration camp.

What the American workers are revolting against since 1936 and holding at bay, this, and nothing else but this, has overwhelmed the Russian proletariat. The rulers of Russia perform the same functions as are performed by Ford, General Motors, the coal operators and their huge bureaucratic staffs. Capital is not Henry Ford; he can die and leave his whole empire to an institution; the plant, the scientific apparatus, the method, the personnel of organisation and supervision, the social system which sets these up in opposition to the direct producer will remain. Not inefficiency of bureaucrats, not "prestige, powers and revenue of the bureaucracy", not consumption but capital accumulation in its specifically capitalist manner, this is the analysis of the Russian economy.

To think that the struggle in Russia is over consumption not only strikes at the whole theory of the relationship of the superstructure to the productive mechanism. In practice, to-day, the crisis in Russia is manifestly the crisis in production. Whoever is convinced that this whole problem is a problem of consumption is driven away from marxism, not towards it.

It was Marx's contention that the existence of a labouring force compelled to sell its labour-power in order to live meant automatically the system of capitalist accumulation. The capitalist was merely the agent of capital. The bureaucrats are the same. Neither can use nor knows any other mode of production. A new mode of production requires. primarily that they be totally removed or totally subordinated.

At this point it is convenient to summarise briefly the abstract economic analysis of state-capitalism. We have never said that the economy of the United States is the *same* as the economy of Russia. What we have said is that, however great the differences, the fundamental laws of capitalism operate. It is just this that Marx indicated with his addition to *Capital* dealing with complete centralisation of capital "in a given country".

"A given country" meant one specific country, i.e. the laws of the world-market still exist. If the whole world became centralised, then there would be a new society (for those who want it) since the *world-market* would have been destroyed. Although *completely centralised* capital "in a given country" can plan, it cannot plan away the contradicitions of capitalist production. If the *organic composition* of capital on a world scale is 5 to 1, moving to 6 to 1, to 7 to 1, etc., centralised capital in a given country *has to keep pace with that*. The only way to escape it would be by a productivity of labour so great that it could keep ahead of the rest and still organise its production for use. Such a productivity of labour is impossible in capitalism which knows only the law of value and its consequence, accumulated labour and sweating proletarians. That is precisely why Engels wrote that though formally, · i.e. abstractly, complete state-property could overcome the contradictions, actually it could not, the "workers remain proletarians". The whole long dispute between underconsumption and rate of profit theorists has now been definitively settled precisely by the experience of Russia.

Lenin in 1917 repeated that state-capitalism without the Soviets meant "military penal labour" for the workers. The Soviet power was the road to socialism. The struggle in Russia and outside is the struggle against "military penal labour" and for the Soviet power. The revolt which gave birth to the CIO prevented American capital from transforming the whole of American production and society into the system which Ford and Bennett had established. This monstrous burden would have driven capital still further along the road of accumulation of capital, domination over the direct producer or accumulation of misery, lowered productivity, barbarism, paralysis and gangrene in all aspects of society. That was Germany. That would be the plan, the plan of capital, and with state property it is more free than before to plan its own ruin.

The totalitarian state in Russia prevents the workers from

making their social and political experiences in open class struggle. But by so doing, it ensures the unchecked reign of capital, the ruin of production and society, and the inevitability of total revolution.

The decisive question is not whether centralisation is complete or partial, heading towards completeness. The vital necessity of our time is to lay bare the violent antagonism of labour and capital at this definitive stage of centralisation of capital. Whether democratic or totalitarian, both types of society are in permanent decline and insoluble crisis. Both are at a stage when only a total reorganisation of social relations can lift society a stage higher. It is noteworthy that in the United States the capitalist class is aware of this, and the most significant work that is being done in political economy is the desperate attempt to find some way of reconciling the working class to the agonies of mechanised production and transferring its implacable resistance into creative co-operation. That is of educational value and many of its findings will be used by the socialist proletariat. In Russia this resistance is labelled "remnants of capitalist ideology" and the whole power of the totalitarian state is organised to crush it in theory as well as in fact.

We shall see that upon this theoretical analysis the whole strategy of revolutionary politics is qualitatively differentiated from stalinism, inside and outside Russia. The stalinists seek to establish themselves in the place of the rival bureaucracy. The rival bureaucracy seeks to substitute itself in the place of stalinism. The Fourth International must not seek to substitute itself for either of these, not after, not during nor before the conquest of power. Theory and practice are governed by the recognition of the necessity that the bureaucracy as such must be overthrown.

We can now come to a theoretical conclusion about the question of plan and with it, nationalisation. For the capitalist mode of labour in its advanced stages, the bureaucratic-administrative plan can become the greatest instrument of torture for the proletariat that capitalism has yet produced. State property and total planning are nothing else but the complete subordination of the proletariat to capital. That is why in *The Invading Socialist Society* we summed up our total theory in two points, the first of which is:

> "1. It is the task of the Fourth International to drive as clear a line between bourgeois nationalisation and proletarian nationalisation as the revolutionary Third International drove between bourgeois democracy and proletarian democracy."

All theory for our epoch must begin here.

But aren't state property and the plan progressive?

State property as such and plan as such are metaphysical abstractions. They have a class content. Aren't trusts progressive, Lenin was asked in 1916. He replied:

"It is the work of the bourgeoisie to develop trusts, to drive children and women into factories, to torture them there, corrupt them and condemn them to the utmost misery. We do not 'demand' such a development; we do not 'support' it; we struggle against it. But *how* do we struggle? We know that trusts and factory work of women are progressive. We do not wish to go backwards to crafts, to pre-monopolist capitalism, to domestic work of women. Forward through the trusts, etc., and beyond them toward socialism!" (*The Bolsheviks and the World War*).

We reply similarly. This is marxism — the antagonism of classes. Under capitalism, private or state, all science, knowledge, organisation, are developed only at the expense and degradation of the proletariat. But at the same time capitalism organises the proletariat for struggle. We do not "demand" or "support" plan. We proposed to substitute proletarian power and subordinate plan to the revolutionary struggle of the proletariat.

Where does orthodox trotskyism stand on this? Every member knows the answer. Nowhere. Its conception of plan is summarised in the slogan in the Transitional Programme: "The plan must be revised from top to bottom in the interests of the producers and consumers."

The capitalist plan cannot be revised except in the interests of capital. It is not the plan that is to be revised. It is the whole mode of production which is to be overthrown.

The whole analysis is in terms of (to use the underlined phrases of the Transitional Programme) *"social inequality"* and *"political inequality"*. In *The Revolution Betrayed* the chapter entitled "The Struggle for Productivity of Labour" deals with money and plan, inflation, rehabilitation of the ruble. It says that analysis of Stakhanovism proves that it is a vicious form of piecework. But it soon returns to the question of the ruble. And it finally ends on the note that the Soviet administrative personnel is "far less adequate to the productive tasks than the workers". Therefore, what is needed is more competence, more efficiency, less red tape, less laziness, etc. If the Russian bureaucracy were more efficient, more scientific, etc., the results for the Russian proletariat would be worse.

The chapter "Social Relations in the Soviet Union" in *The Revolution Betrayed* deals with the privileges, wages, etc. of the bureaucracy in relation to the workers. Neither in the Transitional Programme nor *The Revolution Betrayed* does analysis of the worker in the production process find any place, except where in the Programme the slogan is raised, "factory committees should be returned the right to control production". In the analyses of orthodox trotskyism there are a few references here and there to creative initiative being needed at this stage. That is all.

All the slogans in the Transitional Programme do nothing more than demand the restoration of democracy to where it was in 1917, thereby showing that the whole great experience of thirty years has passed orthodox trotskyism by. World capitalism has moved to the crisis and counter-revolution in production. The programme for the reintroduction of political democracy does no more than reintroduce the arena for the reintroduction of a new bureaucracy when the old one is driven out.

But, after all, production relations must include somewhere workers, labour, the labour process — the place where the population is differentiated by function. The World Congress Resolution (*Fourth International*, June 1948) quotes from *The Revolution Betrayed* an elaborate summary by Trotsky of his own position in 1936. The worker in the labour process is not mentioned. The resolution asks: what alterations have to be made in the analysis following the development of the past eleven years? It begins:

". . . the social differentiation is the result of bourgeois norms of *distribution*; it has not yet entered the domain of ownership of the means of production."

The struggle out of which the CIO was born, the domination of the machine, the drive for greater productivity, what about that? The orthodox trotskyist in 1950 would have to reply: the question is not a question of production. It is a question of collective ownership; it is a question of the thieving bureaucracy taking for itself consumption goods which belong to the workers; it is a question of whether the bureaucracy passes laws of inheritance; it is a question in 1950 as it was in 1934 of whether the tendency to primitive accumulation will restore private property, etc. etc. Is this an injustice to orthodox trotskyism? If it is, then *what* would it reply, and where is any other reply to be found?

1950

11

Fiction and Reality

[*This is a chapter drawn from* Mariners, Renegades and Castaways, *a full-length study of Herman Melville which James wrote during his internment on Ellis Island in 1952. It was published privately in New York the following year, immediately before his expulsion from the country; he added an appendix pointing out the contrast between the charge of "unamerican activities" lodged against him and his interest in and concern for American culture, as demonstrated in the book. James says: "I had read* Moby Dick *in Trinidad when I was about twenty-one. The book had been too much for me . . . I suppose my mind was too concerned with more immediate things. But I went to the United States in 1938: I read* Moby Dick *and saw the life, read the history of the United States, and realised what a masterpiece of fiction it was — in my opinion the greatest single piece of creative writing after Shakespeare."*]

The question of questions is: how could a book from the world of 1850 contain so much of the world of the 1950s?

The best answer is given by Melville himself. He once explained how great writers wrote great books. A character like Ahab is an original character. And by original character Melville meant a type of human being that had never existed before in the world. Such characters come once in many centuries and are as rare as men who found new religions, philosophers who revolutionise human thinking, and statesmen who create new political forms. Melville mentions three: Satan from Milton's *Paradise Lost*, Hamlet from Shakespeare's play and the Don Quixote of Cervantes. That is how rare they are. According to Melville, many a gifted writer can create dozens of interesting, sprightly, clever, intriguing characters. But original characters? No. A writer is very lucky if in his lifetime he creates one.

Where does a writer find such characters? And here Melville is categorical. He finds them in the world around him, in the world *outside*. They do not originate in his head.

The process seems to be as follows. The originality, the newness, in the actual human beings a great writer sees, are half-formed, partial, incomplete. Starting from these hints, the great writer creates the type as it would be if its originality were perfected. As a fully developed human personality, a character like Hamlet, Don Quixote, Ahab never existed, and in fact could not exist. He is a composite of a realistic base from which imagination and logic build a complete whole. But if something new in personality has really come into the world, if the writer observes closely enough, and his creative power is great enough, then future generations will be able actually to see and recognise the type in a manner the author himself was not able to do.

But almost as important is the second aspect of the process. As the artist clarifies the newness, the originality of the character, the character itself becomes a kind of revolving light illuminating what is around it. Everything else grows and develops to correspond to this central figure so that the original character, so to speak, helps the artist to create a portrait not only of a new type of human being but also of the society and the people who correspond to him.

Melville does not say this about Ahab and *Moby Dick* in so many words. But the evidence is overwhelming that when writing about characters like Hamlet and Don Quixote, and how they were created, he was drawing on his own experience in creating Ahab. Except for Aristotle, nearly 2,500 years ago, and Hegel who wrote a generation before Melville, no critic of literature has written so profoundly of the art of great writing.

What is more important in this theory is the idea that the great tragic writer has to work out an adequate conception of the character, to create the character in its perfection. It is a process that lasts for years until finally a great masterpiece is written. To follow this in the case of Melville, we need only the bare elementary facts of his life before *Moby Dick* and these can be told in less than a hundred words.

Melville was born in New York in 1819, of a good family. But his people lost their money and after doing various odd jobs, he went to sea as a common sailor, first to England and then to the Pacific on a whaling-vessel. He deserted, lived among the natives, and finally, after four years, came home as a seaman on board a ship of the United States Navy. He was twenty-five years old. He began to write, his first book was a success, and between 1845 and 1850 he published five books. In 1851 he wrote *Moby Dick*.

No one except scholars and people specially interested in literature need read any of these books. They are not worth it. But it is in them that lies the answer as to how Melville came to write *Moby Dick*. It is no miracle. You can trace the same process in the writings of Shakespeare.

The first book, *Typee*, is an account of Melville's life among that cannibal people. But quite early in the book we who are familiar with *Moby Dick* come across the following episode.

The hero is plotting to escape from the ship, and he decides to ask another man to accompany him, one Toby. Toby

> "was one of that class of rovers you sometimes meet at sea, who never reveal their origin, never allude to home, and go rambling over the world as if pursued by some mysterious fate they cannot possibly elude. . . . He was a strange wayward

being, moody, fitful, and melancholy — at times almost morose. He had a quick and fiery temper too, which, when thoroughly roused, transported him into a state bordering on delirium. It is strange the power that a mind of deep passion has over feebler natures. I have seen a brawny fellow, with no lack of ordinary courage, fairly quail before this slender stripling, when in one of his furious fits. . . .

No one ever saw Toby laugh. . . ."

Now there was a real person, Toby, who shared Melville's adventure. He settled down on land. He lost no leg, captained no ship and pursued no whales. But here, already, Melville's mind is struck by the type of person who will eventually become Ahab. Deep resentment against the world, solitude, gloom, power over men.

At the same time his mind thus early is open. In *Typee* he holds up to admiration the civilisation of the Typees and makes the most damaging comparisons with Western civilisation. Melville says that during the weeks he lived among the Typees, no one was ever put on trial for any public offence. As far as he could see there were no courts of law or equity. No police. Yet everything went on in the valley with a perfect harmony and smoothness. He denounces missionaries, white traders and government officials for degrading and corrupting this ideal civilisation, cannibalistic as it was.

"I will frankly declare," he writes, "that after passing a few weeks in this valley of the Marquesas, I formed a higher estimate of human nature than I had ever before entertained. But alas! since then I have become one of a crew of a man-of-war and the pent-up wickedness of five hundred men has nearly overturned all my previous theories."

The book was a success both in England and the United States and Melville immediately began a continuation, *Omoo*. This one, as he says in the introduction, is to describe the whale-fishery and the sailors who work at it.

The attack upon the crew is even more savage than in *Typee*:

"The crew manning vessels like these are for the most part villains of all nations and dyes; picked up in the lawless ports of the Spanish Main, and among the savages of the islands. Like galley-slaves, they are only to be governed by scourges and chains. Their officers go among them with dirk and pistol — concealed, but ready at a grasp."

Among the sailors there is one memorable figure — a native harpooneer, powerful, fearless and ferocious. Being insulted by a seaman, he does his best to wreck the ship with all on board, including himself. Here is another of these Ahab-like types.

Then Melville drops the real business of an artist, the study of human personality and human relations, and writes a book whose special value is that it shows how very close his mind was to ours.

Mardi is an ill-constructed, ill-written book, and on the whole, for the average reader, is today, even more than when it was published, almost unreadable. Its importance is that in the course of writing this book Melville became convinced that the world as he knew it was headed for disaster.

This is the story. An intellectual who is at the same time a common sailor deserts from a ship. This time his companion is an old Scandinavian sailor, Jarl, ignorant and superstitious, but a man of skill, bravery, loyalty and sterling character. In Jarl are the first signs of the crew of *Moby Dick*, except for the fact that he is an individual. Their voyage is also a quest. Here for the first time appears the idea of a ship setting out to search for an answer to the problems of human destiny. After some realistic adventures, they are joined by a native savage, Samoa, a man of great bravery who has lost his arm. Very, very faintly the outline of *Moby Dick* is beginning to appear.

In a fight with natives they gain possession of a beautiful white girl, Yillah. The young man falls in love with her and woos her successfully.

They land on territory inhabited by natives. The young sailor poses as a god, Taji, they are all welcomed by the native ruler, King Media, and entertained in his palace.

While they are there, a body of natives comes to petition King Media, demanding that thereafter all differences between man and man, together with all alleged offences against the state, be tried by twelve good men and true. They are demanding what is in effect trial by jury. King Media laughs long, loudly and scornfully: "I am King, ye are slaves. Mine to command, yours to obey."

Thus we are plunged violently and without warning into a satirical novel whose subject matter is the fundamentals of political democracy.

Yillah is abducted from Media's kingdom by enemies and it is soon clear that Yillah is a symbolic figure, signifying peace, happiness, beauty and whatnot.

To help find her King Media himself sets out with Taji to visit the neighbouring countries. Taji is determined to find his Yillah who for a moment seems to be the answer to his quest. This time he is assisted by philosophy, history, poetry, and experience, in the persons of Mohi the historian, Babbalanja the philosopher, Yoomy the poet, and King Media himself. Together they visit country after country in Poorpheero, which turns out to be Europe, and then they visit Vivenza, which turns out to be America. It is a foretaste of things to come that Jarl, the sailor and Samoa, the native, have no interest in this search for individual happiness. They stay behind and are soon murdered. In the intervals of their examination of these countries and their interview with their rulers, the travellers talk incessantly about religion, philosophy, poetry, history and politics.

Melville's correspondence shows us that when he started *Mardi*, he had seriously intended to write some sort of continuation of *Typee* and *Omoo*. It is obvious therefore that he had yielded to what was an irresistible impulse to write down his views on the philosophy, literature and politics of Europe and America. Melville had been reading hard, ancient and modern history, classical literature, modern literature, philosophy and religion, the arguments for and against Christianity. Since his success as an author he corresponded and talked regularly with educated and informed people. *Mardi* shows the results.

Country after country in Europe is rapidly visited. The poverty of the majority; the tyranny of the rich; aristocracy, organised religion, the Papacy, law, medicine, war, the immoral rivalries of national states, the deception of the people by their rulers, the emptines of philosophy, the uselessness of poetry, all these are mercilessly castigated by Melville. A great deal of it had been said before. Melville's writing is not very brilliant. At times he is quite superficial. But his rejection of what the people of his time were doing and thinking is as complete as he can make it.

How close his experience was to ours is proved by the fact that the two things that interested him most were (a) the world revolution and (b) the future of American democracy.

The travellers visit Vivenza, the United States. No Republican in the campaign of 1952 has said anything so savage against graft, greed and corruption in Washington politics as Melville did. Melville does not denounce one party. He denounces the whole Congress and his attitude is that it is and always will be the same. Downstairs where great affairs of state are being carried out, the party leaders sit around a huge bowl. "They were all chiefs of immense capacity — how many gallons there was no finding out."

Next day they visit that section of Vivenza again. News had just come of the 1848 revolutions in Europe. Here we must remember that when the news of the French revolution of 1848 came to Washingon, not only did the populace rejoice, but the White House itself was illuminated. This is the scene to which Melville is referring. People are delirious, awaiting and greeting with wild cheers and wild excitement the successive news of the fate of monarchical governments. "Who may withstand the people? The times tell terrible tales to tyrants! Ere we die, freemen, all Mardi will be free."

Amidst the tumult the excited people discover a scroll written by an anonymous person, and after much discussion, it is decided to read it aloud. Melville leaves the question of who wrote the scroll a mystery, but there is no doubt that it contains his essential views.

According to the scroll, the great error of the people of the United States is to believe that Europe is now in the last scene of her drama and that all preceding historical events were ordained to bring "a universal and permanent republic". People who think that way are fools. History teaches that everything collapses in the end. It was so with the republic of Rome. It was so with the republic of the French revolution. If America is different, it is only because it has a vast western territory. When that is overrun, the crisis must come. If its population had been packed tight as that of Britain, then the great experiment might have resulted in explosion. The people are free because they are young, but age overtakes all things. Do not think that America will "forever remain as liberal as now."

Equality is an illusion. No equality of knowledge can get rid of the inbred servility of mortal to mortal. Men inevitably are divided into brigades and battalions, with captains at their head.

It is not the primary aim and chief blessing to be politically free. Freedom is only good as a means. It is not an end in itself. If men fought it out against tyrants until the knife was plunged in to the handle, they would not thereby free themselves from the yoke of slavery. In no stable democracy do all men govern themselves. Though an army be all volunteers, it must be ruled by martial law. People who live in association with each other must delegate power.

"Freedom is the name for a thing that is *not* freedom."

All over Europe "poverty is abased before riches . . . everywhere, suffering is found."

"Thus, freedom is more social than political. And its real felicity is not to be shared. *That* is of a man's own individual getting and holding. It is not, who rules the state, but who rules me. Better be secure under one king, than exposed to violence from twenty millions of monarchs, though oneself be of the number."

Though great reforms are needed, nowhere are bloody revolutions required. People believed that the old ages of blood and sword were over and the world was settling down. That is an illusion. The world is on fire once more. America should cut herself away from Europe in deed and word.

When the travellers leave Washington they go to the South where they see slavery. They all burn with anger but they cannot agree on whether revolution by the slaves is justified. And yet, if they do not think it is, they are, they admit, no better than Calhoun, the apologist for slavery. Their anger fizzles out in frustration. It was not the first time that the travellers had been baffled by this question of revolution. When the French revolution of 1848 broke out, they had been torn between fears of the violence and destruction and hope that something valuable for mankind might come of it.

It is obvious that the Universal Republic of 1848 was a far cry from the world revolution as we have known it since 1917. It is also extremely dangerous to take these ideas as specific political policies of Melville. He was an artist, and had made no consistent studies of economics and politics. He was for example an extreme, in fact a fanatical democrat. Some of the views he expressed he would change in his next book. But *Mardi* shows that already he believed that a future of continually expanding democracy was an illusion, for America as for the rest of the world, that he considered politics a game played by politicians, and that he was grappling seriously with the question of what exactly did men mean by freedom. It is not too much to say that he was thinking about the very things that the vast majority of men are thinking about today.

Yillah was never found. Instead Taji is tempted by the dark-haired Hautia who is a very crude symbol for wealth, sensuality, luxury and power. He nearly succumbs, but in the end he flies from her, alone in an open boat, pursued by three of Hautia's soldiers. "And thus, pursuers and pursued, fled on, over an endless sea." That is the last sentence of the novel. What the sailor-intellectual was looking for he has not found.

Mardi was a failure. Melville was now very broke. He had to write for money and write fast. But it is precisely this sitting down and scribbling exactly what is in his mind that allows us to see how he is developing. In his next two books before *Moby Dick* we see him strengthening his rejection of the world as he knows it, and working out what will take its place. And it is here that he begins to work again on the type which will become Ahab.

Redburn is an account of his first voyage to England. Like his first two books it is fiction on a solid groundwork of fact. He is once more living through his early experiences. Dominating *Redburn* is the character of Jackson. Jackson is a man of passion, of spiritual force, and a man in revolt against the whole world for what it has done to him. He is the best seaman on board. Despite physical weakness he is so overpowering a personality that all the men on board are afraid of him. Without education, he is marvellously quick and cunning, and understands human nature and those he has to deal with. And finally there was his eye, "the most deep, subtle, infernal looking eye, that I ever saw lodged in a human head".

He might have been thirty or fifty. He had travelled all over the world as a sailor and had horrible experiences to tell, full of piracies, plagues and poisonings. Broken in health from the consequences of the evil life he had lived, he hated the young and healthy. He seemed determined to die with a curse on his lips. The world seemed to him to be one person, which had done him some dreadful harm and his hatred was rankling and festering in his heart. And Melville gives the reason. One day a sailor, in Jackson's hearing, talks about the heaven which is awaiting all men, including sailors, who will then be repaid for their sufferings on earth. All Jackson's hatred seems to fly out of him at one breath. The sailor is a fool to talk like that. All talk of heaven is lies. "I know it!" And all who believe in it are fools. Heaven for sailors? Will they let a sailor in, with tar on his hands and oil in his hair? Death swallows a sailor as a sailor swallows a pill and he wishes that some tempest would swallow down the whole ship.

Here at first sight is the genuine totalitarian consciousness of injustice, the totalitarian hatred and the totalitarian readiness to destroy the whole world in revenge, which will be the basis of Ahab's character. But Jackson is no Ahab. Jackson is a worker whose evil character Melville attributes to the suffering and misery which society imposed upon the class to which he belonged. Just here some of the greatest writers of the nineteenth century stopped and never went a step further. It is precisely here, however, that Melville's originality begins. Melville knew workers and workers are not people who in revenge wish to destroy the world.

In his account of how a great writer finally arrives at portraying a great character, he had written that, beginning with the character, everything around seems to start up to meet it, to correspond to it. It seems, as far as one can work out such things, that this was the way Melville got to the crew of *Moby Dick*. This much is certain. When the future creator of the crew of *Moby Dick* sat down to write his first book, *Typee*, all he had to say about the sailors was their coarseness of mind and body, their debauchery, their unholy passions, their gross licentiousness, their shameful drunkenness. When he wrote about the whale-fishery and whaling-vessels in *Omoo*, it was worse. In *Mardi*, there is a change. But now in *Redburn* he begins seriously to examine the crew. He still portrays them as ignorant and cruel men, but he begins to talk about their skill. More important, he launches into a long defence of sailors as a class of workers. They carry around the globe missionaries, ambassadors, opera-singers, armies, merchants. The business of the world depends upon them; if they were suddenly to emigrate to the navies of the moon everything on earth would stop except its revolution on its axis and the orators in the American Congress. Respectable people and pious hypocrites give a little charity to sailors and speak of the improvemnt in their condition. There is no real improvement and there can never be. The world is constituted in such a way that the working poor have to bear the burdens, and the sailors are among those who have to bear them.

In *Redburn* also three new things appear. He paints a horrible picture of the misery of the population of Liverpool and the general cruelty. We shall see this again in the opening chapters of *Moby Dick*. The account of the voyage home describes at length the suffering of a body of Irish immigrants, and the cruelty and selfishness of the captain and the cabin passengers.

Also he changes his mind about America cutting itself away from Europe. Now he looks forward to America being in future years a society of liberty and freedom, composed of all the races of the earth:

> "There is something in the contemplation of the mode in which America has been settled that, in a noble breast, should forever extinguish the prejudices of national dislikes. Settled by the people of all nations, all nations may claim her for their own. You cannot spill a drop of American blood without spilling the blood of the whole world. . . . Our blood is as the flood of the

Amazon, made up of a thousand noble currents all pouring into one. We are not a nation, so much as a world . . . Our ancestry is lost in the universal pageantry; and Caesar and Alfred, St Paul and Luther, and Homer and Shakespeare are as much ours as Washington, who is as much the world's as our own. We are the heirs of all time, and with all nations we divide our inheritance. On this Western Hemisphere all tribes and peoples are forming into one federated whole; and there is a future which shall see the estranged children of Adam restored as to the old hearthstone in Eden."

All this we shall meet again in the conception of the crew of the Pequod as an Anacharsis Clootz deputation, seeking the universal republic of liberty and fraternity under the leadership of American officers.

But his main preoccupation is still the individual character of passionate revolt, who for the time being is Jackson.

He compares Jackson to the Emperor Tiberius, an embodiment of evil in ancient times, and to Satan of Milton's *Paradise Lost*. This Yankee sailor, Jackson, he says, is worthy to rank with these historic figures. But Melville is as yet still somewhat confused. He has not seen the character in its perfection. There is, he says, no dignity in evil. Yet is is a credit to Milton's genius that out of such a monster as Satan, he could create so magnificent a poem. Melville has not solved his problem but he is already conscious of what it is. He has to show how genuine and deeply-rooted is this fearful desire for revenge upon the world by embittered men, the men of his century — the Yankees he knows. He feels that this is a mighty force in the world around him, and that the world will have to reckon with it sooner or later. He is already certain that this destructive passion is not characteristic of aristocrats, financiers and property-owners. For them he has a general contempt. It is to be found among men concerned with work.

If you have read *Moby Dick* you can feel the uncertainty in *Redburn*. But the man of passionate revolt who will reorganise or destroy, and the crew, if only in Melville's new attitude to it, are there.

In his next book, *White Jacket*, he crosses the bridge from his own time into ours. His greatest discovery is to push individual characteristics aside and see men in terms of the work that they do. A warship is an organisation where men perform special functions. This man may be a drunkard, that one a thief, the other one writes poetry, another is a splendid, fine sailor, a born leader of men and charming. But a ship is in reality nothing more than various groups of men who do certain types of work, without which there would be complete chaos. It is this specific type of work which determines their social characteristics. And the ship is only a miniature of the world in which we live.

It is this discovery which leads him to perhaps his greatest single

step, taking the character of Jackson from out of the crew and
placing him among the officers, where we will see him as Ahab.

What is the bitterest personal cry of Ahab? It is his isolation, the
isolation inseparable from the function of authority in the modern
world. Melville found it in writing about the officers on the warship. Take the Commodore. He was perhaps dumb, for the author
of the book never heard him utter a word. But not only was he
dumb himself but his mere appearance on the deck seemed to
give everyone the lock-jaw. The real reason was perhaps that like
all high functionaries he had to preserve his dignity, and inasmuch
as apart from the common dignity of manhood, Commodores have
no real dignity at all, Commodores, like crowned heads, general-
issimos, lord-high admirals, have to carry themselves straight, which
is uncomfortable to themselves and ridiculous to an enlightened
generation. Melville is very light-hearted about it but before two
years Ahab will speak from the depths of his heart about the
Guinea-Coast slavery of solitary command.

On the Pequod, Ahab's word is law and it is this which paralyses
resistance. Next to the Commodore on the man-of-war is the captain. His word is law. He never speaks but in the imperative mood.
He commands even the sun. For when the noon observation is
taken, it is officially twelve o'clock only when the captain says
"*Make* it so". Ahab will smash the quadrant and denounce the
whole procedure and all science included.

Ahab's dinner-table is the symbol of his social isolation. The
dinner-table of a man-of-war is the criterion of rank. The Commodore dines alone at four or five o'clock; the captain at three;
the younger men at two. A captain once dined at five when the
Commodore dined at four. A note from the Commodore made him
change to half-past three.

It is the relations between men at work that shape human character. And the most decisive relation on board ship is the relation between officers and men.

There are marines on board. Why? Because the officers want
to use the marines against the sailors and the sailors against the
marines. And Melville condemns the whole system not only as evil
but as incurable.

> "The immutable ceremonies and iron etiquette of a man-of-
> war; the spiked barriers separating the various grades of rank;
> the delegated absolutism of authority on all hands; the impossi-
> bility, on the part of the common seaman, of appeal from
> incidental abuses, and many more things that might be enumerat-
> ed, all tend to beget in most armed ships a general social con-
> dition which is the precise reverse of what any Christian could
> desire. And though there are vessels that in some measure furnish
> exceptions to this; and though, in other ships, the thing may be
> glazed over by a guarded, punctilious exterior, almost completely
> hiding the truth from casual visitors, while the worst facts touch-

ing the common sailor are systematically kept in the background, yet it is certain that what has here been said of the domestic interior of a man-of-war will, in a greater or less degree, apply to most vessels in the navy. It is not that the officers are so malevolent, nor, altogether, that the man-of-war's-man is so vicious. Some of these evils are unavoidably generated through the operation of the naval code; others are absolutely organic to a navy establishment, and, like other organic evils, are incurable, except when they dissolve with the body they live in."

War? "The whole matter of war is a thing that smites common sense and Christianity in the face; so everything connected with it is utterly foolish, unchristian, barbarous, brutal and savouring of the Feejee Islands, cannibalism, saltpetre and the devil." But what if your country is attacked? That has nothing to do with it. If you profess Christianity, be then Christians.

The chaplain is a hypocrite; the surgeon a bloodthirsty maniac and his subordinates cowards and self-seekers; the master-at-arms (the civilian responsible for discipline) is a crook, a smuggler and an unmitigated scoundrel; the purser is a thief.

But Melville's most intriguing step forward is the manner in which he now treats the crew. *White Jacket* is full of their shortcomings and their crimes. But he now gives a detailed description of the various types of work that they do and the kind of men who do it. To give two examples:

The sheet-anchor men are veterans all, fine sailors, feared by the officers and all fanatical worshippers of Andrew Jackson. Three decks down are the troglodytes, people who live below the surface among the water-tanks, casks and cables. You never get to know their names. But: "In times of tempests, when all hands are called to save ship, they issue forth into the gale, like the mysterious men of Paris, during the massacre of the three days of September; every one marvels who they are, and whence they come; they disappear as mysteriously; and are seen no more, until another general commotion."

The reference is of course to the September massacres, one of the best-known events in the French revolution, and it is impossible to believe that Melville is not aware of the overtones of what he is writing.

For him now the crew embodies some type of social order. Their association at work gives them interests, ideas and attitudes that separate them entirely from the rest of society.

He has not got the differences between the crew and officers nearly so clear as he will in *Moby Dick*, where Ahab, Starbuck and Ishmael, on the one hand, and the anonymous crew on the other react to things, large and small, in such consistent opposition. But once you have read *Moby Dick*, then the line of division in *White Jacket* is already clear.

The whole of the last chapter sums up the ship as symbolical of the real world. "Outwardly regarded, our craft is a lie; for all that is outwardly seen of it is the clean-swept deck, and oft-painted planks comprised above the water-line; whereas, the vast mass of our fabric, with all its store-rooms of secrets, forever slides along far under the surface." The great majority are far below deck and no one knows what is happening to them. Commodores and captains and Lord High Admirals parade as leaders, but neither they nor anybody else knows where the vessel is going. Characteristic of Melville's attitude is the fact that he praises the Commodore as a brave old man who had fought gallantly for his country. The captain, as captains go, was not a bad or vindictive man. They lived in a world in which they had to behave as they did. Very striking is his good humour and high spirits which he rarely loses, except on the question of flogging. He does not urge action. As in *Mardi* he is clearing his mind. There is very little of this type of rebelliousness in *Moby Dick*.

Melville is not an agitator. He is a creative artist who is moving steadily towards that rarest of achievements — the creation of a character which will sum up a whole epoch of human history. And twice in *White Jacket* he once more tackles the type.

The first is old Ushant, captain of the forecastle. He is a man in his sixties, always alert to his duty and boldly mounting the fore-yard in a gale. But when not required by duty he was staid, reserved and a majestic old man, who frequently talked philosophy to the men around him:

> "Nor was his philosophy to be despised; it abounded in wisdom. For this Ushant was an old man, of strong natural sense, who had seen nearly the whole terraqueous globe, and could reason of civilised and savage, of gentile and Jew, of Christian and Moslem. The long nightwatches of the sailor are eminently adapted to draw out the reflective faculties of any serious-minded man, however humble or uneducated. Judge, then, what half a century of battling out watches on the ocean must have done for this fine old tar. He was a sort of sea Socrates, in his old age 'pouring out his last philosophy and life', as sweet Spencer has it; and I never could look at him, and survey his right reverend beard, without bestowing upon him that title which, in one of his satires, Persius gives to the immortal quaffer of the hemlock."

Strange and contradictory (but profoundly logical) are the ways by which writers arrive at their masterpieces. The very first reference to Ahab in *Moby Dick* is as follows:

> ". . . a man of greatly superior force, with a globular brain and a ponderous heart; who has also by the stillness and seclusion of many long night-watches in the remotest waters, and beneath constellations never seen here at the north, been led to think untraditionally and independently; receiving all nature's sweet or

savage impressions fresh from her own virgin voluntary and confiding breast, and thereby chiefly, but with some help from accidental advantages to learn a bold and nervous lofty language — that man makes one in a whole nation's census — a mighty pageant creature, formed for noble tragedies."

One model for Ahab is clearly this delightful old man. But this old man too has much of the defiance of Ahab in him. As the ship nears home an order comes down that all beards are to be shaved. The men have been preparing magnificent beards for their homecoming and are furious. An insurrection almost breaks out and is averted in fact only by the experience and popularity of Jack Chase, a sailor beloved by all on board. Finally, however, the men give in, all except Old Ushant. He is threatened with flogging. He replies that his beard is his own. The old man is flogged and placed in irons, and though these are removed after a few days he remains confined for the rest of the voyage. His time of service was up, and when the ship reached port Ushant took a boat and went ashore, amid the unsuppressible cheers of all hands. The episode of the beards and Ushant fills four chapters and is the emotional climax of the book. Somehow that old man's beard had become the test of his manhood. They could have killed him but he would have died with his face unshaven.

The second example is none other than the hero of the book, young White Jacket himself. The young fellow is called up one day to be flogged, as usual before the crew. He is innocent but he explains in vain. The sentence will be carried out. White Jacket, however, is determined not to be flogged. Behind the spot where the captain is standing, there is no rail. He plans to rush at him and sweep him overboard. He himself will go overboard too. But that price he is prepared to pay. However, just as he is preparing to carry out this desperate measure, one of the leading marines does an unheard-of thing. He steps out of the assembled crew and tells the captain that he does not think White Jacket is guilty. The leader of the seamen, encouraged by this, does the same. Taken aback, the captain hesitates for a moment and then dismisses White Jacket and saunters off "while I who in the desperation of my soul had but just escaped being a murderer and a suicide almost burst into tears of thanksgiving where I stood".

Suicide and murder. Destroy yourself and everything you can take with you rather than submit. Even after he had written *Moby Dick*, Melville for years pondered on this peculiar type of character which seemed to him new in the world, and which he thought, and so rightly, would increasingly dominate human society. But *White Jacket* was the end of his apprenticeship.

Is it possible now to have any doubt as to what Melville had in mind when he wrote *Moby Dick*? These early books of his are not an account of his life from 1839, when he first shipped, to 1844 when he returned home. They are an account of the development of a mind from 1844 to 1850, the finest mind that has ever functioned in the New World and the greatest since Shakespeare's that has ever concerned itself with literature. It must not be though that he consciously plotted his course from book to book as it has been described here. But the books show how logically the process developed, and if not at the time, then years after *Moby Dick*, Melville recognised how it had happened and sketched it out in his book, *The Confidence Man.*

Yet the ultimate question is not how Melville did it, but what he did. And the proof of that is in the world around us. It is not what he had in mind when he wrote that is important. If he were to return today, how would the author of *Moby Dick* see the world in which we live and which he divined in relation to the world he actually knew? The answer to that question lies in his books and in the world around us.

As Melville gets rid of traditional conceptions, he begins to re-capture his own individual experiences. He begins to realise that his contact with Nature is made through his work on the ship. And something new is born in literature, as new as Ahab is among men. Redburn climbs the mast in a storm. There is a wild delirium about it, a rushing of the blood, a thrilling and throbbing of the whole system, to find yourself tossed up at every pitch into the clouds of a stormy sky and hovering like a judgment angel between heaven and earth, both hands free, with one foot in the rigging and one somewhat behind you in the air.

The attitude is still romantic. Melville is still describing Red-burn's feelings as a literary intellectual would. But this is not Rousseau flying to Nature from the evils of society, or Words-worth meditating over a yellow primrose, or Shelley pouring out verses about liberty to the West Wind, or Keats following a night-ingale over Hampstead Heath and drowning himself in thoughts of death and countless generations of dead men, or Whitman, shocked at the death of Lincoln, going off by himself to look at the water and dream of death. This is not personal emotion or reflection or play. Redburn has to get up there as a matter of business when-ever it is needed, calm or storm, and, as Melville warned Ishmael dreaming on the mast-head, if he misses, he will fall and lose his life.

By *White Jacket* Melville has moments in which he gets rid of all literary self-consciousness. They are rounding Cape Horn, and on that journey no one ever knows when a destructive squall may leap out of the calm and sink the ship with every soul on board. A storm bursts. The men who are holding the double-wheel are jumping up and down with their hands on the spokes "for the whole helm and galvanised keel were fiercely feverish, with the life imparted to them by the tempest". Fifty men are ordered aloft to furl the main-sail. The rigging is coated with ice. For three-quarters of an hour they remain in the darkness clinging for dear life and finally have to abandon the task. But they cannot get back so easily. Some have to throw themselves prostrate along the yard, and embrace it with arms and legs and just hold on. Yet no one was afraid:

"The truth is, that, in circumstances like these, the sense of fear is annihilated in the unutterable sights that fill all the eyes, and the sounds that fill all the ear. You become identified with the tempest; your insignificance is lost in the riot of the stormy universe around."

You cannot find anything like this in all the Romantic wrters, from Rousseau to Whitman.

And, very significantly, the next paragraph is:

"Below us, our noble frigate seemed thrice its real length — a vast black wedge, opposing its widest end to the combined fury of the sea and wind."

No wonder in *Moby Dick* and elsewhere Melville makes jokes at Byron with his rhapsodic:
"Roll on, thou dark and deep blue ocean, roll,
Ten thousand fleets roll over thee in vain."
But as with so many of Melville's jokes, new conceptions of the world lay behind them. In the world which Melville saw, and more particularly saw was coming, there was no place any more for these outpourings of the individual soul. The dissatisfied intellectual would either join the crew with its social and practically scentific attitude to Nature or guilt would drive him to where it drove Ishmael. Hence Melville's totally new sense of Nature, as incessantly influencing men and shaping every aspect of their lives and characters. Nature is not a background to men's activity or something to be conquered and used. It is a part of man, at every turn physically, intellectually and emotionally, and man is a part of it. And if man does not integrate his daily life with his natural surroundings and his technical achievements, they will turn on him and destroy him. It was Ishmael who was tortured by the immensity of the universe and Ahab by the magnetic lights and the thunder. Not Tashtego.

Ishmael is a character in *Moby Dick* and sometimes it is impossible to tell whether Ishmael is writing or Melville himself is speaking in his own name. But by *Moby Dick* Melville has created for himself a total philosophy of life to replace the one he has rejected. It is not organised, but it is not in the slightest degree unconscious. This, one of the best-read of all Americans, says that if he should ever leave any literary work of importance behind him, the honour should go to whaling for "a whale-ship was my Yale college and my Harvard". These are not passing words. His qualification for attempting the enormous but neglected task of classifying the whales of the ocean is that he had read enormously and: "I have had to do with whales with these visible hands". He will try to portray the whale as he appears to the eye of the whale-man when the whale is moored alongside the whaleship. Most draw-ings and paintings of the whale he denounces as inaccurate and fanciful — the living whale in his full majesty and significance is to be seen at sea only in unfathomable waters. So with scientific writers. They have seldom had the benefit of a whaling voyage. Pictures of whales and whaling he judges as an expert whaleman would; his standard is the fidelity with which they represent the facts and the spirit of whaling. It is common sailors, he finds, who with their simple jack-knife will carve and engrave sketches of whaling-scenes, not quite up to the mark technically but close-packed in design and full of barbaric spirit and suggestiveness.

It might be thought that this undeviating reference back of everything to a body of men working would result in narrow-ness and limitation. The exact opposite is the case. It is he who attempts the first classification of the sperm whale because as he says the sperm whale lives not complete in any literature neither as science nor as poetry. He begins his book with some seventy quotations about whales, from the literature of the world. His analysis of the anatomy and physiology of every separate part of the whale is as complete as he can make it. But always from the point of view of men working with whales every day.

He is inexhaustible at the business of using his practical experiences and knowledge of whaling to make sometimes serious, at other times deliberately fanciful interpretations of ancient mythology and history. In the end the whale and whaling turn out to be a thread on which is hung a succession of pictures portray-ing the history of the world; before time; the mating and birth and domesticity of whales as they must have been before man; the social habits of whales and the cannibal savagery of sharks, in all of which sailors can see daily the primary instincts and the drives of what has become civilised man; the primitive aboriginalness of early civilisations; phallic-worship; the civilisations and writers of Greece and Rome; the succession of modern European nations who as whalemen ruled the seas. He wishes to include in his book everything:

> "Friends, hold my arms! For in the mere act of penning my thoughts of this Leviathan, they weary me, and make me faint with their outreaching comprehensiveness of sweep, as if to in-clude the whole circle of the sciences, and all the generations of whales, and men, and mastodons, past, present, and to come, with all the revolving panoramas of empire on earth, and throughout the whole universe, not excluding its suburbs."

But it is all as a whale-man, a common sailor, one who writes and reads and studies but always on the basis of "the living expe-riences of living men", and by this he means people who work with their hands. Man has to become a total, complete being, par-ticipating in all aspects and phases of a modern existence or the modern world would crush his divided personality.

He ranges the universe, groping down into the bottom of the sea where he has his hands "among the unspeakable foundations, ribs and very pelvis of the world". And from there he soars into the lyric outbursts which none of the Romantics can exceed.

> "At some old gable-roofed country houses you will see brass whales hung by the tail for knockers to the roadside door. . . . On the spires of some old-fashioned churches you will see sheet-iron whales placed there for weather-cocks; . . .
>
> In bony, ribby regions of the earth, where at the base of high broken cliffs masses of rock lie strewn in fantastic groupings upon the plain, you will often discover images as of the petrified forms of the Leviathan partly merged in grass, which of a windy day breaks against them in a surf of green surges.
>
> Then, again, in mountainous countries where the traveller is continually girdled by amphitheatrical heights; here and there from some lucky point of view you will catch passing glimpses of the profiles of whales defined along the undulating ridges. But you must be a thorough whaleman, to see these sights. . . .
>
> Nor when expandingly lifted by your subject, can you fail to trace our great whales in the starry heavens, and boats in pursuit of them; as when long filled with thoughts of war the Eastern nations saw armies locked in battle among the clouds. Thus at the North have I chased Leviathan round and round the Pole with the revolutions of the bright points that first defined him to me. And beneath the effulgent Antarctic skies I have boarded the Argo-Navis, and joined the chase against the starry Cetus far beyond the utmost stretch of Hydrus and the Flying Fish."

And here the poet of an industrial civilisation speaks.

> "With a frigate's anchors for my bridle-bitts and fasces of harpoons for spurs, would I could mount that whale and leap the topmost skies, to see whether the fabled heavens with all their countless tents really lie encamped beyond my mortal sight!"

Only a man who has thoroughly integrated his conception of life into modern industry could create so simple and yet so daring an image. Beginning with a certain type of mind, the mind of a man of genius, and fortunate enough to live at a time when some new type of personality has come into the world, Melville worked out an entirely new conception of society, not dealing with profits and the rights of private property (Ahab was utterly contemptuous of both), but with new conceptions of the relations between man and man, between man and his technology and between man and Nature. We can see Melville, in book after book, working them out until he arrives at the ultimate profundities of *Moby Dick*.

Melville is not only the representative writer of industrial civilisation. He is the only one that there is. In his great book the division and antagonisms and madnesses of an outworn civilisation are mercilessly dissected and cast aside. Nature, technology, the community of men, science and knowledge, literature and ideas are fused into a new humanism, opening a vast expansion of human capacity and human achievement. *Moby Dick* will either be universally burnt or be universally known in every language as the first comprehensive statement in literature of the conditions and perspectives for the survival of Western civilisation.

1953

12

Every Cook Can Govern: A Study of Democracy in Ancient Greece

[*Lenin's famous remark about the Russian masses' capacity to run their own society by themselves is the inspiration for James's most concentrated attempt to set down his appraisal of Greek democracy, a theme which runs through much of his work. It was first published in June 1956, in the Detroit-based journal* Correspondence.]

The Greek form of government was the city-state. Every Greek city was an independent state. At its best, in the city-state of Athens, the public assembly of all the citizens made all important decisions on such questions as peace or war. They listened to the envoys of foreign powers and decided what their attitude should be to what these foreign powers had sent to say. They dealt with all serious questions of taxation, they appointed the generals who should lead them in time of war. They organised the administration of the state, appointed officials and kept check on them. *The public assembly of all the citizens was the government.*

Perhaps the most striking thing about Greek democracy was that the administration (and there were immense administrative problems) was organised upon the basis of what is known as sortition, or, more easily, selection by lot. The vast majority of Greek officials were chosen by a method which amounted to putting names into a hat and appointing the ones whose names came out.

Now the average CIO bureaucrat or Labour member of parliament in Britain would fall in a fit if it was suggested to him that any worker selected at random could do the work that he is doing. But that was precisely the guiding principle of Greek democracy. And this form of government is the government under which flourished the greatest civilisation the world has ever known.

Modern parliamentary democracy elects representatives and these representatives constitute the government. Before the democracy came into power, the Greeks had been governed by various forms of government, including government by representatives. The democracy knew representative government and rejected it. It refused to believe that the ordinary citizen was not able to perform practically all the business of government. Not only did the public assembly of all the citizens keep all the important decisions in its own hands. For the Greek, the word *isonomia*, which meant equality, was used interchangeably for democracy. For the Greek, the two meant the same thing. For the Greek, a man who did not take part in politics was an *idiotes,* an idiot, from which we get our modern word "idiot", whose meaning, however, we have limited. Not only did the Greeks choose all officials by lot. They limited their time of service. When a man had served once, as a general rule, he was excluded from serving again because the Greeks believed in rotation, everybody taking his turn to administer the state.

Intellectuals like Plato and Aristotle detested the system. And Socrates thought that government should be by experts and not by the common people. For centuries, philosophers and political writers, bewildered by these Greeks who when they said equality meant it, have either abused this democracy or tried to explain that this direct democracy was suitable only for the city-state. Large modern communities, they say, are unsuitable for such a form of government. We of *Correspondence* believe that the larger the modern community, the more imperative it is for it to govern itself by the principle of direct democracy (it need not be a mere copy of the Greek). Otherwise we face a vast and ever-growing bureaucracy. That is why a study, however brief, of the constitution and governmental procedures of Greek democracy is so important for us today.

Let us see how Greek democracy administered justice.

The Greek cities for a time had special magistrates and judges of a special type, like those that we have today. When the democracy came into power, about the middle of the fifth century B.C., there began and rapidly developed a total reorganisation of the system of justice. The quorum for important sessions of the assembly was supposed to be six thousand. The Greek democracy therefore at the beginning of each year, chose by lot twelve groups of five hundred each. These five hundred tried the cases and their decisions were final.

The Greek democracy made the magistrate or the judge into a mere clerk of the court. He took the preliminary information and he presided as an official during the case. But his position as presiding officer was merely formal. The jury did not, as in our courts today, decide only on the facts and look to him for information on the law. They decided on the law as well as on the facts. Litigants pleaded their own case, though a litigant could go to a man learned in the law, get him to write a speech and read it himself. The Greeks were great believers in law, both written and unwritten. But the democrats believed not only in the theory of law, but in the principles of equity and we can define equity as what would seem right in a given case in the minds of five hundred citizens chosen by lot from among the Athenian population.

He would be a very bold man who would say that that system of justice was in any way inferior to the modern monstrosities by which lawyers mulct the public; cases last interminably, going from court to court, and matters of grave importance are decided by the position of full stops and commas (or the absence of them) in long and complicated laws and regulations which sometimes have to be traced through hundreds of years and hundreds of law books. When the Russian revolution took place and was in its heroic period, the Bolsheviks experimented with People's Courts. But they were timid and in any case, none of these experiments lasted for very long. The essence of the Greek method, here as elsewhere, was the refusal to hand over these things to experts, but to trust to the intelligence and sense of justice of the population at large, which meant of course a majority of the common people.

We must get rid of the idea that there was anything primitive in the organisation of the government of Athens. On the contrary, it was a miracle of democratic procedure which would be beyond the capacity of any modern body of politicians and lawyers, simply because these believe that when every man has a vote, equality is thereby established. The assembly appointed a council of five hundred to be responsible for the administration of the city and the carrying out of decisions.

But the council was governed by the same principle of equality. The city was divided into ten divisions and the year was divided into ten periods. Each section of the city selected by lot fifty men to serve on the council. All the councillors of each section held office for one tenth of the year. So that fifty people were always in charge of the administration. The order in which the group of fifty councillors from each section of the city should serve was determined by lot. Every day, the fifty who were serving chose someone to preside over them and he also was chosen by lot. If on the day that he was presiding, the full assembly of all the citizens met, he presided at the assembly.

The council had a secretary and he was elected. But he was elected for the duration of one tenth of the year. And (no doubt to prevent bureaucracy) he was elected not from among the fifty, but from among the 450 members of the council who were not serving at the time.

When members had served on the council, they were forbidden to serve a second time. Thus every person had a chance to serve. And here we come to one of the great benefits of the system. After a number of years, practically every citizen had had an opportunity to be a member of the administration. So that the body of citizens who formed the public assembly consisted of men who were familiar with the business of government.

No business could be brought before the assembly except it had been previously prepared and organised by the council.

When decisions had been taken, the carrying out of them was entrusted to the council.

The council supervised all the magistrates and any work that had been given to a private citizen to do.

The Greeks had very few permanent functionaries. They preferred to appoint special boards of private citizens. Each of these boards had its own very carefully defined sphere of work. The co-ordination of all these various spheres of work was carried out by the council. A great number of special commissions helped to carry out the executive work. For example, there were ten members of a commission to see after naval affairs, and ten members of a commission to hear complaints against magistrates at the end of their term. One very interesting commission was the commission for the conduct of religious ceremonies. The Greeks were a very religious people. But most of the priests and officials of the temples were elected and were for the most part private citizens. The Greeks would not have any bunch of bishops, archbishops, Popes and other religious bureaucrats who lived by organising religion. Some of these commissions were elected from the council. But others again were appointed by lot.

At every turn we see the extraordinary confidence that these people had in the ability of the ordinary person, the grocer, the candlestick-maker, the carpenter, the sailor, the tailor. Whatever the trade of the individual, whatever his education, he was chosen by lot to do the work the state required.

And yet they stood no nonsense. If a private individual made propositions in the assembly which the assembly considered frivolous or stupid, the punishment was severe.

Here is some idea of the extent to which the Greeks believed in democracy and equality. One of the greatest festivals in Greece, or rather in Athens, was the festival of Dionysus, the climax of which was the performance of plays for four days, from sunrise to evening. The whole population came out to listen. Officials chose the different playwrights who were to compete. On the day of the performance, the plays were performed and, as far as we can gather, the prizes were at first given by popular applause and the popular vote. You must remember that the dramatic companies used to rehearse for one year and the successful tragedians were looked upon as some of the greatest men in the state, receiving immense honour and homage from their fellow citizens. Yet it was the public, the general public of fifteen or twenty thousand people, that came and decided who was the winner.

Later, a committee was appointed to decide. Today such a committee would consist of professors, successful writers and critics. Not among the Greeks. The committee consisted first of a certain number of men chosen by lot from each section of the city. These men got together and chose by lot from among themselves ten men. These ten men attended as the judges. At the end of the performances, they made their decision. The ten decisions were placed in the hat. Five were drawn out. And the one who had the highest vote from among these five received the prize. But even that does not give a true picture of the attitude of the Greeks towards democracy.

Despite the appointment of this commission, there is evidence that the spectators had a preponderant influence on the judges. The Greek populace behaved at these dramatic competitions as a modern crowd behaves at some football or baseball game. They were violent partisans. They stamped and shouted and showed their likes and dislikes in those and similar ways. We are told that the judges took good care to notice the way in which popular opinion went. Because, and this is typical of the whole working of the democracy on the day after the decision, the law allowed dissatisfied citizens to impeach the members of the commission for unsatisfactory decisions. So that the members of the commission (we can say at least) were very much aware of the consequences of disregarding the popular feeling about the plays.

Yet it was the Greeks who invented playwriting. In Aeschylus, Sophocles and Euripides, they produced three tragedians who, to this day, have no equals as practitioners of the art which they invented. Aristophanes has never been surpassed as a writer of comic plays. These men obviously knew that to win the prize, they had to please the populace. Plato, the great philosopher, was, as can easily be imagined, extremely hostile to this method of decision. But the Greek populace gave the prize to Aeschylus thirteen times. They were the ones who repeatedly crowned Aeschylus and Sophocles, and later Euripides, as prizewinners. It is impossible to see how a jury consisting of Plato and his philosopher friends could have done any better. There you have a perfect example of the Greek attitude to the capacities, judgement and ability to represent the whole body of citizens, which they thought existed in every single citizen.

There are many people today, and some of them radicals and revolutionaries, who sneer at the fact that this democracy was based on slavery. So it was, though we have found that those who are prone to attack Greek democracy on behalf of slavery are not so much interested in defending the slaves as they are in attacking the democracy. Frederick Engels in his book on the family makes an analysis of slavery in relation to Greek democracy and modern scholars on the whole agree with him. In the early days, Greek slavery did not occupy a very prominent place in the social life and economy of Greece. The slave was for the most part a household slave. Later, the slaves grew in number until they were at least as many as the number of citizens.

In later years, slavery devoloped to such a degree, with the development of commerce, industry, etc., that it degraded free labour. And it is to this extraordinary growth of slavery and the consequent degradation of free labour that Engels attributes the decline of the great Greek democracy.

However, it is necessary to say this. In the best days of the democracy, there were many slaves who, although denied the rights of citizenship, lived the life of the ordinary Greek citizen. There is much evidence of that. One of the most important pieces of evidence is the complaint of Plato that it was impossible to tell a slave to go off the pavement to make way for a free citizen (especially so distinguished a citizen as Plato) for the simple reason that they dressed so much like the ordinary citizen that it was impossible to tell who was a citizen and who was a slave. In fact, Plato so hated Greek democracy that he complained that even the horses and the asses in the streets walked about as if they also had been granted liberty and freedom. Near the end of the period of radical democracy, Demosthenes, the greatest of Athenian orators, said that the Athenians insisted on a certain code of behaviour towards the slaves, not because of the slaves, but because a man who behaved in an unseemly manner to another human being was not fit to be a citizen. There were horrible conditions among the slaves who worked in the mines. But on the whole, the slave code in Athens has been described by competent authorities as the most enlightened the world has known.

It was also stated by many that the position of women in Athens during the democracy was very bad. Naturally in those days, they did not have the vote. But for many centuries we were taught that the women of the Greek democracy were little better than bearers of children and housekeepers for their husbands. Yet some modern writers, on closer examination of the evidence, have challenged the old view, and we believe that before very long, the world will have a more balanced view of how women lived in the Greek democracy.

Now if the ancient Greeks had done little beside invent and practise this unique form of human equality in government, they would have done enough to be remembered. The astonishing thing is that they laid the intellectual foundation of Western Europe. Today when we speak about philosophy, logic, dialectic; when we speak of politics, democracy, oligarchy, constitution, law; when we speak of oratory, rhetoric, ethics; when we speak of drama, of tragedy and comedy; when we speak of history; when we speak of sculpture and architecture; in all these things we use the terms and build on the foundations that were discovered and developed by the Greeks.

Correspondence is not sure about science, but in every other sphere of human endeavour, whatever the methods, routines, procedures, etc. that are used by people in intellectual and political association with each other, these were discovered, invented, classified and analysed by the people of ancient Greece.

They not only invented or discovered these things. The men who invented and discovered and developed them, sculpture, politics, philosophy, art and literature, medicine, mathematics, etc., these men are still to this day unsurpassed as practitioners of the things that they invented or discovered. If you were writing a history of modern civilisation, you might find it necessary to bring in perhaps half a dozen Americans. Let us be liberal. A dozen. You will be equally in difficulty to find a dozen Englishmen. But in any such history of Western civilisation, you would have to mention some 60 or 80 Greeks.

Here are some of the names. Epic poetry — Homer. Dramatic

poetry — Aeschylus, Sophocles and Euripides. Comedy — Aristophanes. Lyric poetry — Pindar and Sappho. Statesmen — Solon, Themistocles and Pericles. Sculpture — The Master of Olympia and Phidias. Oratory — Demosthenes. History — Thucydides and Herodotus. Philosophy — Socrates, Aristotle and Plato. Science and mathematics — Pythagoras and Archimedes. Medicine — Hippocrates.

These are only some of the best known names. And the fact which should never be forgotten and which indeed we should make the foundation of all our thinking on Greece is that by far the greatest number of them lived, and their finest work was done, in the days when the Greek democracy flourished.

This is the greatest lesson of the Athenian democracy for us today. It was in the days when every citizen could and did govern equally with any other citizen, when in other words, equality was carried to its extreme, that the city produced the most varied, comprehensive and brilliant body of geniuses that the world has ever known. The United States today has a population of 155 million people. In other words, 1,500 times the population of Athens. In economic wealth, any two-by-four modern city of 20,000 people probably contains a hundred times or more of the economic resources of a city like Athens in its greatest days. Furthermore, for a great part of its existence, the total citizen population of Athens could be contained in Ebbets Field or at any of a dozen football grounds in England. This will give you some faint idea of the incredible achievements not of ancient Greece in general, but of Greek democracy. For it was the democracy of Greece that created these world-historical achievements and they could not have been created without the democracy.

Greece did not only produce great artists, philosophers and statesmen at a time when their work laid the foundation of what we know as civilisation. The Greeks fought and won some of the greatest battles that were ever fought in defence of Western civilisation. At the battles of Marathon, Plataea and Salamis, a few thousand Greeks, with the Athenian democrats at their head, defended the beginnings of democracy, freedom of association, etc., against the hundreds of thousands of soldiers of the Oriental despotic monarchy of Persia. In those battles in the fifth century, oriental barbarism, which aimed at the destruction of the Greeks, was defeated and hurled back by the Greeks fighting against odds at times of over twenty to one. The oriental despots knew very well what they were doing. They came determined to crush the free and independent states of Greece. Never before and never since was so much owed by so many to so few, and as the years go by the consciousness of that debt can only increase.

This has always been an important question, but at the stage of society that we have reached it is the fundamental question: what kind of a man was this Greek democrat? Karl Marx has stated that the future type of man, the man of a socialist society, will be a "fully developed individual, fit for a variety of labours, ready to face any change of production, and to whom the different social functions he performs are but so many modes of giving free scope to his own natural and acquired powers".

Here is how Pericles, one of the greatest statesmen of the Greek democracy, described the ordinary Greek citizen:

> "Taking everything together then, I declare that our city is an education to Greece, and I declare that in my opinion each single one of our citizens, in all the manifold aspects of life is able to show himself the rightful lord and owner of his own person, and do this, moreover, with exceptional grace and exceptional versatility."

Marx and all the men who have written of a society of democracy and equality had to place it in the future. For our Greek, this conception of the citizen was not an aspiration. It was a fact. The statement occurs in perhaps the greatest of all the Greek statements on democracy, the speech of Pericles on the occasion of a funeral of Athenians who had died in war.

The Greek democrat achieved this extraordinary force and versatility because he had two great advantages over the modern democrat. The first was that in the best days of the democracy, he did not understand individualism as we know it. For him an individual was unthinkable except in the city-state. The city-state of democracy was unthinkable except as a collection of free individuals. He could not see himself or other people as individuals in opposition to the city state. That came later when the democracy declined. It was this perfect balance, instinctive and unconscious, between the individual and the city-state which gave him the enormous force and the enormous freedom of his personality.

Pericles shows us that freedom, the freedom to do and think as you please, not only in politics but in private life, was the very life-blood of the Greeks. In that same speech, he says:

> "And, just as our political life is free and open, so is our day-to-day life in our relations with each other. We do not get into a state with our next-door neighbour if he enjoys himself in his own way, nor do we give him the kind of black looks which, though they do no real harm, still do hurt people's feelings. We are free and tolerant in our private lives; but in public affairs we keep to the law. This is because it commands our deep respect.
>
> We give our obedience to those whom we put in positions of authority, and we obey the laws themselves, especially those which are for the protection of the oppressed, and those unwritten laws which it is an acknowledged shame to break."

Those simple words need hard thinking for us to begin to understand them today. The United States is notorious among modern nations for the brutality with which majorities, in large things as in small, terrorise and bully minorities which do not conform; in Great Britain, the conception of "good form" and "what is not done" exercises a less blatant but equally pervasive influence. The Greek democrat would have considered such attitudes as suitable only for barbarians. One reason why the Greeks so hated the Persians was that a Persian had to bow down and humble himself before the Persian King — the Greek called this "a prostration" and this too he thought was only fit for barbarians. Instead, in the midst of a terrible war, he went to the theatre (which was a state-theatre) and applauded a bitterly anti-war play by Aristophanes, and on another occasion, when the ruler of Athens, accompanied by foreign dignitaries, attended the theatre in his official capacity, Aristophanes ridiculed him so mercilessly in the play that he sued the dramatist — and lost the case.

Another great advantage of the Greek democrat was that he had a religion. The Greek religion may seem absurd to us today, but any serious study of it will show that it was as great an example of their genius as their other achievements. Religion is that total conception of the universe and man's place in it without which a man or a body of men are like people wandering in the wilderness. And the religious ideas of a people are usually a reflection and development of their responses to the society in which they live. Modern man does not know what to think of the chaotic world in which he lives and that is why he has no religion.

So simple and easy to grasp in all its relations was the city-state that the total conception which the Greeks conceived of the universe as a whole and man's relation to it was extremely simple and, despite the fact that it was crammed with absurdities, was extremely rational. The Greek gods were essentially human beings of a superior kind. The Greeks placed them on top of a mountain (Olympus) and allowed them their superiority up there. But if any citizen looked as if he was becoming too powerful and might establish himself like a god in Athens, the Athenian democracy handled him very easily. They held a form of referendum on him and if citizens voted against him, he was forthwith banished for ten years, though when he returned, he could get back his property. Gods were strictly for Olympus.

Around all religions there is great mystery and psychological and traditional associations which are extremely difficult to unravel. But, although the Greek no doubt recognised these mysteries, his relation to them was never such as to overwhelm him.

Thus in his relation to the state, and in his relation to matters beyond those which he could himself handle, he understood what his position was and the position of his fellow men in a manner far beyond that of all other peoples who have succeeded him.

In strict politics the great strength of the system was that the masses of the people were paid for the political work that they did. Politics, therefore, was not the activity of your spare time, nor the activity of experts paid specially to do it. And there is no question that in the socialist society the politics, for example, of the workers' organisations and the politics of the state will be looked upon as the Greeks looked upon it, a necessary and important part of work, a part of the working day. A simple change like that would revolutionise contemporary politics overnight.

The great weakness of the system was that, as time went on, the proletariat did little except politics. The modern community lives at the expense of the proletariat. The proletariat in Greece and still more in Rome lived at the expense of the community. In the end, this was a contributory part of the decline of the system. But the system lasted nearly two hundred years. The empires of France and Britain have not lasted very much longer, and America's role as a leader of world civilisation is mortally challenged even before it has well begun.

It is obvious that we can give here no more than a general account of Greek democracy. There are great gaps in our knowledge of many aspects of Greek life; and even the facts that scholars have patiently and carefully verified during centuries can be, and are, very variously interpreted. There is room for differences of opinion, and Greek democracy has always had and still has many enemies. But the position we take here is based not only on the soundest authorities, but on something far more important, our own belief in the creative power of freedom and the capacity of the ordinary man to govern. Unless you share that belief of the ancient Greeks, you cannot understand the civilisation they built.

History is a living thing. It is not a body of facts. We today who are faced with the inability of representative government and parliamentary democracy to handle effectively the urgent problems of the day, we can study and understand Greek democracy in a way that was impossible for a man who lived in 1900, when representative government and parliamentary democracy seemed securely established for all time.

Take this question of election by lot and rotation so that all could take their turn to govern. The Greeks, or to be more strict, the Athenians (although many other cities followed Athens), knew very well that it was necessary to elect specially qualified men for certain posts. The commanders of the army and of the fleet were specially selected, and they were selected for their military knowledge and capacity. And yet that by itself can be easily misunderstood. The essence of the matter is that the generals were so surrounded by the general democratic practices of the Greeks, the ordinary Greek was so vigilant against what he called "tyranny", that it was impossible for generals to use their positions as they might have been able to do in an ordinary bureaucratic or representative form of government.

So it was that the Greeks, highly sophisticated in the practice of democracy, did not, for example, constantly change the men who were appointed as generals. Pericles ruled Athens as general in command for some thirty years. But although he ruled, he was no dictator. He was constantly re-elected. On one occasion, he was tried before the courts but won a victory. On another occasion, Aspasia, the woman with whom he lived, was brought before the court by his enemies. Pericles defended her himself. He was a man famous for his gravity of deportment, but on this occasion, Aspasia was so hard pressed that he broke down and cried. The jury was so astonished at seeing this, that it played an important role in the acquittal of Aspasia. Can you imagine this happening to a modern ruler? Whether democratic or otherwise?

The Greek populace elected Pericles year after year because they knew that he was honest and capable. But he knew and they knew that if they were not satisfied with him, they were going to throw him out. That was the temper of the Greek democracy in its best days.

This democracy was not established overnight. The early Greek cities were not governed in this way. The landed aristocracy dominated the economy and held all the important positions of government. For example, rich and powerful noblemen, for centuries, controlled a body known as the Areopagus, and the Areopagus held all the powers which later were transferred to the council. The magistrates in the courts were a similar body of aristocrats who functioned from above with enormous powers such as modern magistrates and modern judges have. The Greek democracy had had experience of expert and bureaucratic government.

It was not that the Greeks had such simple problems that they could work out simple solutions or types of solutions which are impossible in our more complicated civilisations. That is the great argument which comes very glibly to the lips of modern enemies of direct democracy and even of some learned Greek scholars. It is false to the core. And the proof is that the greatest intellectuals of the day, Socrates, Plato, Aristotle and others (men of genius such as the world has rarely seen), were all bitterly opposed to the democracy. To them, this government by the common people was wrong in principle and they criticised it constantly. More than that, Plato spent the greater part of his long life discussing and devising and publishing ways and means of creating forms of society, government and law which would be superior to the Greek democracy. And yet, Plato owed *everything* to the democracy.

He could think and discuss and publish freely solely because he lived in a democracy. We should remember too that the very ideas of what could constitute the perfect society he was always seeking, came to him and could come to him only because the democracy in Greece was itself constantly seeking to develop *practically* the best possible society. It is true that Plato and his circle developed theories and ideas about government and society which have been of permanent value to all who have worked theoretically at the problems of society ever since. Their work has become part of the common heritage of Western civilisation.

But we make a colossal mistake if we believe that all this is past history. For Plato's best known book, *The Republic*, is his description of an ideal society to replace the democracy, and it is a perfect example of a totalitarian state, governed by an élite. And what is worse, Plato started and brilliantly expounded a practice which has lasted to this day among intellectuals — a constant speculation about different and possible methods of government, all based on a refusal to accept the fact that the common man can actually govern. It must be said for Plato that, in the end, he came to the conclusion that the radical democracy was the best type of government for Athens. Many intellectuals today do not do as well. They not only support but they join bureaucratic and even sometimes totalitarian forms of government.

The intellectuals who through the centuries preoccupied themselves with Plato and his speculations undoubtedly had a certain justification for so doing. Today there is none. What all should study first is the way in which the Greeks translated into active concrete life their conception of human equality. The Greeks did *not* arrive at their democracy by reading the books of philosophers. The common people won it only after generations of struggle.

It would seem that somewhere between 650 and 600 B.C., the first great stage in the development of Greek democracy was reached when the laws were written down. The people fought very hard that the law should be written so that everyone should know what it was by which he was governed.

But this was not accidental. As always, what changed the political situation in Greece were changes in the social structure. Commerce and (to a degree more than most people at one time believed) industry, the use of money, played great roles in breaking down aristocratic distinctions, and over the years there was a great social levelling, social equality, due to the growth of merchant and trading classes, to the increases of the artisan class, of workmen in small factories and sailors on the ships. With these changes in Greek society, the merchants made a bid for power in the manner that we have seen so often in recent centuries in European history and also in the history of oriental countries. Solon was the statesman who first established a more or less democratic constitution and, for that reason, his name is to this day famous as a man of political wisdom. We see his name in the headlines of newspapers, written by men who we can be pretty sure have little sympathy with what Solon did. But the fact that his name has lasted all these centuries as a symbol of political wisdom is significant of the immense change in human society which he inaugurated. A few years before the end of the sixth century B.C., we have the real beginning of democracy in the constitution of Solon.

The citizens of the city-state were not only those who lived in the city, but the peasants who lived around. Solon was supported by the merchants and the urban classes, and also by the peasants. The growth of a money economy and of trade and industry, as usual, had loaded the peasants with debt and Solon cancelled the burden of debt on them. So that in a manner that we can well understand, the growth of industry and trade, and the dislocation of the old peasant economy provided the forces for the establishment of Solon's great constitution. *It was the result of a great social upheaval.*

To give you some idea of the state of the surrounding world when Solon was introducing his constitution, we may note that thirty years after Solon's constitution, we have the death of Nebuchadnezzar, the king in the Bible who was concerned in that peculiar business of Shadrack, Meshak and Abednego. And this is the answer to all who sneer about the greatness of Greek democracy. You only have to look at what the rest of the world around them was doing and thinking.

But although Solon's constitution was a great and historic beginning, the democracy that he inaugurated was far removed from the radical democracy, the direct democracy of later years. For at least a century after Solon, the highest positions of the state could only be filled by men who had a qualification of property and this property qualification was usually associated with men of noble birth. The constitution in other words, was somewhat similar to the British constitution in the eighteenth century. The real relation of forces can be seen best perhaps in the army. In cities like Athens, the whole able-bodied population was called upon to fight its wars. Political power, when it passed from the aristocracy, remained for some decades in the hands of those who were able to supply themselves with armour and horses.

About ninety years after Solon, there was another great revolution in Athens. It was led by a radical noble, Cleisthenes by name. Cleisthenes instituted a genuinely middle-class democracy. As in Western European history, the first stage in democracy is often the constitution. Then later comes the extension of the constitution to the middle classes and the lower middle classes. That was what took place in Greece.

The great masses of the people, however, the rank and file, were excluded from the full enjoyment of democratic rights. The ordinary citizen, the ordinary working man, the ordinary artisan, did not have any of the privileges that he was to have later. The way he gained them is extremely instructive.

The development of commerce gradually transformed Athens first into a commercial city, and then into a city which did a great trade in the Mediterranean and the other lands around it. But a few years after the establishment of this middle class democracy by Cleisthenes, we have the period of the great Persian invasion. In 490 B.C. we have the battle of Marathon, in 480 the battle of Salamis, and in 479 the battle of Plataea, in which the whole population fought. Much of this war was fought at sea. Thus, commercially and militarily, Athens became a naval power. But the ships in those days were propelled by the men who rowed them. Thus the rowers in the fleet became a great social force. The Greeks always said that it was the growth of democracy which had inspired the magnificent defence of Greece against Persia. But after that victory was won, the rowers in the fleet became the spearhead of the democracy and they were the ones who forced democracy to its ultimate limits.

The port of Athens was, as it is to this day, the Piraeus. There, for the most part, lived the sailors of the merchant fleet and the navy and a number of foreigners, as takes place in every great naval port. The leaders in the popular assembly were sometimes radical noblemen and later were often ordinary artisans. But the proletarians of the Piraeus were the driving force and they were the most radical of the democrats.

The struggle was continuous. The battle of Plataea took place in 479 B.C. A quarter of a century later, another revolution took place and power was transferred definitely from the nobles who still retained some of it, to the radical democracy. Pericles, an aristocrat by birth, was one of the leaders of this revolution. Five years after, the lowest classes in the city gained the power of being elected or chosen for the Archonship, a very high post. It was Pericles who began to pay the people for doing political work. From 458, the radical democracy continued until it finally collapsed in 338 B.C.

The struggle was continuous. The old aristocratic class and some of the wealthy people made attempts to destroy the democratic constitution and institute the rule of the privileged. They had temporary successes but were ultimately defeated every time. In the end, the democracy was defeated by a foreign enemy and not from inside. One notable feature of Athenian democracy was that, despite the complete power of the popular assembly, it never attempted to carry out any socialistic doctrines. The democrats taxed the rich heavily and kept them in order, but they seemed to have understood instinctively that their economy, chiefly of peasants and artisans, was unsuitable as the economic basis for a socialised society. They were not idealists or theorisers or experimenters, but sober, responsible people who have never been surpassed at the practical business of government.

How shall we end this modest attempt to bring before modern workers the great democrats of Athens? Perhaps by reminding the modern world of the fact that great as were their gifts, the greatest gift they had was their passion for democracy. They fought the Persians, but they fought the internal enemy at home with equal, if not greater determination. Once, when they were engaged in a foreign war, the anti-democrats tried to establish a government of the privileged. The Athenian democrats defeated both enemies, the enemy abroad and the enemy at home. And after the double victory, the popular assembly decreed as follows:

"If any man subvert the democracy of Athens, or hold any magistracy after the democracy has been subverted, he shall be an enemy of the Athenians. Let him be put to death with impunity, and let his property be confiscated to the public, with the reservation of a tithe to Athene. Let the man who has killed him, and the accomplice privy to the act, be accounted holy and of good religious odour. Let all Athenians swear an oath under the sacrifice of full-grown victims in their respective tribes and demes, to kill him. Let the oath be as follows: 'I will kill with my own hand, if I am able, any man who shall subvert the democracy at Athens, or who shall hold any office in the future after the democracy has been subverted, or shall rise in arms for the purpose of making himself a despot, or shall help the despot to establish himself. And if any one else shall kill him, I will account the slayer to be holy as respects both gods and demons, as having slain an enemy of the Athenians. And I engage, by word, by deed, and by vote, to sell his property and make over one-half of the proceeds to the slayer, without withholding anything. If any man shall perish in slaying, or in trying to slay the despot, I will be kind both to him and to his children, as to Harmodius and Aristogeiton and their descendants. And I hereby dissolve and release all oaths which have been sworn hostile to the Athenian people, either at Athens, or at the camp (at Samos) or elsewhere.' Let all Athenians swear this as the regular oath immediately before the festival of the Dionysia, with sacrifice and full-grown victims; invoking upon him who keeps it good things in abundance, but upon him who breaks it destruction for himself as well as for his family."

That was the spirit of the men who created and defended the great democracy of Athens. Let all true believers in democracy and equality today strengthen ourselves by studying what they did and how they did it.

1956

13

The Workers' Councils in Hungary

[*The appearance of the workers' councils in Hungary and Poland in 1956 soon brought the utmost contemporary relevance to James's previous essay "Every Cook Can Govern".* Facing Reality, *from which this extract is taken, was published first in 1958, and discussed the new stage in world politics to which the Hungarian councils, among other things, had contributed.*]

The secret of the workers' councils is this. From the very start of the Hungarian revolution, these shop-floor organisations of the workers demonstrated such conscious mastery of the needs, processes, and inter-relations of production, that they did not have to exercise any domination over *people*. That mastery is the only basis of political power against the bureaucratic state. It is the very essence of any government which is to be based upon general consent and not on force. The administration of things by the workers' councils established a basic coherence in society and from this coherence they derived automatically their right to govern. Workers' management of production, government from below, and government by consent have thus been shown to be one and the same thing.

The actual resort to arms has obscured the social transformation that took place from the first day of the revolution. Along with the fighting the workers took over immediate control of the country. So complete was their mastery of production that large bodies of men, dispersed over wide areas, could exercise their control with the strategy of a general deploying troops, and yet with the flexibility of a single craftsman guiding his tools. The decision to carry out a general strike was not decreed by any centre. Simultaneously and spontaneously in all industrial areas of the country, the decision not to work was taken, and the strike organised itself immediately according to the objective needs of the revolutionary forces. On the initiative of the workers' councils in each plant, it was possible to come to a general decision, immediately acceptable to all, as to who should work and who should not work, where the goods produced should go and where they should not go. No central plan was needed. The plan was within each individual factory. General strikes have played a decisive role in bringing down governments in every modern revolution, but never before has the general been initiated and controlled so completely by the particular. It was not merely unity against the common enemy which made this cohesion possible. The strike, as well as the whole course of the revolution, demonstrated how deep were its roots in the mastery over production and social processes, which is the natural and acquired power of modern workers.

All great revolutions have obtained arms from soldiers who joined the revolution, and by taking them from the police and the arsenals of the state. In this the Hungarian revolution was no exception. The difference is that in Hungary, despite the fact that the whole army came over to the revolution, the workers' councils proceeded immediately to manufacture their own arms. The decision was immediately taken that these newly-produced arms should be distributed to the striking workers in other industries who were to withdraw themselves into an army of defence. Production for use was for them not a theory but an automatic procedure from the moment they began to govern themselves.

At a certain stage the miners' council decided to work in order to keep the mines from flooding. At another, they informed the Kadar government precisely how much they would produce in exchange for precise political concessions. At the same time they opened out to all a vision of the future by stating boldly and confidently that once all their political demands were realised they would produce at a rate that would astonish the world. Thus they established that the secret of higher productivity is self-government in production.

Previous revolutions have concentrated on the seizure of political power and only afterwards faced the problems of organising production according to new procedures and methods. The great lesson of the years 1923-1956 has been this, that degradation in production relations results in the degradation of political relations and from there to the degradation of all relations in society. The Hungarian revolution has reversed this process. As a result of the stage reached by modern industry and its experience under the bureaucratic leadership of the party and its plan, the revolution from the very beginning seized power in the process of production and from there organised the political power.

The workers' councils did not look to governments to carry out their demands. In the Hungarian revolution the workers' councils not only released the political prisoners, as in all revolutions. They immediately rehired them at their old plants without loss of pay. Even while they were demanding that the government abolish the system of norms and quotas, they were themselves establishing how much work should be done and by whom, in accordance with what was needed. They demanded increases in wages, but they assumed the responsibility not only for paying wages but for increasing them by 10%. From the moment that they took the apparatus of industry under their control, they began to tear off the veils which hide the essential simplicity of the modern economy.

The parties, the administrators and the planners have claimed always that without them society will collapse into anarchy and chaos. The workers' councils recognised the need for an official centre and for a head of state. Early in the revolution, because they believed Nagy to have the confidence of the people, they proposed that he assume the national leadership. But the councils finished once and for all with the delegation of powers to a centre while the population retreats into passive obedience. Thus the workers' councils and the Nagy government were not a dual power in the classical sense of that phrase. The Nagy government proposed to legalise the revolutionary councils by incorporating them into the existing administration. The workers' councils made it clear, in reply, that *they* were the legal administration, and that the power to legalise, incorporate, indeed dis-establish an official centre, rested with them. They drew no distinction between the work of production and the work of government. They decided who should occupy government posts, who should be dismissed, which ministries should be retained, which should be dissolved.

Everyone knows that the revolution attacked without mercy the infamous stalinist secret police. But people have not concerned themselves with the far more important judicial actions of the workers' councils. It is traditional with revolutions to place on trial those members of the old régime whom popular opinion holds most responsible for its crimes. In the last twenty-five years, however, the trials of political enemies and vengeance against them have become inseparable in the public mind from the brutalities of the totalitarian and imperialistic states. Conscious that they represented a new social order, and never forgetting, in their own words, *why* they were fighting, the Hungarian revolutionaries renounced terror and vengeance. Characteristically they carried out their judicial functions within the framework of the plant itself. The councils constituted themselves into courts to discuss, one by one, the directors of the plant, the trade union officials, and the party officials, to decide which should be expelled from the plant and which allowed to remain. They dissolved and destroyed the records of the personnel departments which had become, as in plants the world over, centres of blacklisting and spying.

One of the greatest achievements of the Hungarian revolution was to destroy once and for all the legend that the working class cannot act successfully except under the leadership of a political party. It did all that it did precisely because it was not under the leadership of a political party. If a political party had existed to lead the revolution, that political party would have led the revolution to disaster, as it has led every revolution to disaster during the last thirty years. There was leadership on all sides, but there was no party leading it. No party in the world would have dared to lead the country into a counter-attack in the face of thousands of Russian tanks. Nothing but an organisation in close contact with the working-class population in the factory, and which therefore knew and felt the strength of the population at every stage, could have dared to begin the battle a second time. Still later, after the military battle had been lost, no organisation except workers' councils would have dared to start a general strike and carry it on for five weeks, unquestionably the most astonishing event in the whole history of revolutionary struggles.

In these unprecedented examples of leadership the workers' councils put an end to the foolish dreams, disasters, and despair which have attended all those who, since 1923, have placed the hope for socialism in the élite party, whether communist or social-democrat. The political party, as such, whatever type it is, con-stitutes essentially a separation of the organising intellectuals and workers with an instinct for leadership, from the masses as force and motive power. As long as the real centres of administration were the private capitalists in their various spheres, the apparatus of government was relatively simple. Political parties as such could represent the opposing classes and in their conflicts with one another and their bids for popular support, clarify the choices be-fore society, and educate the population as a whole. But with the growth of large-scale production, the state apparatus controls the national economy in fact, and whichever party comes to power inherits and becomes the agent of an existing apparatus.

Control over production means first and foremost control over the workers, and the modern state can function only if the decisive trade unions are incorporated into it, or are prepared at critical moments to submit to it. The powerful labour organisations, there-fore, by their very existence, must suppress those creative energies which the reconstitution of society demands from the mass of the people. The workers' councils in Hungary instructed the workers to put aside party affiliations and elect their delegates according to their judgement of them as workers in the plant. At the same time no worker was discriminated against either in his work or in his election to the workers' councils because of his party affiliations. The traditional political parties take their political differences into the factories, breaking the unity of the workers according to these divisions. They make of individual workers representatives of a political line, corrupting relations between people by transform-ing them into relations of political rivalry. Once the powers of government were with the shop-floor organisations, the objective relations of the labour process provided all the discipline required. On the basis of that objective discipline, the widest variety of views and idiosyncracies could not only be tolerated but welcomed.

So confident were the workers' councils that the workers' mastery over production would be decisive in the solution of all important questions, that they proposed a great "party of the revolution" This was to include all who had taken part in the revolution, the clerical and petty-bourgeois right, former members of the Small Proprietors' Party, Social-Democrats and Communists. Before these and other proposals could be worked out and tried, the Russian tanks suppressed the revolution.

Once the Hungarian people erupted spontaneously, the rest followed with an organic necessity and a completeness of self-organisation that distinguishes this revolution from all previous revolutions and marks it as specifically a revolution of the middle of the twentieth century. So obviously were the workers' councils the natural and logical alternative to the totalitarian state, that the traditional demand for a constituent assembly or convention to create a new form of government, was not even raised. So deep is the consciousness in modern people that organisation of production is the basis of society, that the whole population mobilised itself around the workers' councils as the natural government.

It is not excluded that in their search for ways and means to organise a new state, political parties might have been formed. But with the state founded on workers' councils, no political parties could assume the powers, suppress the people, or make the mischief that we have seen from all of them in the last thirty years.

Capitalism has created and steadily deepened the gulf between workers and the intelligentsia (technicians and intellectuals). These have been incorporated by capitalism into the directing apparatus of industry and the state. There they administer and discipline the working population. The Hungarian workers, conscious that technicians are part of the labour process, gave to technicians and intellectuals their place on the workers' councils. The majority on the councils were fittingly production workers, who constitute the majority in the plant itself. But in these all-inclusive workers' councils, the technician could be functionally related to the activities and attitudes of the plant community, instead of being isolated from the mass of the people, as he is on both sides of the iron curtain today.

In previous revolutions, particularly the Russian, it was necessary to state and restate and underline the power of the working class. The very emphasis testified to the weakness of the proletariat in the social structure of the nation. The modern world has understood, after three decades of bitter experience, that the socialist revolution is a national revolution. Recognised at home and abroad as the leader of the nation, the Hungarian workers called for the establishment of "workers' councils in every branch of the national activity". Thus not only white collar workers in offices, but all government employees, including the police, should have their own councils.

The Hungarian intellectuals heroically defied stalinism. Yet even after the revolution began, all that they could demand was the democratisation of the party and the government, freedom of speech, honesty in placing the economic situation before the people, Nagy in power, etc. Within a week they had come to the conclusion that the workers' councils should form the government of the country with Zoltan Kodaly, the composer, as president, because of his great national and international reputation. It was the Hungarian workers and not they who showed the form for the new society.

The Hungarian peasants showed how far society has progressed in the last thirty years. They broke up the collective farms which were in reality factories in the field, owned and run by the state, the party, and the plan. But at the same time they immediately organised themselves to establish contact with the workers and others in the towns on the basis of social need. They organised their trucks to take them food, did not wait to be paid but went back to the countryside to bring in new loads, risking their lives to do so.

So confident were they that the only power against the totalitarian state was the workers, that the peasants did not wait to see if the workers would guarantee them the land before committing themselves to the active support of the workers' councils. What revolutionary governments have usually striven in vain to win, the confidence of the peasants, was here achieved in reverse — the peasant took all risks in order to show his confidence in the worker.

These objectively developed relations of co-operation have now passed into the subjective personality of people, their instinctive responses and the way they act. Released from the fear that art and literature must serve only politics, sensing all around them the expansion of human needs, human capacities, and co-operation, the Hungarian people created twenty-five new newspapers overnight, the older artists, and the younger talent pouring out news, articles, stories, and poems, in a flood-tide of artistic energy.

The Hungarian workers' councils not only made appeals to the Russian troops to cease fire and go home. They entered into negotiations and made direct arrangements with Russian commanders to retire. At least one council not only negotiated the removal of a garrison of Russian troops but arranged for it to be supplied with food. This was not just fraternisation. It was the assumption of responsibility by the workers' councils for foreign affairs. The simplicity with which the negotiations were carried out reflects the education which the post-war world has received in the futile bickering and cynical propagandising of ceasefire conferences in Korea, Big Four meetings in London and Paris, and Big Two meetings in Geneva. Russian troops mutinied and deserted to fight under the command of the Hungarian councils. When the hospital at Debrecen radioed its needs for iron lungs, the workers' councils at Miskolc undertook to get these from West Germany and by radio organised the landing of the lung-bearing plane at the Debrecen airport. The Hungarian revolution transcended that combination of threats, snarls, lies, hypocrisy, and brutality which today appear under the headlines of foreign affairs.

The Hungarian people welcomed such medical aid and supplies as they received from abroad. But, as they explained to their Czech brothers, it was not assistance or charity which they needed as much as understanding by the world that they fought not only for themselves but for Europe. To a world which is constantly being offered bribes of economic aid and promises of a higher standard of living, these words ring with a new morality. The Hungarian people were not begging for handouts from the Romanian, Serb, or Slovak workers. They wanted them to join in the common struggle for a new society.

The neutrality which the Hungarian people demanded was not the neutrality of a Switzerland. The revolution had in fact begun by a mass demonstration of solidarity with the Poles. They did not want their country to be the battleground of the struggle between America and Russia for mastery of the world, but they themselves were prepared to lay down their lives in the struggle to build a new society, side by side with the other peoples of Europe on both West and East.

The urgent appeals for arms in the final days of the military battle, the voices fading from the radio with cries for help, must be seen against this awareness by the Hungarian population that they were in the forefront of a world movement to build a new civilisation, as profoundly different from American materialism as from Russian totalitarianism. Such confidence in the ideals and aims by which men live can come in the modern world only from a material foundation. The material foundation of the Hungarian workers was their natural and acquired capacity to organise production, and their experience of the centralised plan and the whole bureaucratic organisation which has reached its ultimate in the one-party state but which is characteristic of modern society the world over.

Helpless before this new civilisation, so weak in logistics but so powerful in appeal to the peoples of the world, aware that it is just below the surface in all Europe and is ready to destroy both American and Russian imperialism, the Western powers hesitated for a moment and then turned their vast propaganda machine to one single aim, to transform the content of the Hungarian revolution into a problem of refugees. The poor, the needy, the supplicating, the weak and helpless, these the American welfare state can deal with by charity and red tape. Thus, as in the East, Russia applied herself to the systematic destruction of the workers' councils by deportation to labour camps, the American government in the West began the break-up by organising refugee camps. The Hungarian people have not been deceived by this characteristic American manoeuvre. The failure of the Hungarian revolution they have placed squarely at the door of both the Russian *and* the American governments.

The complete withdrawal of the Russian troops from all Hungary was on the surface a national demand. But in reality, that is, in the concrete circumstances, the whole population realised that the Russian tanks were the only force inside the country able to crush the workers' councils. To speak of a civil war between right and left in Hungary once the Russian troops had left, in the classical style of national revolutions, is to misunderstand completely the stage to which the mastery of production by the workers has reached in modern society and the understanding of this by the whole population.

In the Hungarian revolution there was no divorce between immediate objectives and ultimate aims, between instinctive action and conscious purpose. Working, thinking, fighting, bleeding Hungary, never for a moment forgot that it was incubating a new society, not only for Hungary but for all mankind. In the midst of the organisation of battle, the workers' councils organised political discussions not only of the position of the particular plant in relation to the total struggle, but of the aims which the councils should achieve. They carried on incessant political activity to root out the political and organisational remnants of the old régime and work out new politics. They knew that the danger to the workers' councils lay, not in the middle classes outside the factory, but from the state, the communist party, and the trade-union bureaucrats, all trying to remove the power from the shop floor. At the very beginning of the revolution, the Gero government, recognising that the party and the unions had collapsed, called upon the party cadres in the plants to form councils and to mobilise them against the revolutionary population in the streets. The workers in the streets returned to the factories, threw out the party cadres and re-elected their own councils on the shop floor. Then they issued the announcement, "We have been elected by the workers and not by the government". They knew whence came their strength and the certainty of correct decision so crucial in the lightning speed of revolution. The trade unions instructed them to return to work and elect workers' councils. The workers replied, "We will elect our councils at our place of work but the strike will continue". Even during the most bitter street fighting, workers returned to their plants to take stock of the situation and delegate responsibility.

The final proof that the Hungarian people were conscious of their responsibiltiy for building a new society is the role that was played by the youth in the revolution. In the plants the workers elected youth in the majority to the councils. Modern society has transformed the youth into displaced persons, rebels without a cause, angry men, juvenile delinquents. The youth, in the United States as in Russia, is in this condition of permanent crisis because it does not know where it has come from and where it is going. So confident were the Hungarian workers that the future belonged to them, so certain were they as to where they stood, that these adults could place upon the young people of the country the responsibiltiy for driving the revolution forward.

The miracle of the Hungarian revolution lies not in the heroism of their struggle for freedom. It lies rather in the certainty, the completeness, and the confidence with which, in the midst of battle and on the shortest notice, they laid the basis of an entirely new society.

1958

14

The Artist in the Caribbean

[*In 1959 James was invited to give a lecture (subsequently published as a pamphlet) at the Mona, Jamaica, campus of the University of the West Indies. According to James, his intention was to demonstrate how "the analysis of the artist in the Caribbean, properly done, was a pointer to the general social and political problems there."*]

This being a university audience, I shall take much for granted. The artist is a human being who uses usually one, sometimes more than one medium of communication with exceptional force and skill. I think that is as far as we need to go to begin with. There are such people in the Caribbean and our society has now reached a stage in which they have scope. How much exactly? To my mind it is the question of the medium which at the present time is crucial, It may be remote, as architecture on the grand scale or the human far more for the Caribbean than for the artist, who usually does the best that he can with what is to hand.

An artistic medium is a thoroughly artificial construction, through which an individual is able to see and to express the world around him. It may be very intimate, as the human voice. and material equipment at the disposal of the movie director. It may be subtle and complicated as the prose of the *Ulysses* of James Joyce or the overtones of Eliot's *Four Quartets*. Without being unsubtle, it can be bold and aggressive as the orchestration of Wagner or the early Stravinsky.

Yet despite this bewildering variety I think I have observed that exceptional mastery in the medium is intimately related to the natural surroundings in which the artist has grown up, to the society in which he lives, and his national or even regional ancestry; these may or may not be directly related to the specific artistic tradition which he has inherited or encounters in his search for a mode of expression, but they most often are. A few years ago I was wandering in the south of France and reading about Cézanne. I spent some time in the district to which he had returned for the last years of supreme achievement. I emerged finally with the impression of a man with generations of southern France behind him, who had studied in Paris and learned what the artists of his time had to teach him in technical knowledge and discovery, but who finally returned to the neighbourhood of his early youth and there found the new objective circumstances which enabled him to give a new direction to modern painting.

How long and in what form had these early impressions been a part of his artistic consciousness?

I am very much concerned this evening with the great artist. The period in which Shakespeare lived is the period in which the Bible was written. It is the period of the marriage of native English with the Latin incorporations which the developing civilisation needed. Nevertheless the impression that I now have of the greatest master of language with whom I am able to have acquaintance is this. He was an Englishman, of yeoman lineage, who was born and grew to manhood in the Midlands of Elizabethan England, for whom thought and feeling were always experienced in terms of nature, the physical responses of human beings and the elemental categories of life and labour. This is the basis of his incomparable vividness and facility of expression and the source of his universality. On Shakespeare's language Mr F. R. Leavis has written some illuminating pages.

Racine was at the opposite pole in verbal refinement and sophistication. No Englishman ever wrote like Racine. No Englishman could. Pascal and Racine gave the French language a form which moulded French thought (and therefore French life) for well over a century, until a great writer who heralded a great social revolution expanded the range and opened up new modes of feeling and expression for the French people, whence they spread to the rest of the world. That is how I think of Rousseau.

The question around which I am circling is this: is there any medium so native to the Caribbean, so rooted in the tight association which I have made between national surroundings, historical development and artistic tradition, is there any such medium in the Caribbean from which the artist can draw that strength which makes him a supreme practitioner? (We can for the time being sum up the whole under the term artistic tradition, which as you see I use in a very wide sense to include all that goes to making it. I may mention in passing that it is never more powerful than when the artist is consciously breaking with it or some important aspect of it.)

I shall not keep you in suspense. So far as I can see, there is nothing of the kind in the Caribbean and none in sight to the extent that I, at any rate, can say anything about it. So far as I can see in the plastic arts, in musical composition, as well as in literature, we are using forms which have been borrowed from other civilisations. Language for us is not a distillation of our past. *Robinson Crusoe, Paul et Virginie,* even Gauguin are only on the surface exotic. They have no roots among people like ourselves, nothing from which we can instinctively draw sustenance. For us and for people like us there is no continuous flow such as for instance the Bachs into Haydn into Mozart into Beethoven . . . ; or in literature, Shakespeare, Milton, the Augustans, the Romantics, the Victorians, the Georgians and the revolt against them all of T. S. Eliot. There is no Donne in our ancestry for us to rediscover and stimulate the invention of new forms and new symbols. You will remember that to clarify his own style Eliot found it necessary to launch an assault upon Milton that nearly (but not quite) toppled that master from the throne on which he had sat unchallenged for 250 years. All that is not for us. It is by this lack that I think I can account for the astonishing barrenness (in the sense that I am speaking here) of the artistic production of Canada, of Australia, of New Zealand, of South Africa. The United States has overcome this defect in literature. In music, in painting. it is as poverty-stricken as the others. Where it has created in the arts, it has broken new ground, new and popular. We can console ourselves that in this matter of shallow origins which prevent our artistic talents from striking the deep roots which seem necessary to full development and towering efflorescence, we are not alone. Size has nothing to do with it. Look at Ibsen and Kierkegaard, and the Greek city-state.

I do not know that it is to be regretted. And before we draw the extreme lugubrious conclusions, we should remember (this is the only absolute in these remarks) that artistic production is essentially individual and the artistic individual is above all unpredictable. Who could have predicted Moussorgsky?

It may seem that I am laying an undue emphasis on the great, the master artist. I am not chasing masterpieces. I have made clear that in my view the great artist is the product of a long and deeply rooted national tradition. I go further. He appears at a moment of transition in national life with results which are recognised as having significance for the whole civilised world. By a combination of learning (in his own particular sphere), observation, imagination and creative logic, he can construct the personalities and relations of the future, rooting them in the past and the present. By that economy of means which is great art, he adds to the sum of knowledge of the world and in doing this, as a general rule, he adds new range and flexibility to the medium that he is using. But the universal artist is universal because he is above all national. Cézanne was the product of the French Impressionists of the French nineteenth century and of Poussin, a French master of two centuries before.

If it takes so much to produce them, the results are commensurate.

A supreme artist exercises an influence on the national consciousness which is incalculable. He is created by it but he himself illuminates and amplifies it, bringing the past up to date and charting the future. We tend to accept this in general. Few, particularly university men, will question the influence of Shakespeare on the intellectual, the psychological and even the social development of the English. Such a writer is a pole of reference in social judgement, a source of inspiration in concept, in language, in technique (not always beneficial), to succeeding generations of artists, intellectuals, journalists, and indirectly to ordinary citizens. That view is traditional in academic circles though they may not carry it to the extremes that I do. I, however, am concerned with something else.

The Greeks and the Florentines of the great period understood the direct, the immediate influence of the great artist upon the society in which he actually lived. But today in particular he is a tremendous force while he lives, and particularly to people like us, with our needs.

I do not think we appreciate the influence which Shakespeare and Burbage must have had on the shaping of Elizabethan London. Quite recently I spent six months in a small town in the south of Spain. I had little time to read, except *Don Quixote*, and we had with us a small volume containing reproductions by Goya. Book and pictures seemed to us merely illustrations of what we saw all around us the moment we put our foot outside the house. If I could see it, surely men of that particular time must have seen it themselves and been affected by it in a manner quite impossible for us today. Read again Ben Jonson's tribute to Shakespeare. Nothing of the kind written since has ever exceeded it. And I am sure, though I cannot stay to prove it here, that the Shakespeare Ben Jonson saw was not the Shakespeare that we see today. We have certain advantages, I admit, but for Jonson and the masses of working people who were Shakespeare's fans, he was new and exciting, with an impact that he could never have for us who have already absorbed indirectly so much of what he brought into the world. The Mannerists were a school of painters who succeeded Michelangelo and have recently come into their own. The critics now tell us that they were not exaggerators of Michelangelo's "idiosyncracies". Their style was an independent style with its own values. Another master who came into his own only about half a century ago is Greco. When you go to the Vatican, ask for permission to see the last two paintings Michelangelo ever did; they are in a private chapel of the Pope's in the Capella Paolina. I shall not try to go into detail about them, but at first sight you will see a strange landscape recalling the paintings Greco did at Toledo, apart from the fact that we know that Greco had made contact with Angelo's work during a stay at Rome. Yet another modern critical discovery is a man named Michelangelo Caravaggio. I, who have spent much of such time that I could spare for these matters in studying and restudying the work of Michelangelo, am acutely conscious of the affinity of Caravaggio with the great master whose name he bore. We discover all these relations and affinities centuries after the works appeared. We do not know the half of what the men of that time felt and thought.

And now. Is everything historical, the whole history of art, against us of the Caribbean? I don't think so. You will have noticed the references I make to Greece, where the political form was the city-state; to Florence, to Rome, to Toledo. I state further centrated in London. These were cities in which it was possible my belief that the influence of Shakespeare was most heavily confor the impact of the artist to be felt by a substantial number of the population. This world in little concentrated his own impressions and theirs. I believe that this was the environment which created more men of genius in a Greek or Florentine city of 50,000 citizens than in modern societies of 150 million. Michelangelo's Rome had only 40,000 people. Our situation in the Caribbean is very similar. Trinidad and Barbados are already very close in their demographic structure to the cities of ancient Greece or the Italian towns of the middle ages. There is an urban centre and agricultural areas closely related. I can only say that I believe this form of social existence will condition to a substantial degree the development of art in the Caribbean. In fact I think this advantage will ultimately outweigh all other disadvantages. Our world is small but it is (or soon will be) complete, and we can all see all of it.

But you may ask me: what about the artist in the Caribbean? I would not have come all this distance to deliver encomiums or disapprovals of West Indian writers and artists. If I emphasise what seem to me heights which today they cannot reach, it is because of my conviction that it is only when we are able to give them the concrete freedom of the conditions I have sketched that we shall get from them the best of which they are capable and, more important, get from them what at this stage of our existence we so much need. On our workers in the plastic arts, I have no judgements to pass. I have not the qualifications for doing so. But we have some very distinguished writers. I shall mention only three: Lamming the Barbadian, Naipaul the Trinidadian, and Vic Reid of *The Leopard* from Jamaica. These are very gifted men. I believe that Lamming is as gifted for literature as Garfield Sobers is for cricket, and I do not believe that in the whole history of the game (with which I am very familiar) there are more than half a dozen men who started with a physical and mental equipment superior to that of young Sobers. But Sobers was born into a tradition, into a medium which though transported was so well established that it has created a Caribbean tradition of its own. This is what I am talking about. There are no limits to what Sobers can achieve. Lamming I believe to be objectively circumscribed. Still more limited are our painters and musicians.

There are things we can do. If there were not I would not speak about this at all. In the age in which we live and in the present social and political stage of the underdeveloped countries, we cannot leave these (and other) matters to an empirical growth which took centuries to develop in other countries. We cannot force the growth of the artist. But we can force and accelerate the growth of the conditions in which he can make the best of the gifts that he has been fortunate enough to be born with. Of that I have no doubt whatever; but the details are mundane and will have to wait for the discussion.

Let me stick to the strictly artistic aspects. This is a university and I expect this audience to have actual or psychological affinities with academic activities directed towards the Caribbean. Let me end with what I am thinking about at the present time since my return to Trinidad some eighteen months ago. The ideas that I have expressed here are, as I think should be obvious, the result of years of observation and reflection on art abroad. Since I have been living in Trinidad, I have observed what is going on there in the light of these general ideas. I have been much struck by the work, first, of Beryl McBurnie. You will no doubt have been delighted by the reception which she and her group received at an international festival in Canada not so long ago. Her success in my view is due to the fact that with the necessary training and experience abroad she has dug deep into the past history of the island, observed closely the life around her. Her inventions, the confidence from successes, the reconsiderations which failures bring, have been fed and have grown in the national tradition and under the scrutiny and responses of a national audience. That is the source of her strength.

There is another artist in Trinidad who performs in a medium that would be ranked not very high in the hierarchy of the arts, although I believe Shakespeare would have listened very carefully to him, and Aristophanes would have given him a job in his company. I refer of course to Sparrow. The importance of Sparrow for what I am saying this evening is that he uses a medium which has persisted in Trinidad, in spite of much official and moral discouragement, and has survived to become a world favourite. I am myself continually astonished and delighted at the way in which Sparrow uses the calypso tradition, the way in which he extends it, the way in which he makes it a vehicle for the most acute observations on the social life and political developments around him, for his genuine musicianship, his wit and his humour. I believe that in addition to his natural gifts, he is enormously helped by the fact that he is using a national form and that his audience is a national audience. This is the origin of what has made calypso so popular abroad. Local men playing for the local people. Every calypsonian who stays abroad too long loses the calypso's distinctive quality. When our local dramatists and artists can evoke the popular response of a Sparrow, the artists in the Caribbean will have arrived.

My conclusion, therefore, is this. At this stage of our existence our writers and our artists must be able to come home if they want to. It is inconceivable to me that a national artistic tradition, on which I lay so much stress as an environment in which the artist must begin, it is inconceivable to me that this can be established by writers and artists, however gifted, working for what is essentially a foreign audience. I think I could prove that already their work is adversely affected by it. They can live where they please. It is not for me to tell an artist how to direct his personal life; I would as soon try to tell him how to write or what to paint. But their books should, I think, be printed at home. Kipling's finest work was first published in the India of some seventy-five years ago. The books most certainly must be published at home. I have no doubt in my own mind that they must be written and printed and published for the national audience. If I say this with such confidence it is because I know that the writers themselves are thinking in similar terms if not exactly for the same reasons. The finest piece of writing that to my knowledge had come from the West Indies is a poem which bears the significant title, *Cahier d'un Retour au Pays Natal*. It is the desperate cry of a Europeanised West Indian poet for reintegration with his own people. The most successful evocation of the West Indian atmosphere that I know is a recent winner of the Prix Renaudot, *La Lézarde*, by a young Martiniquan, Edouard Glissant. Yet his style is more traditionally French than that of Césaire. He lives in Paris. I cannot believe that the last resources of West Indian artistic talent can be reached under these conditions.

That is what the nation needs at the present time, and that is what the artist needs, the creation of a national consciousness. Perhaps the most important thing I have to say this evening is that if the threads of a tradition can be discovered among us and made into a whole, if we are to be shocked into recognition of what we are, and what we are not, with the power that this will bring, it is the great artist who will do it. He may by fiction or drama set our minds at rest on the problem which intrigues so many of them: what is Africa to us? He may be a great historian. (His history might be denounced by professional historians and justly. It would not matter. It would have served the national need: look at the illusions most of these European nations have had of themselves.) But such work cannot be created under the conditions in which our artists work today.

These conditions can be changed. Lack of money is too facile an explanation. It is lack of that very national consciousness, lack of that sense of need; we lack that impulse towards a more advanced stage of existence which sees material obstacles in terms of how to overcome them. Today we can no longer compare ourselves in artistic (as well as in other) matters with the barrenness of twenty-five years ago. The time for that is past. Our sights now should be trained twenty-five years ahead. In the Caribbean there are many things that are denied to us and will be denied for a long time to come. But the production of a supreme artist and all that he or she can give to us (including what lesser artists will gain), that we need not despair of. The rapidity of all modern developments is on our side. Our native talent is astonishing — it continually astonishes me. And in these matters we never know. Life is continually causing us to revise our most carefully based judgements. Let us do what we can do. Let us create the conditions under which the artist can flourish. But to do that, we must have the consciousness that the nation which we are hoping to build, as much as it needs the pooling of resources and industrialisation and a higher productivity of labour, needs also the supreme artist.

1959

15

The Mighty Sparrow

[*The great calypsonian, discussed at the close of "The Artist in the Caribbean", was given a chapter to himself — reproduced here — in* Party Politics in the West Indies, *which was first published in Port of Spain in 1961. James has this to say of Sparrow: "I found Sparrow the most alert and the most intelligent person I met in the Caribbean. He had a great mastery of West Indian speech, and as for his music — I thought it was remarkable. I used to talk with him, and I even used to go and hear him record. . . . We were very friendly. I said once that they should have asked Sparrow to write the national anthem that Trinidad was going to have. He would have written a proper national anthem, in words and music. . . ."*]

A native West Indian talent. Born and bred in the West Indies and nourished by the West Indies. What he lacks is what we lack, and if we see that he gets it, the whole nation will move forward with him: Francisco Slinger, otherwise known as the Mighty Sparrow, the most remarkable man I have met during four years in the West Indies.

Sparrow is a Grenadian who lived as a youth in Grenada. Obviously he was born with an exceptional gift for music, for words and for social observation. If he had gone to America he would have sung (and composed) American songs, like Brook Benton, Ben E. King, Sam Cooke and many others. Not one of them, not one, surpasses him in anything that he does. He came to Trinidad and found in Trinidad a medium, the calypso, in which his talents could have full play.

Where have we won creative national distinction in the past? In two spheres only, the writing of fiction, and cricket. Cricketers and novelists have added a new dimension, but to already established international organisations. Not so the Mighty Sparrow, and here he is indeed mighty. His talents were shaped by a West Indian medium; through this medium he expanded his capacities and the medium itself. He is financially maintained by the West Indian people who buy his records. The mass of people give him all the encouragement that an artist needs. Although the calypso is Trinidadian, Sparrow is hailed in all the islands and spontaneously acknowledged as a representative West Indian. Thus he is in every way a genuinely West Indian artist, the first and only one that I know. He is a living proof that there is a West Indian nation.

I do not propose any critical review of his music. This is work for a trained musician. There is only one quality which I wish to elaborate here.

In the famous "Jean and Dinah", Sparrow immortalises the attitude of the ordinary people to the Americans at the base:

> It's the glamour boys again
> We are going to rule Port-of-Spain
> No more Yankees to spoil the fete. . . .

If that is not a political statement, then, after thirty years of it, I don't know what politics is. He relates how the Yankee dollars have brought some ancient performers once more into the ring, and then:

> But leave them alone, don't get in a rage
> When a Yankee drunk he don't study age
> For whether she is twenty-four, twenty-five or eighty
> I am sure it would not interest a drunken Yankee
> For when you drink Barbados nectar is doesn't matter
>   How old she is
> As long as the Yankee get what is his.

Sparrow is uninhibited about what he sees. He doesn't get in a rage. But he views the world with a large detachment. His irony and wit are the evidence.

In strict politics he shows an extraordinary sensitivity to public moods, with the same ironical detachment; this time, however, not merely as an observer but as one of the people. He begins by rejoicing at the victory of Dr Williams in 1956:

> For we have a champion leader
> William the Conqueror.

But he believes that the victory of the PNM has raised the taxi fares and the price of milk. He sings "No, Doctor, No". He philosophises on the curious behaviour of politicians in general but this verse was omitted in a later edition, so I shall leave it where it is. However, he says that he still supports PNM though he will see how things go: he has in reserve his piece of mango wood.

Then follows his superb "You Can't Get Away from the Tax". He tells the public that they must accept. He expresses popular resentment at "Pay As You Earn", but in the end his father sells the revolutionary axe to pay the income tax. Despite the pervading irony he is performing a public service. He is making the unpleasant palatable with wit and humour.

Then Sparrow expresses perfectly the attitude of the ordinary man to PNM in 1959:

> Leave the damn Doctor
> He ain't trouble all you
> Leave the damn Doctor
> What he do he well do.

Not too long ago, Sparrow becomes aware that things are not
going well. He blames the Opposition. What is notable is his sense
of the political confusion in the country:

> The island as you see
> Suffering politically
> Because the present Government
> Have some stupid opponent
> Oh, Lord, man, they ignorant . . .
> Causing they own self embarrassment.

I believe here he faithfully reports public sentiment. Things are
in a mess and the reason is that the Opposition are objecting to
everything.

Finally there is his magnificent "Federation" calypso, a triumph.
I was in the tent the night he returned and first sang it. When it
became clear what he was saying, the audience froze. Trinidad
had broken with the Federation. Nobody was saying anything
and the people did not know what to think, far less what to say.
At the end of the last verse on that first night Sparrow saw that
something was wrong and he added loudly: "I agree with the
Doctor". But the people of Trinidad and Tobago only wanted a
lead. Sparrow divined their mood, for henceforth he became increasingly bold and free. When he sang at the Savannah he put
all he had into it and the public made a great demonstration. They
wanted, how they wanted somebody to say something, and Sparrow
said something. He attacked Jamaica and Jamaica deserved to be
attacked. But Sparrow said what people wanted to hear: "We failed
miserably".

He went further:

> Federation boil down to simply this
> It's dog-eat-dog, and survival of the fittest.

The scorn, the disappointment he poured into those words did
for the whole population what it wanted done and could not do
for itself. The response of the public was greater than anything I
have ever heard in the West Indies.

But Sparrow is a very clever man. Note the insoluble ambiguity
of the last verse. He was singing before a Trinidad audience for
whom a political position on federation had been taken.

> Some may say we shouldn't help part it
> But is Jamaica what start it.

There he introduces the all-important question: was Trinidad
right to leave, and he says that after all it was Jamaica which
started this leaving business. He does not comment himself, but he
has registered that some Trinidad people are against Trinidad
leaving. Now comes a masterpiece of political statement.

Federation boil down to simply this
It's dog-eat-dog, and survival of the fittest
Everybody going for independence
    Singularly
Trinidad for instance
And we'll get it too, boy, don't bother
But I find we should all be together
Not separated as we are
Because of Jamaica.

What does this verse mean? I have asked a score of people and
nobody can say for certain. Let us look at it. The dog-eat-dog
includes everybody, and is savage enough. Then the lines which say
that everybody is "going for independence Singularly Trinidad for
instance", can be related to dog-eat-dog. But he says quickly that
we in Trinidad will get it. Which does not modify the ferocity of
dog-eat-dog by a single comma. But Trinidad will get it. There must
be no doubt about that so he puts in an encouraging "don't
bother". Then comes the mysterious

But I find we should all be together
Not separated as we are
Because of Jamaica.

It can mean "I think we should all, all of us in the British West
Indies, be together, and not separated as we are because Jamaica
left us". But it could easily mean, "I think that we who remain
behind should all be together and not be separated as we are because Jamaica left".

What do I think? I think first that politically the statement is a
masterpiece. But I can go a little further. I cannot ignore the savage
contempt of dog-eat-dog, and I find the musical tone of "Everybody going for independence/Singularly/Trinidad for instance"
very revealing. If Sparrow liked that move politically, or if he
thought that his public liked it, he would have written and sung
differently. There I have to leave it.

There is more to Sparrow, much more. There is that comic
episode of the Governor who was crazy, and changed the law for
a lady, the lady in the short little shorts. There is the same amused
and ironical detachment as when he is describing the social tastes
of the Yankees.

At times he explodes. In "Leave the Damn Doctor", there suddenly stands out this verse:

They makin' so much confusion
'Bout race riot in England
They should kick them from Scotland Yard
We have the same question in Trinidad.

That can mean a lot of things.

Then comes this skilful and ferocious verse:

> Well, the way how things shapin' up
> All this nigger business go' stop
> I tell you soon in the West Indies
> It's please Mr Nigger please.

The ways of an artist are his own. You can only judge by the result. I once told him that I thought his "Gunslingers" was a picture of violent and rebellious sentiments simmering in the younger generation. He said he didn't think of it that way. Everybody was going around saying, "Make your play" and on that he built up the whole. This is an old problem. I told him: "I accept what you say. But that would not alter the fact that such a calypso would spring only from a feeling that similar sentiments were rife among the younger generation". He reflected a second and then said, "I see what you mean." And I had no doubt that he saw exactly what I meant: that an artist draws or paints a single episode which he sees in front of him, but that he has chosen it or shapes it from pervading sentiments of which he is not necessarily conscious.

Another more pointed instance of his attitudes is his calypso on the marriage of Princess Margaret. It is most brilliantly done and for comic verse this one stands high on my list:

> Long ago in England
> You couldn't touch the princess' hand
> Unless, well, you able
> Like the Knights of the Round Table
> If you want she real bad
> You had to beat Ivanhoe or Sir Galahad
> Mount your horse with your spear in hand
> Who remain alive that's the princess' man.

Again:

> Some people real lucky
> Take for instance Anthony

And again:

> If the Princess like you
> Boy, you ain't have a thing to do

That single word, "Boy", is loaded.

And here in my view is an example of the real social value of Sparrow. I didn't know what he was getting at until after conversations in Jamaica with ordinary citizens. Now I have been a republican since I was eight years old. An Englishman, William Makepeace Thackeray, taught it to me. But the British people respect and some even love the Royal Family, and we revolutionists don't make a fuss about it. What to my surprise I discovered in Jamaica among the ordinary people was a deep regard for the British Royal Family, combined with nationalism. How widespread that is among the ordinary people in Trinidad I do not know, but Sparrow's song on the marriage was the song of a man whose inner conceptions of royalty had received a violent shock.

For a young man he shows an exceptional maturity and detachment in the way he views the life around him. As he grows older he can become a guide, philosopher and friend to the public. Some of his songs are very improper, but the West Indian audience takes them in its stride, and I could mention some world-famous novelists who excel Sparrow in impropriety. But what attracts and holds me is his social and political sense, and his independence and fearlessness. Such men are rare. At critical moments he can say, to the people or on their behalf, what should be said. Will Rogers was such a one in the United States. But I am afraid for Sparrow, mortally afraid. Such a man should be left alone to sing what he likes when he likes; he should be encouraged to do so. But West Indian governments help those who praise them and can be as savage and vicious as snakes to those who are not helping them to win the next election.

I used to listen to Sparrow before I came here and was very much impressed with his records. As soon as I saw and heard him in person, felt his enormous vitality and gathered some facts about him I recognised that here was a man who comes once in fifty years. In November 1959 I was invited to speak at UCWI on "The Artist in the Caribbean". I want to refer to how I approach the question. I spoke of art in general through the ages, of Cézanne, of Shakespeare, of Michelangelo; of the Greek city-state, of the cities of the Middle Ages. I made it clear that while I spoke about Cézanne and Michelangelo, historical figures, I was not going to express any opinions about West Indian painters because I had no qualification for doing so.

Then I moved straight to Beryl McBurnie and Sparrow, West Indian artists playing for West Indian audiences. To that university audience, after a passage on our novelists and the need to get them home, I said finally:

"When our local artists can evoke the popular response of a Sparrow, the artist in the Caribbean will have arrived."

Everything that I really think about the West Indies, not only its art, is contained in that lecture and particularly in that sentence.

Sparrow has it in him to go much further and take the West Indian nation with him. He is fully able to carry a full-length West Indian show first all over the West Indies and then to London and New York. He could write most of it, words and music. Of that I am absolutely confident. And if he were to spend some time in England his satirical eye would not fail to add to the gaiety of nations. But that undertaking is not one to be lightly embarked upon. And I am yet to find any educated West Indians in the West

Indies who are educated enough to put their education at the disposal of the Mighty Sparrow. At any rate Sparrow knows those who do not like him and when he sings he doesn't mince words about them. He knows that *"they"* will do *"anything"*. He sticks to the people. Let us hope that, difficult as it may become, he will continue to be *vox populi*.

Note for 1962

I will go fully into it and devil take the hindmost.

There is much more to Sparrow than I have said above. Prejudice is eating away at the vitals of West Indian progress, race prejudice, class prejudice stimulated and fortified by race prejudice, and intellectual prejudice. Sparrow is fighting it all gamely but he doesn't know the full extent of what he is fighting against and the allies he has.

Let us forget Sparrow for a bit. You have to begin with Haiti, a West Indian island as we are. After the successful revolution for Haitian independence in 1802, the Haitian intelligentsia tried for nearly a hundred years to build a model of French civilisation and culture in the West Indies. Their failure is of great importance to us today. They produced some fine scholars and some gifted writers, but a civilisation, a culture of any kind, far less French, that they failed utterly to do. Recognising this failure to make themselves French, they turned back home. What they found and built up was the African heritage which the Haitian peasants, more than all others in the West Indies, had preserved. Dr Price Mars was the originator of this movement and a world-famous sociologist he became. His influence and the influence of his followers last in Haiti to this day. Without exaggeration it can be entitled "Africa in the West Indies".

Future events were to show that this was no accidental explosion of an individual personality. A few years after Price Mars began, Marcus Garvey, a West Indian from Jamaica, achieved the heroic feat of placing Africa and Africans and people of African descent upon the map of modern history. Before him they were not there. They have been there ever since. After Garvey followed George Padmore, a political organiser and theoretician, and West Indians should know that no names of non-Africans stand higher in Africa today in intellectual and political circles (in Ghana among the people too) than these two West Indians, Marcus Garvey and George Padmore. (You are wondering what all this has to do with Sparrow? If the strain is too much for you, go back to the study of all those wars fought by the British and French which fill up books purporting to be West Indian history.)

Just before World War II another African-orientated manifestation appeared in the West Indies. Aimé Césaire, the Martinique politician and writer, in 1939 published the most famous poem ever written about Africans. He called it "Statement on a Return to My Native Country".* Although he is writing about Martinique, the main theme of the poem is African. He says that the poverty-stricken Negroes of Martinique can only arrive at full self-expression by recognising and appreciating what they owe to their African ancestry. In the poem Césaire uses the word *Négritude*, a very important word today. It symbolises respect for the black man's past, above all for his African contributions to civilisation, without which he cannot make any real progress personal or social. *Négritude* is widely known throughout Africa and Western Europe, and the debate on it is hot, world-wide and continuous.

What emerges from all that is this, a profoundly remarkable historical fact. The recognition of Africanism, the agitation for recognition of Africa, the literary creation of an African ideology, one powerful sphere of African independence, all were directly the creation of West Indians. The exact proportion of their contribution need not be estimated. The undisputable fact is that able and powerful West Indians concentrated their exceptional familiarity with Western thought, expression and organisation on Africa and Africans when these qualities were urgently needed both in Africa and elsewhere. This is a part of the history of the West Indies, a very important part. But West Indians do not study this.

Why they did this I shall not go into here. What we have to note is that about 1950, five years after the shaking-up the world got in World War II, and following upon the mass political upheavals in the West Indies in 1937-38 and its consequences, this African orientation came to a pause. It was succeeded, superseded I should say, by another powerful orientation. First of all arose our British West Indian novelists, a splendid bunch. Two of them, Lamming and Naipaul, have no superiors of their age and time. Our writers have to live abroad to do their work. But the greater part of their work and by far the best of it is concerned with the West Indian peasant and the West Indian ordinary man. What Price Mars, Garvey, Padmore, Césaire could not find at home, with the development of history and the development of the West Indies, our writers have found. Of their world-wide significance there is no space to speak here, but I believe it is destined to be as famous as *Négritude* has become.

In the same period we have the emergence of West Indian cricketers who add something new and particularly West Indian to cricket. The position had to be fought for, some magnificent West Indians were deprived of making the contribution they could have made. But it was done and a West Indian style has been established.

Latest to join the new emergence is Derek Walcott, a West Indian poet, not a writer of some poems, but a poet who has made poetry in the West Indies his vocation. He is doing a tremendously difficult job and knows what he is doing.

*Cahier d'un Retour au Pays Natal.

The year 1950, therefore, marks a definitive change in West Indian thought and its expression. It is to this outburst of West Indianism after 1950 that Sparrow belongs. With him and the steelband the West Indian masses have joined the new West Indian procession. It is not his unusual personal gifts that are decisive here, though without them he would be nothing. It is that he is so obviously a man of the people, using a people's medium and cherished by the people as one of their own. He is in reality a very curious historical figure and one whose work and influence deserve serious study. It can be very instructive about the type of development the West Indian nation is destined to undergo. For in most nations the popular music and the popular song come first, are usually centuries old, and the artists and intellectuals often build their national creations upon these age-old roots.* I am sure that it is not at all accidental that in the very same decade that the West Indian artists are finding West Indianism, the native popular music and the native popular song find their most complete, their most vigorous expression and acceptance. Here I tread very cautiously but I think I see that our own historical existence and the kind of world in which we live, are forcing upon us a rapid combination of historical stages which took centuries in the older nations. Ghana, Ceylon, India do not have the same premises. They have a native language, native religion, native way of life. We haven't. We are Western, yet have to separate what is ours from what is Western, a very difficult task. Sparrow in the popular sphere is doing that with a dedication, even an obstinacy which is very exciting to see. He found a medium already established. But he is making it a genuinely national expression and possession.

He is not educated in the ordinary sense and I think, though I am not sure, that this helps him in what he is doing. It is to me a striking and magnificent demonstration of West Indians finding themselves in all sorts of fields, that the common people have produced the steelband and now as I have tried to show, have found and support a local ballad singer.

The fields he opens up are immense. Sparrow's use of the language over and over again makes memorable lines of ordinary Trinidad speech. He represents, makes known what the people really think, what they really are and how they speak. Through him the ordinary West Indian speech is given its place and some good portion of it is very effective and powerful speech. That part of our nation is usually ignored or neglected among us, because intellectually we are a very backward people who have no conception of the greatest discovery of modern times, the positive role of the masses of the people in all phases of national develop-

---

*The real originator of the importance of popular story and popular song in a national development is a German, Herder. We are unfortunately not very familiar with the German language. However, Rousseau, here as almost everywhere else in what is modern, is an ancestor.

ment. Sparrow is seeing to it that this aspect of our contemporary life is not by-passed.

I may have given the impression that he is primarily interested in politics. That would be quite false. He is interested in the life around him, all aspects. I could write about his versification, the subjects he chooses, his handling of narrative. But I prefer to hope that others will do it. Most usefully, Mr Derek Walcott has recently given us his reflections on the West Indian poet and the English language (*Trinidad Guardian*, 18 June 1962). I hope that the whole will be published. He understands the significance of the calypso, the troubles of all poets in our age and much else of importance to us, but all that I shall leave you to find out for yourself from him. I want to make urgent reference to only one point. The quotation is long but I don't want you to miss a word:

> "For if we accept that poetry has its origins in the myth of the race, in the heredity of the folk imagination, then the poet in the West Indies, exiled from a mythically fertile past, must first explore his origins before he can purify the dialect of the tribe. And those origins are not only political but ancestral, they are subdued in the blood and he must provoke them to speak. The language in which they speak will be the one he has learnt by imitation, and it is one of immense flexibility and power, but the feelings must be his own, they must have their roots in his own earth."

The English language has its roots in a country very different from ours. In the most profound sense of the word it is not our language, particularly their poetry is not a model for our poets. But Mr Walcott has learnt that he has to master a poetic language which is the creation of men who are using their own language in their own country. Then he has to use whatever he has worked out to express poetically the deepest feelings and instincts of a very different environment. The process is more complicated than I have stated it here. But in any case it is a special West Indian problem. What makes it worse, the West Indies have little of the past historical experience which the painter in Mexico for instance finds ready to hand. We have not had much of a past of our own, and what we have had we know little of. What Sparrow is doing is to make alive, to develop and to establish what the ordinary people of the West Indies are now doing. Better late than never. For the first time in their lives modern engineering technique and a certain amount of political freedom make this possible. And that they have found a man, one of their own, to devote great powers to this is immensely to their credit, and to the advantage of all of us. I hinted to UCWI that they should pay attention to his work. I had in mind his use of language, and his musical use of traditional cadences, musical tones, intervals and transitions. If you listen to his very early records you will hear much that he has since worked over and developed into masterpieces. Thus you can hear in "Race Track" the original ideas which finally blossomed into "Jean and Dinah". It would be most interesting to know, and only a trained musician can tell us this, what are the purely musical changes by which he develops the early statement of an idea into its maturer form. Informed but sympathetic criticism of his words and his music can be of great value not only to Sparrow himself but to the more traditional type of poet and popular composer.

Today I do not know one popular composer whom I find more attractive, more inventive and with a finer sense of correspondence between words and music and meaning.* But though I would welcome critical studies, I would say that above all Sparrow must be left alone to find his own way, using whatever is done, ignoring it or denouncing it as he pleases. Behind him, and Mr Walcott's analysis, there emerges a fact and direction that summarises the whole West Indian position as I see it, politics, economics, art, everything. That was the main point of my lecture at UCWI in 1959 on "The Artist in the Caribbean". We have to master a medium, whatever it is, that has developed in a foreign territory and on that basis seek and find out what is native, and build on that. It is obvious that our present race of politicians are too far gone ever to learn that. But there are signs that this truth is penetrating younger people. It is the West Indian truth that matters above all. Perhaps Sparrow will make a calypso on it.

1961

---

*Someone once told him in my hearing: "The music of the last line of 'Royal Jail' doesn't seem as good as the rest." Very amicably Sparrow started to think. "How can I change those words?" he said. The critic said, "Not the words, the music." As if it were obvious to everybody, as no doubt it was to him, he replied, "If something is wrong with the music, something is wrong with the words."

16

W. E. B. Du Bois

[*James wrote this essay as an introduction to a 1965 republication of W. E. B. Du Bois's* The Souls of Black Folk. *He says: "Dr Du Bois has always been put forward as one of the great black men and one of the great leaders of the black people. But I have said that he is one of the great intellectuals — American intellectuals — of the twentieth century, and today and in years to come his work will continue to expand in importance while the work of others declines."*]

It is more than a misjudgement to think of W. E. B. Du Bois as a great leader of Negroes or as some type of spiritual African expatriate. To do so is not only to subject him to racialist connotation; it is to circumscribe and to limit the achievements of one of the greatest American citizens of his time. For that is what Du Bois was, an American scholar and public man who could have done the work he did only as an American with the opportunities and needs and world-wide scope that only America could have given him. A mere listing of his achievements will demonstrate his Americanism without possibility of argument.

1. He educated and organised black people in the United States to claim, and white people to acknowledge, that racial prejudice in the United States was a disease against the material well-being and moral health of the American people.

2. More than any other citizen of Western civilisation (or of Africa itself) he struggled over many years and succeeded in making the world aware that Africa and Africans had to be freed from the thraldom which Western civilisation had imposed on them.

3. As a scholar he not only initiated the first serious study of the American slave trade; in his studies of the Civil War, and of the Negro in the United States after the Civil War, he also laid foundations and achieved monumental creations surpassed by no other scholar of the period.

To this may be added the fact that in the beginning, the development and the conclusion of his life's work, he symbolised certain stages in the development of American thought which are a pointer to the examination of dominant currents in the role that the United States is now playing in the world.

There is no need to subscribe to all that Dr Du Bois has said and done. But long before the rulers and leaders of thought in the United States grasped the essentials of the world in which they lived,

Dr Du Bois did, and to look upon him just as a great leader of the Negro people or just a true son of Africa is to diminish the conceptions and mitigate the impact of one of the great citizens of the modern world.

1. *He educated and organised black people in the United States to claim and white people to acknowledge that racial prejudice in the United States was a disease against the ·material well-being and moral health of the American people.*

Born in 1868, in 1903 Dr Du Bois was 35 years old. In this year a growing reputation reached a climax in *The Souls of Black Folk*. He had been educated at Fisk, a Negro university, and then at Harvard, where he was the first Negro to take a doctorate of philosophy. He followed this with post-graduate studies in Berlin. To the end of his days he remained a man of a fantastic range of accomplishments — he was Professor of Greek and Latin at Wilberforce University from 1894-1896; he was Assistant Instructor of Sociology at the University of Pennsylvania whence he went to Atlanta to become Professor of Economics and History. In his last year at Pennsylvania he published his *Suppression of the Slave Trade* where American historicism for the first time lifted this substantial phase of American history out of the limitations of sociology and ethics and established it within economic relations. The book was not merely, as it has been hailed, "the first scientific historical work" written by a Negro. It marked a new stage in the development of American historical study and thought. Fifteen years afterwards the road paved out by Du Bois was followed by Charles Beard with his epoch-making book, *The Constitution, an Economic Interpretation*.

With his sociological studies of *The Philadelphia Negro* in 1899 and the sociological studies of the Negro which followed, Gunnar Myrdal, author of the monumental study of Negro life in the United States, *An American Dilemma*, says of Du Bois that he produced work which is still viable to-day "while white authors . . . have been compelled to retreat from the writings of earlier decades". Gunnar Myrdal notes that the secret of Du Bois's success was that he proceeded on the assumption later formulated by Du Bois himself that "the Negro in America and in general is an average and ordinary human being". For Du Bois this was not merely a way of thinking but a way of life, his own life. During his years at Atlanta he refused to travel in a segregated transport system and could always been seen walking on his journeys from one part of the city to another.

In 1895 Booker T. Washington, President of Tuskegee Institute, had accepted segregation as an inevitable and necessary stage of the Negro's status in American Society. "In all things purely social we can be as separate as the fingers. Yet (here he balled his fingers into a fist) one, as the hand, in all things essential to mutual progress."

Du Bois at first joined in the enthusiastic reception given to these words by the whole nation. But by 1903 Du Bois's study of Negro Americans had made it clear to him that the hope of creating an independent Negro peasantry was vain. Heavy capital investment in agriculture was turning increasingly large numbers of Negroes into demoralised sharecroppers, now experiencing the added weight of legalised persecution by all the state governments of the South. A number of educated Negroes had long resented the policy of Booker T. Washington and the immense recognition which increasingly represented him as the voice of the Negro people. In the essay "On Booker T. Washington and Others" Du Bois broke shatteringly with the programme and policies of Washington. With a formidable dignity which strengthened his opposition, Du Bois ended his piece as follows:

"The black men of America have a duty to perform, a duty stern and delicate, a forward movement to oppose a part of the work of their greatest leader. So far as Mr Washington preaches Thrift, Patience, and Industrial Training for the masses, we must hold up his hands and strive with him, rejoicing in his honours and glorying in the strength of this Joshua called of God and of man to lead the headless host. But so far as Mr Washington apologises for injustice, North or South, does not rightly value the privilege and duty of voting, belittles the emasculating effects of caste distinction, and opposes the higher training and ambition of our brighter minds, so far as he, the South, or the nation, does this, we must unceasingly and firmly oppose them. By every civilised and peaceful method we must strive for the rights which the world accords to men, clinging unwaveringly to those great words which the sons of the Fathers would fain forget: 'We hold these truths to be self-evident: That all men are created equal; that they are endowed by their Creator with certain unalienable rights; that among these are life, liberty, and the pursuit of happiness.' "

By its mastery of economic and social movement and the general humanity and personal distinction of its style, the book at once gained a recognition which it has never lost. From that time Du Bois steadily grew into the leader of the opposition to Washington who was by now an established consultant to Congressmen, Senators and the White House on all problems affecting Negroes in the United States. While sticking in principle to the theory that all men were created equal, Du Bois characteristically made what will have appeared to him a necessary concession to objective fact. In his study of the Philadelphia Negro he had unearthed the rise to comparative well-being and at least self-respect of a Negro class of house servants. Du Bois now advocated the conception of the Talented Tenth, by which he sought to clear the road of the educated Negro to full citizenship and to stimulate among the masses of Negroes a passionate belief in education as the curative of all social ills. This was a conception gaining ground in the United

States under the powerful advocacy of the philosopher, John Dewey.

The Du Bois who preferred to walk rather than use a Jim Crow car in Atlanta was not the type of political thinker to be satisfied with the mere statement of a position whatever its acceptance. In July 1905 he helped to inaugurate a meeting at Buffalo, New York; the first stage in what became known as the Niagara Movement. Next year the protagonists met at Harper's Ferry, the scene of the martyrdom of John Brown. In his address Du Bois declared:

> "We will not be satisfied to take one jot or tittle less than our full manhood rights. We claim for ourselves every single right that belongs to a free-born American, political, civil, and social; and until we get these rights we will never cease to protest and assail the ears of America. The battle we wage is not for ourselves alone, but for all true Americans."

These were not mere phrases. In 1910 Du Bois founded *The Crisis* as the monthly organ of the National Association for the Advancement of Coloured People. The organisation and the journal were devoted to equality for Negroes, but distinguished white people, John Dewey, Frank Boas the anthropologist, and Mary Ovington the social worker, were staunch and active supporters of Du Bois. Due Bois, however, always remained the dominant figure. The national membership of the organisation, 9,282 in 1917, by 1919 was 91,000. The circulation of *The Crisis*, 1,750 in 1910, was by 1919 over 100,000. Du Bois continued as editor for a quarter of a century when his by no means infrequent disputes with what he considered the conservatism of the organisation ended in his resignation. In 1944 he once more joined the staff of the NAACP as Director of Studies. This lasted until 1948 when his break with the organisation became final. The news that he had died in Accra, Ghana, came during the preparation for the great march on Washington in 1963, led by Negro organisations including the NAACP. Many realised that the road America was travelling had not only been charted but its foundations laid by W. E. Burghardt Du Bois.

2. *More than any other citizen of Western civilisation (or of Africa itself) he struggled over many years and succeeded in making the world aware that Africa and Africans had to be freed from the thraldom which Western civilisation had imposed on them.*

Du Bois had conquered Booker T. Washington. Before long he was in conflict with a far more formidable rival for the allegiance of Negroes in the United States and elsewhere, the celebrated West Indian agitator, Marcus Garvey. In the conflict and contrast between these two men, both in their own way great fighters for African independence, can be seen a great deal of neglected world history and the peculiar qualities which characterised Du Bois: belief in the ultimate power of the intellect, an instinct for political activity on the largest or smallest scale, both inspired and maintained by a tenacity that never admitted defeat.

As early as 1911, just a year after the founding of *The Crisis*, Du Bois took part in the First World Races Congress in London. The congress grew out of the suggestion of Dr Felix Adler, the founder of the Ethical Cultural movement, that a congress of races of the world be held

> "to discuss, in the light of science and the modern conscience, the general relations subsisting between the peoples of the West and those of the East, between so-called whites and so-called coloured peoples, with a view to encouraging between them a fuller understanding, the most friendly feelings, and a heartier co-operation."

The Congress was attended by representatives of most of the peoples of the world. Dr Du Bois represented the NAACP and, supposedly, American Negroes. The sessions were devoted largely to such topics as the meaning of the concept of race; political, economic, social and religious conditions in the colonial areas; miscegenation; inter-racial conflicts; the role of the Jew and the Negro in the world scene, and methods of abolishing the international "evils" of indentured labour and drink. The Races Congress was an example of that rationalistic liberalism which placed great faith in scientific interchange as an adequate method of social progress.

Du Bois was an active member of the Congress, being one of its secretaries and delivering one of its major addresses.

At the end of World War I, Du Bois instituted a movement for a Pan-African Congress to be held in Paris during the sessions of the peace conference in 1919, in order to pressure peacemakers to internationalise the former German colonies in Africa in a way that would best serve the needs of the growing African nationalism. Du Bois and the NAACP worked under the assumption that the Negroes of the world represented a unified pressure group.

Not only did Du Bois and the NAACP hope that such a congress would lead to "self-determination" for the African natives, but also that it would "serve, perhaps better than any other means that could be taken, to focus the attention of the peace delegates and the civilised world on the just claims of the Negro everywhere".*

Du Bois's reminiscences twenty years later concerning the motives of this first congress may be taken as an accurate portrayal of his actual intentions in 1919. In 1940, Du Bois wrote in *Dusk of Dawn*:

> "My plans as they developed had in them nothing spectacular nor revolutionary. If in decades or a century they resulted in such world organisation of black men as would oppose a united front to European aggression, that certainly would not have been be-

---

*Du Bois, *Dusk of Dawn*, 275.

yond my dream. But on the other hand, in practical reality, I knew the power and guns of Europe and America and what I wanted to do was in the face of this power to sit down hand in hand with coloured groups and across the council table to learn of each other, our condition, our aspirations, our chances for concerted thought and action. One of this there might come, not race war and opposition, but broader co-operation with the white rulers of the world, and a chance for peaceful and accelerated development of black folk."

Du Bois experienced opposition from both the French Government and the American State Department but through the intercession of Blaise Diagne, an African member of the French Assembly from Senegal, Clemenceau granted permission to hold the First Pan-African Congress at the Grand Hotel in Paris. Fifty-seven delegates finally attended the Congress, including sixteen American Negroes, twenty West Indian Negroes, and twelve Africans.

From the beginning, Diagne, who was chosen as the President of the Congress, and Du Bois, its Secretary, were at odds, for Diagne was a Frenchman before being a Pan-African, and insisted upon praising French colonial rule, while attacking the other European powers' operations in Africa. However the Congress did pass a series of resolutions calling for the creation of an "internationalised" African state, consisting of the one million square miles and twelve and one-half million inhabitants of the former German colonies, the 800,000 square miles and nine million inhabitants of Portuguese Africa, and the 900,000 square miles and nine million inhabitants of the Belgian Congo, this state to be ruled by the League of Nations. That the range, however remote, of Du Bois's activity was governed by the possible was shown by the fact that the Congress demanded action only on the territory of the defeated enemy and the possessions of the two smaller colonial powers, while not mentioning the lands of France or Britain for inclusion in this new state.

The Congress resolutions went on to demand safeguards against economic exploitation, cultural subjection and for increased self-rule, educational and medical facilities for all Africa. These resolutions, drawn up largely by European and American university-trained Negroes placed emphasis upon the development of a Negro cultural and intellectual élite in whose hands the development of Africa was to be placed. Du Bois applied the same doctrine of the "upper tenth" to the African Negroes as he had earlier done in reference to the advancement of the American Negro people.

This Pan-African Congress met with support in the United States. On 6 January 1919, a "mass meeting for the Pan-African movement" was held at Carnegie Hall, New York, under the auspices of NAACP. Two resolutions showed the way Du Bois habitually thought. The first resolution demanded that the German colonies in Africa be turned over to the natives, while the second resolution declared that if lynchings of Negroes were not stopped in America, "a revolution of twelve million Negro citizens might be used to stop it".

The Second Pan-African Congress was held in the early autumn of 1921, sponsored by the NAACP, i.e. initiated by Du Bois. He always saw the movement for African independence as an international movement. Therefore the Second Congress met successively in the capitals of three European nations which had African colonies — London, Brussels, and Paris. This Congress had 113 accredited delegates including 35 from the United States, mainly, though not all, Negro.

At this Congress the dissension between Du Bois and Blaise Diagne came to a head. The Brussels meeting watered down the more radical statements and resolutions passed at the London meeting, in particular removing all specific attacks on French and Belgian imperialism. However, the Congress did agree to petition the League of Nations to set up a special Negro section of the International Labour Organisation, to appoint a Negro to the Mandates' Commission, and to put pressure on public opinion through an educational programme to end racial discrimination. A manifesto declared that in the process of raising the Africans "to intelligence, self-knowledge and self-control, their (Negro) intelligentsia of right ought to be recognised as the natural leaders of their groups".

A Third Congress was held in 1924 in London and Lisbon but even though the London meeting attracted people like Harold Laski and H. G. Wells, the movement was obviously on the decline.

A Fourth Congress was held in New York City in 1927 sponsored by the Council of the Women of the Darker Races. A great deal of time was spent in the discussion of the work of American Negro Christian missionaries in Africa. Professor Melville Herskovits of Columbia University was a notable participant.

An attempt was made to organise a Fifth Congress in Tunis, North Africa, in 1929, but it failed.

From start to finish Du Bois was the moving spirit and active organiser of these congresses. Much later he was to claim that the Mandates' Committee of the League of Nations came out of the Congress proposal that the German colonies be turned over to an international organisation. That claim may or may not be justified. That is not important. What matters is this clear vision and persistent attempt, long before all other statesmen and political thinkers, to apply to Africa the type of thought and action with which the world is now familiar, not so much from the League of Nations as from the United Nations. Du Bois was limited to support from mainly Negro intellectuals, for the most part American and this interest in Africa of many of them was stimulated directly or indirectly by their belief in the repercussion of African progress on their own situation in the United States.

Du Bois did not have only to stimulate Negro intellectuals whose ideas were not as comprehensive as his own. He had to battle with hostile imperialist powers. What he was preaching and trying to do must be seen side by side with another American movement, the movement of Marcus Garvey.

Garvey, a Jamaican by birth, achieved the astonishing feat of building a mass movement of millions of Negroes in the United States. He also impressed upon world opinion the conception that the subordination of Africa to foreign powers could not continue, its regeneration would come from Negroes in the Western world whom Garvey was to lead back to Africa. Long before Garvey, Du Bois in *The Souls of Black Folk* had noted the resentment bottled up in large sections of the Negro population of the South. The needs of war propelled a mass migration of more than a million of these Negroes to the North and they formed the basis of Garvey's United Negro Improvement Association. Garvey declared Negro opposition not only to white oppression but to the Negro middle classes of whom Du Bois as the originator of the conception of the Talented Tenth was the accepted chief. Du Bois at first did not attack Garvey. As late as December 1922 he wrote in *The Crisis* that Garvey was "essentially an honest and sincere man with a tremendous vision, great dynamic force, stubborn determination, and unselfish desire to serve". But Du Bois, struggling against the enormous vested interests that impeded his Pan-African Congresses and finding that his movement was being linked with Garvey's Back-to-Africa movement, and no doubt stimulated by Garvey's unbridled attacks against him, turned against Garvey and in 1924 declared that "Marcus Garvey is, without doubt, the most dangerous enemy of the Negro race in America and in the world. He is either a lunatic or a traitor for he believes that forcible separation of the races and the banishment of Negroes to Africa is the only solution of the Negro problem."

Thus the two most dedicated movements for the emancipation of Africa originated among Negroes in the United States and were in mortal opposition to each other. Long before 1930 Garvey's movement came to an end and when Garvey was deported back to his native Jamaica Du Bois led the movement for the rehabilitation of his aims if not his methods.

Pan-Africanism seemed to have died in 1927. In the thirties it was revived by a West Indian in London, George Padmore. In association with Kwame Nkrumah and Jomo Kenyatta the new Pan-Africanism held a great conference at Manchester in 1945. Du Bois came from the United States to preside over the conference which launched the political movement that ended in the achievement of independence by the Gold Coast under the leadership of Kwame Nkrumah. The United States government prevented Du Bois from accepting Nkrumah's invitation to attend the celebration of the independence of the new state of Ghana in 1957. But as during the 1963 March on Washington the celebration was pervaded by the spirit of the far-seeing and doughty pioneer.

3. *As a scholar he not only initiated the first serious study of the American slave trade; in his studies of the Civil War, and of the Negro in the United States after the Civil War, he also laid foundations and achieved monumental creations surpassed by no other scholar of the period.*

In *The Crisis* Du Bois wrote constantly about Africa and published a volume devoted to the history of African civilisations. But, as he had done in every sphere of endeavour he touched, Du Bois broke new ground in one of the most important fields of modern history — the history of the United States itself. In 1909 before the American Historical Association Du Bois delivered an address on John Brown which startled all historians and students of history. Brown, Du Bois declared, had been the protagonist of a movement of active revolutionaries in American history. "Slavery," he declared, "had to die by revolution and not by milder means. And this men knew and they had known it for a hundred years. Yet they shrank and trembled." Readers of his address could not escape the implication that the whole character of Du Bois's interpretation of John Brown had contemporary connotations. A piquant situation now developed. Oswald Garrison Villard, editor of the liberal journal, *The Nation*, bore the family name of the Abolitionist Movement and would soon give years of devoted service as head of the NAACP. Villard challenged Du Bois's interpretation and in time produced his own volume on Brown in which the death of Brown at Harper's Ferry is reduced to an episode. Liberal opinion welcomed this recovery of John Brown from the explosive pen of Du Bois. Little did American historical study know what was in store for it. In 1935 Du Bois produced his *Black Reconstruction*, subtitled *An essay toward a history of the part which black folk played in the attempt to reconstruct democracy in America, 1860-1880.*

The time was the tumultuous thirties when revolutionary ideas were in the air even of universities. Du Bois, however, had raised his banner since 1909, twenty-six years before. He was sixty-seven when the book was published and its over 700 pages embodied a mastery of detail which could only have been the work of a lifetime. The book for the first time established the elevated aspirations and genuine social and educational achievements of the post-Civil War Negro-dominated government of the South. Du Bois showed that what he called the Great Strike of the slaves, their carefully-timed but incessant pouring from slavery into Union lines, had created a condition in which emancipation had become the price and only guarantee of victory.

But this material with which he was so familiar Du Bois placed within a framework which embraced his life's studies, his political work and his hopes for the future. Slavery and slave revolts, American society inside and out of the South, the military and political features of the Civil War, the grandeur and decadence of Reconstruction, were fitted into a comprehensive view of world politics, including Marx's International Workingmen's Association, the Paris Commune, World War I, the crash of 1929, the rise of fascism, the threat of World War II. Some of these relations he established were in 1935 startling enough, though time and the violent historical changes in the contemporary world have made much that in 1935 seemed wanton not at all remote thirty years later. Only the future can tell to what degree the historical audacities of Du Bois are viable. Quotation can scarcely do him justice but his awareness of the intricacies and subtleties of politics and social movement on an international scale rest firmly on a deep and passionate humanity.

> "There was to be a new freedom! And a black nation went tramping after the armies no matter what it suffered; no matter how it was treated, no matter how it died. First, without masters, without food, without shelter; then with new masters, food that was free, and improvised shelters, cabins, homes; and at last, land. They prayed; they worked; they danced and sang; they studied to learn: they wanted to wander. Some for the first time in their lives saw Town; some left the plantation and walked out into the world; some handled actual money, and some with arms in their hands, actually fought for freedom. An unlettered leader of fugitive slaves pictured it: 'And then we saw the lightning — that was the guns! and then we heard the thunder — that was the big guns; and then we heard the rain falling, and that was the drops of blood falling; and when we came to git in the crops it was dead men that we reaped.'
> The mass of slaves, even the more intelligent ones, and certainly the great group of field hands, were in religious and hysterical fervour. This was the coming of the Lord."

Black Reconstuction is and is likely to continue to be one of the finest history books ever written.

It is also the climax of Du Bois's work and the herald of the surprising activities of his last years. In 1948 when he was eighty years of age he was forced out of the NAACP and until his death in 1963 Du Bois became an avowed propagandist of socialism. The communist states gave him an ecstatic welcome during his visits to their territories and to his unrestrained advocacy of their cause at home and abroad.

It is easy to understand how he made this transition. At the end of World War II he had written:

> "Accomplish the end which every honest human being must desire by means other than communism, and communism need not be feared. On the other hand, if a world of ultimate democracy, reaching across the colour line and abolishing race discrimination, can only be accomplished by the method laid down by Karl Marx, then that method deserves to be triumphant no matter what we think or do."

All his life he had seen whatever activity he had taken part in within the context of the movement of world forces. After World War II it must have seemed to him that the communist world with its denunciations of the old order and its sponsorship of a new order for all peoples represented the approach to an ideal which had inspired all his life.

Du Bois was persecuted for the transfer of his allegiance to socialism. He disdained to disguise his views and faced trial and the danger of imprisonment with fortitude and dignity undiminished. World-wide protest came to his rescue.

In 1961 he accepted an invitation from President Nkrumah of Ghana to undertake and direct plans for an Encyclopaedia Africana, a project for which he was well suited. With his wife, he moved to Ghana and was active in this work until the end. On 13 February 1963 he became a citizen of Ghana. He died on 27 August of the same year, five months before his ninety-sixth birthday.

This was the day of the great Civil Rights March on Washington. Du Bois's death was announced to the crowd at the foot of the Lincoln Memorial, when Roy Wilkins, Executive Secretary of the NAACP, said: "The true leader of this march is W. E. Burghardt Du Bois."

In his constant energy, his deep respect for the history and learning of the old world, his audacity and readiness to venture into uncharted seas, he was a true son of the intellectuals who founded the United States in 1776. Devoted as he was to righting the injustices of coloured people, he came in time to see his famous aphorism, that the problem of the twentieth century was the problem of the colour line, in a wider context. In his retrospect to *The Souls of Black Folk* he wrote:

> "So perhaps I might end this retrospect simply by saying: I still think today as yesterday that the colour line is a great problem of this century. But to-day I see more clearly than yesterday that back of the problem of race and colour, lies a greater problem which both obscures and implements it: and that is the fact that so many civilised persons are willing to live in comfort even if the price of this is poverty, ignorance, and disease of the majority of their fellowmen; that to maintain this privilege men have waged war until today war tends to become universal and continuous, and the excuse for this war continues largely to be colour and race."

Yet it was his consciousness of race which widened his vision and deepened his sensitivity. Africa can rightly claim him as a son and it is fitting that his dust should rest there, but for three-quarters of a century he strove to adapt the impulses of 1776 to the world of the twentieth century. He represents a current of American effort which will have much to do with the establishment of peace and progress not only to Africans and all people of colour but to the whole troubled world.

1965

17

Garfield Sobers

[*This is one of two contributions made by James to an anthology entitled* The Great All-Rounders *(Pelham Books, 1969), edited by John Arlott. James gives what he calls "historically opposite presentations of two remarkable cricketers . . . Learie Constantine was at the beginning of the West Indies' entry into big cricket; Garfield Sobers was at the high peak which Worrell had taken them to. He was a West Indian living in the modern age of highly developed technology, and had a scientific attitude towards the game."*]

The pundits colossally misunderstand Garfield Sobers — perhaps the word should be misinterpret, not misunderstand. Garfield Sobers, I shall show, is a West Indian cricketer, not merely a cricketer from the West Indies. He is the most typical West Indies cricketer that it is possible to imagine. All geniuses are merely men who carry to an extreme definitive the characteristics of the unit of civilisation to which they belong and the special act or function which they express or practise. Therefore to misunderstand Sobers is to misunderstand the West Indies, if not in intention, by inherent predisposition, which is much worse. Having run up the red flag, I should at least state with whom I intend to do battle. I choose the least offensive and in fact he who is obviously the most well-meaning, Mr Denys Rowbotham of the *Guardian* of Friday, 15 December 1967. Mr Rowbotham says of Sobers: "Nature, indeed, has blessed Sobers liberally, for in addition to the talents and reflexes, conditioned and instinctive, of a great cricketer, he has the eyes of a hawk, the instincts and suppleness of a panther, exceptional stamina, and apparently the constitution of an ox."

I could not possibly write that way about Garfield Sobers. I react strongly against it. I do not see him that way. I do not see Hammond that way. I see Sobers always, except for one single occasion, as exactly the opposite, the fine fruit of a great tradition. That being stated, let us now move on to what must always be the first consideration in writing about a cricketer, what he has done and what he does: that is, a hard look at Sobers on the field of play.

For Sobers the title of all-rounder has always seemed to me a circumscription. The Sobers of 1966 was not something new: that Sobers of 1966 has been there a long time. The truth is that Sobers for years now has had no superior in the world as an opening fast bowler.

Here are some facts to substantiate this apparently extravagant claim: which even today many of the scribes (and there are among them undoubted Pharisees) do not yet know.

It is the business of a fast bowler opening the innings, to dismiss for small scores two or three of the first line batsmen on the opposing side. If he does this and does it dramatically, then good captaincy will keep him in trim to make short work of the last two or three on the side, so ending with five or six wickets.

In 1964, his last session for South Australia, Sobers, against Western Australia, bowled batsman No. 1 for 12, and had batsman No. 2 caught by wicket-keeper Jarman for 2. Against Queensland Jarman caught No. 2 off Sobers for 5, and Sobers bowled No. 3 for 1. Against the history-making New South Wales side, Sobers had Thomas, No. 1, caught by Lill for 0. He had No. 2, Simpson, caught by Jarman for 0. He then had Booth, No. 4, caught by Jarman for 0. He thus had the first three Australian Test players for 0 each. In the second innings he bowled Thomas for 3.

South Australia's last match was against the strong Victoria side. Sobers had Lawry, No. 1, caught by Jarman for 4; Potter, No. 3, caught by Lill for 0; Stackpole, No. 5, caught by Lill for 5. In the second innings Redpath, No. 2, was caught by Jarman for 0; Cowper, No. 4, was caught by Hearne for 0; Lawry, No. 1, was caught by Jarman off Sobers for 22. (Let us note in passing that in this match against Victoria, Sobers scored 124 and had also scored 124 in the game against New South Wales, the same in which he dismissed the three Test batsmen each for 0.)

It is impossible to find within recent years another fast bowler who in big cricket so regularly dismissed for little or 0 the opening batsmen on the other side.

His action as a pace bowler is the most orthodox that I know. It is not the classical perfection, above all the ease, of E. A. McDonald. Sobers gathers himself together and is obviously sparing no effort (a rare thing with his cricket) to put his whole body into the delivery. The result is that the ball leaves the ground at a pace quite inconsistent with what is a fast-medium run-up and delivery. It would be worthwhile to get the pace of his delivery mechanically timed at different stages, as well as the testimony of observant batsmen and observant wicket-keepers.

There is nothing of the panther in the batting of Sobers. He is the most orthodox of great batsmen. The only stroke he makes in a manner peculiar to himself is the hook. Where George Headley used to face the ball square and hit across it, Denis Compton placed himself well outside it on the off-side, and Walcott compromised by stepping backwards but not fully across and hitting, usually well in front of and not behind square leg, Sobers seems to stand where he is and depend upon wrist and eyesight to swish the short fast ball square to the leg boundary. Apart from that, his method, his technique is carried to an extreme where it is indistinguishable from nature.

You see it in both his defensive and offensive strokes. He can, and usually does, play back to anything about which he has the slightest doubt. More rarely he uses a forward defensive stroke. But he never just plays forward to put the bat on the ball and kill it. He watches the ball off the pitch and even in the most careful forward defensive, plays the ball away; very different from that modern master of the forward defensive, Conrad Hunte. Hunte from the advanced front foot (never advanced too far) plays what Ranjitsinhji used to insist on calling a back stroke. His type of mastery of the forward defensive gives us the secret of the capacity of Sobers to punish good length bowling on anything like a reasonable wicket. He does not need the half-volley of a fast or fast-medium bowler to be able to drive. From a very high backlift he watches the ball that is barely over the good length, takes it on the rise and sends it shooting between mid-on and mid-off. That is a later acquisition to a stroke that he has always had: to move back and time the good length through the covers.

The West Indian crowd has a favourite phrase for that stroke: 'Not a man move.' That stroke plus the ability to drive what is not a half-volley is the basis of the combination that makes Sobers the orthodox attacking player that he is. His aggressive play is very disciplined, which is shown by his capacity to lift the ball straight for six whenever he feels like it. But as a rule he reserves these paroxysms for occasions when the more urgent necessities of an innings have been safely fulfilled. It is possible that Sobers at times plays forward feeling for a slow ball, more often to a slow off-spin bowler, pitching on or just outside his off-stump, going away. But I have to confess that I saw this and remembered previous examples when I was searching for a way in which as a captain I would plan to get him out.

Yet I have seen the panther in Sobers. Not when he opened in a Test and hit Miller and Lindwall for 43 runs in fifteen minutes. The balls were just not quite there and this neophyte justly put them away. No. The panther one day saw the cage door open. In 1959-60, MCC visited Trinidad in the course of the tour of the West Indies. In between the match against the territory and the Test match the players of the Test side had a practice game, Hall on one side and Sobers on the other. Ramadhin was on the side of Sobers and Hall bowling to him was extremely careful to bowl not too slow but not too fast and always at a good length: he was not going to run the risk of doing damage to one of the main West Indies bowlers. But when he bowled at Sobers, Hall made up for the restraint enforced when bowling to Ramadhin. He ran to the wicket and delivered as fast as he could, obviously determined not to forgo the pleasure of sending Sobers' wicket flying.

Sobers returned in kind. I have never seen a fast bowler hit back so hard. It was not a forward push, it was not a drive. It was a hit. Sobers lifted his bat right back and did not lift the ball. He hit one or two of these balls to the on-boundary, almost straight drives. Hall did not fancy it and bowled faster. Sobers hit him harder. But in competitive cricket Sobers did not play that way. I saw on the screen shots of the famous century in the first Test against Australia in Brisbane in 1961 and also in the latter part of a day's play at Sydney in the third Test. All have agreed, and I agree with them, that at no time was there anything but orthodoxy carried to the penultimate degree when orthodoxy itself disappears in the absolute. There is no need here to give figures. One episode alone will show what the batting of Sobers can mean not only to spectators but to seasoned Test players. The episode will, I am certain, live in the minds of all who saw it. In a recent series, West Indies were striving to force a win against Australia in Barbados. On the last day with less than an hour to go, West Indies had to make some 50 runs.

Sobers promoted himself in the batting order, and as he made his way to the wicket, as usual like a ship in full sail, the feeling in the crowd grew and expressed itself that if this was to be done, here was the man to do it. But somebody else was thinking the same. Simpson, the Australian captain, put Hawke on to bowl; he himself stood at slip and he distributed the other eight men about the boundary. Obviously Simpson felt that if he left one gap in the field unprotected, Sobers would be able to find the boundary through it. I have never seen or heard before of any such arrangement or rather disarrangement of a cricket field.

Sobers had a look at the eight men strewn about the boundary, then had a look at Simpson standing at slip. He accepted Simpson's homage with a great grin which Simpson suitably acknowledged, altogether quite a moment. And an utterly spontaneous obeisance before the fearsome skill of the super batsman.

Two more points remain of Sobers on the field, his close fielding and his captaincy. Sobers has one most unusual characteristic of a distinctive close fielder. The batsman is probably aware of him at short-leg, most probably very much aware of him. But the spectator is not. Constantine in the slips and at short leg prowled and pounced like a panther. Sobers did not. Of all the great short-legs, he is the most unobtrusive that I can bring to mind. To Gibbs, in particular, he seems to stand where there is no need for him to move; in making the catch he will at most fall or rather stretch his length to the right, to the left or straight in front of him. But he is so close and so sure of himself that I for one am not aware of him except to know that he will be there when wanted.

His captaincy has the same measured, one might say classical character. Don Bradman has written how embarrassing it is for a junior cricketer, even a Bradman by 1938, to captain a side containing his seniors. Sobers has had to contend with similar pressures native to West Indies society. I awaited his handling of the captaincy with some trepidation. Not in any doubt about his strategic or tactical ability, not at all. I could not forget a conversation (one of many) with Frank Worrell, immediately after the return from Australia. We had talked about the future captaincy of the West Indies. Worrell was as usual cautious and non-committal: yes, so-

and-so was a good man and capable; and so on. Then when that stage of the conversation was practically at an end, he suddenly threw in:

"I know that in Australia whenever I had to leave the field, I was glad when I was able to leave Sobers in charge." The timing, the style of the remark was so pointed that I felt I could push the unlocked door right open.

"He knows *everything*?" I asked.

"Everything," Worrell replied. For me that settled one aspect of the question. The other I would be able to see only on the field. I saw it at Sabina Park at the first Test against Australia in 1965. Sobers was completely master of the situation from the moment he stepped on to the field, most probably before. He was aware of everything and at no time aware of himself. He was more in command of his situation than the far more experienced Simpson, though he did not have to face the onslaught that Simpson had to face, a problem not only collective but personal, Hall at one end and Griffith on the other. To see in the course of one day Sobers despatch the ball to all parts of the field with his bat, then open the bowling, fielding at slip to Hall or Griffith, change to Gibbs and place himself at short-leg, then go on to bowl slows, meanwhile placing his men and changing them with certainty and ease, this is one of the sights of the modern cricket field. I cannot visualise anything in the past that corresponds to it.

It was jealousy, nay, political hatred which prompted Cassius to say of Caesar:

> Why, man, he doth bestride the narrow world,
> Like a Colossus, and we petty men
> Walk under his huge legs and peep about,
> To find ourselves dishonourable graves.

Certainly in the Press-box watching Sobers a mere scribe is aware of Hazlitt's: "Greatness is great power, producing great effects. It is not enough that a man has great power in himself, he must show it to all the world in a manner that cannot be hid or gainsaid." Of a famous racket-player: "He did not seem to follow the ball, but the ball seemed to follow him." Hazlitt would not have minded the appropriation of this acute simplicity for Sobers at short-leg to Gibbs.

At the end of 1966 Sobers had scored over 5,000 runs in Tests and taken well over 100 wickets. Prodigious! Is Sobers the greatest all-rounder ever? The question is not only unrhetorical. It is un-historical. Is he? I do not know. And nobody knows. I go further. Alert I always am to the reputation of West Indian cricketers; about this I do not even care. Sobers exceeds all I have seen or read of. That for me is enough, but I keep that well within bounds. There are pedants who will claim that he does not face bowling or batting of the temper and skill of previous generations. The argument errs on the side opposite to that which bravely asserts "the greatest ever". Sobers has so far met and conquered all opposition in sight. How can anyone say that if he had met this bowling quartet or that batting trio he could not have conquered them too? My presumption is to presume that he would have dealt adequately with whatever problems he faced. Sir Donald Bradman is reported to have contested strongly Sir Stanley Jackson's dictum that George Lohmann was the greatest of medium pace bowlers. Sir Donald gave first place to O'Reilly because O'Reilly bowled the googly and Lohmann did not. Despite the eminence of these two gentlemen I beg to disagre with both. Lohmann had no need to bowl the googly. He had enough in his fingers to dismiss the men whom he bowled at. He needed nothing else. To compare him with other bowlers who had other problems and solved them can lead to missing what really matters and what cries for comparison. And what really matters is this: I believe Garfield Sobers has it in him, has already done enough to become the most famous, the most widely known cricketer of the century and of any century barring of course the Telstar of all cricket, W.G. This is not so much a quality of Sobers himself, though without his special qualities he could not fill the position. It is rather the age we live in, its material characteristics and its social temper.

Let us go back to the weekend, more precisely the Sunday, following the first three days of the Oval Test in 1966. West Indies, in their second innings, had lost wickets and still had to make runs to avoid an innings defeat.

On that Sunday over half the world, was that a topic of discussion? Not at all.

The topic was: would Sobers make 200, vitalise his side and so enable West Indies to win? That he could no one doubted, a situation that only one word can express — the word *formidable* as the Frenchman uses it, vocally and manually.

I borrow here a thought from Sir Neville Cardus. Visualise please. Not only in the crowded towns and hamlets of the United Kingdom, not only in the scattered villages of the British Caribbean, people were discussing whether Sobers would make the 200 or not. In the green hills and on the veldt of Africa, on the remote sheep farms of Australia, on the plains of Southern and the mountains of Northern India, on vessels clearing the Indian Ocean, on planes making geometrical figures in the air above the terrestrial globe. In English clubs in Washington and in New York, there that weekend at some time or other, they were all discussing whether Sobers would make the 200 required from him for the West Indies to win the match.

Would he? No one knew. But everyone knew that he could. And this was no remote possibility. It was not even 50-50. It was nearer 60-40. I have never known or heard anything like it, though I suspect that in 1895 when W.G. approached the hundredth century the whole cricket world stood on its toes and held its breath. But the means of communication in 1895 were not what they were in

1966. A man must fit into the expanded technicalities of his age. Garfield Sobers does. We are the second half of the twentieth century, heading for the twenty-first and the word global has shrunk to a modest measure.

In 1967 I saw Garfield Sobers captaining a World XI at Lords. He not only had been appointed. He fitted the position. No one would challenge either his competence or his moral right to the distinguished position. I confess I was profoundly moved as he led his team on to the ground and fixed his field.

I thought of cricket and the history of the West Indies. I cannot think seriously of Garfield Sobers without thinking of Clifford Goodman, Percy Goodman, H. B. G. Austin (always H. B. G. Austin), Bertie Harragin and others "too numerous to mention" (though not very numerous). They systematically built up the game, played inter-island matches, invited English teams to the West Indies year after year, went to England twice before World War I. I remember too the populace of Trinidad & Tobago subscribing a fund on the spot so that "Old Cons" would not miss the trip to England; and that prodigious St Vincent family of the Ollivierres. The mercantile planter class led this unmercantile social activity and very rapidly they themselves produced the originator of West Indian batting, George Challenor. In 1906 he was a boy of eighteen and made the trip to England. He saw and played with the greatest cricketers England has ever known, the men of the Golden Age. Challenor returned to set a standard and pattern for West Indian batting from which at times it may have deviated, but which it has never lost. That history is a history of its own, going deep, too deep for the present area of discourse.

The local masses of the population, Sobers' ancestors and mine, at first looked on; they knew nothing about the game. Then they began to bowl at the nets, producing at that stage fine fast bowlers. Here more than anywhere else all the different classes of the population learnt to have an interest in common.

The result of that consummation is Garfield Sobers. There is embodied in him the whole history of the British West Indies. Barbados has estabished a tradition that today is the strength, not only of Barbados, but of the West Indian people. But if there is the national strength there is also the national weakness. Sobers, like the other great cricketers of the present day West Indies, could develop his various gifts and bring them to maturity only because the leagues in England offered them the opportunity to master English conditions, the most varied and exacting in the world. Without that financial backing, and the opportunity systematically to consolidate potential, to iron out creases, and to venture forth on the sea of experiment, there would be another fine West Indian cricketer but not Garfield the ubiquitous. When Sobers was appointed captain of the West Indies he was the first genuine native son to hold that position, born in the West Indies, educated in the West Indies, learning the foundations of his cricket there without benefit of secondary school, or British university. And there he was, just over thirty, with no serious challenge as the greatest cricketer of his generation.

The roots and the ground he now covers (and can still explore further) go far down into our origins, the origins of all who share in the privileges and responsibilities of all who constitute the British version of Western civilisation.

For to see Sobers whole one must place him in a wider framework than meets the eye. Research shows that cricket has been a popular game in England for centuries, but the modern game that we know came into its own, at the end of the eighteenth century, and the beginning of the nineteenth. It was part of the total change of an agricultural type of society that was developing into what are now known as the advanced countries. Perhaps a most unexpected and therefore arresting exemplification of the change is to be found in a famous piece of writing.

Few books in English literature are more noteworthy than *The Lyrical Ballads,* a joint publication in 1798 of William Wordsworth and Samuel Taylor Coleridge. In addition to the poems, known today to every schoolboy, Wordsworth wrote a preface, now classical, in which he said what he and Coleridge were trying to do and what had impelled them to do it.

Civilisation had reached a certain stage of decay and they set out to offer an alternative. It reads as if written yesterday:

> "For the human mind is capable of being excited without the application of gross and violent stimulants and he must have a very faint perception of its beauty and dignity who does not know this, and who does not further know, that one being is elevated above another, in proportion as he possessed this capability.
>
> It has therefore appeared to me, that to endeavour to produce or enlarge this capability is one of the best services in which at any period a writer can be engaged; but this service, excellent at all times, is especially so at the present day.
>
> For a multitude of causes unknown to former times, are now acting with a combined force to blunt the discriminating powers of the mind and unfitting it for all voluntary exertion to reduce it to a stage of almost savage torpor.
>
> The most effective of these causes are the great national events which are daily taking place and the increasing accumulation of men in cities where the uniformity of their occupations produces a craving for extraordinary incident, which the rapid communication of intelligence hourly gratifies."

To meet these new chaotic conditions, Wordsworth and Coleridge wrote about simple things with a simplicity that sought to counteract these new dangers. Wordsworth was certain that there were "inherent and indestructible qualities of the human mind"

which would survive "this degrading thirst after outrageous stimulation".

That was the period and those the circumstances in which
modern cricket was born. In its own way it did what Wordsworth
was trying to do.

And this is the enlargement of our historical past and the savan-
nahs of the future which this young man now impels into our
vision of ourselves. For he is one of us. We are some of him. I have
met his people, listened to his mother talk about her son; he is a
West Indian of the West Indies. But he is also a citizen of the
world today. Sobers has played not only in the cricketing countries
of the wide, wide world. E. W. Swanton has taken him to Malaya
and, the other day, Yorkshire took him to play in Canada and
the United States.

More than ever today the English game is a most powerful
resistant to the "outrageous stimulation" of our age, stimuli far
more powerful and far more outrageous than they were in Wordsworth's time.

And of all those who go forth the world over to maintain and
develop the beauty and dignity of the human mind which Wordsworth was so certain would survive all challenges, cricketers are
not the least. This is the age of Telstar and whatever the engineers
do for cricket, there is one all-rounder whom we may be certain will
meet their challenge. Such is the social temper of our age that
of all cricketers, the ubiquitous all-rounder Sobers, native West
Indian, sprung from the people and now treading the purple with
unfaltering steps, is the cricketer with whom people living over
thousands and thousands of far-removed square miles, in London,
Birmingham, Sydney, Calcutta, Nairobi and Capetown can most
easily identify.

In writing about cricket you have to keep an eye on the game,
your own eye on the game that is before you, not on any other.
Sometimes it is, it has to be, play and players reconstructed in the
imagination. Garfield Sobers as a small boy most certainly played
cricket barefooted in the streets with a sour orange for a ball
and a piece of box or a coconut branch hacked into an approximation of a bat. All of us in the West Indies did that. I have
owned a bat since I was four years of age and I do not remember
ever being in a situation where I did not own a pair of shoes. But
in the early years of this century there were not many, if any,
motor cars about, cork balls were easily lost and could be bought
only at the nearest small town; and to this day, far less than thirty
years ago when Sobers was a boy, from convenience or necessity,
future players at Lord's may be seen playing barefooted with a
piece of wood and a sour orange in some village or the back street
of a small town in the Caribbean. In the larger islands, once you
show unusual capacity, people begin to watch you and talk about
you. Sobers stood out easily and people have told me that even as
a lad he conferred distinction on his club and people were on the

lookout to help in any way he needed. In the West Indies the sea
divides us and, in any case, when Sobers at the age of sixteen played for Barbados, I could not possibly see him because I was far
away in England. Though as a personality he could mean little
to me, I read the accounts, as I always did (and always will if I
live in Tierra del Fuego). I couldn't help noting that he was only
sixteen years old and that he had taken seven wickets. The scores
showed that all were bowled or lbw. Very interesting but no more.

Later, however, I saw what I did not see at the time. In the
second innings he bowled sixty-seven overs with thirty-five maidens
for ninety-two runs and three wickets, this when India scored
445 for 9. This was a boy of sixteen, obviously someone that would
attract special notice. But in those days Valentine filled the bill for
slow left-arm bowling. He took twenty-eight wickets in the series
so that one could not take Sobers very seriously as a slow left-
arm bowler.

Followed the visit of MCC to the West Indies. Sobers did little
for Barbados with the ball, but this youth, it seemed, could bat.
His forty-six in the first innings was the second highest score and
he made twenty-seven in the second. After the third Test, Valentine
did not play and Sobers came into the fifth Test, taking four
wickets in one innings and scoring fourteen and twenty-six not out.
So far, very useful but nothing to strike the eye of anyone far away.
He goes into the list of youngest Test players. When he played
at Kingston he was only seventeen years and 245 days.

So far there was to the reading eye only promise, but now against
the Australians in the West Indies there could be no failure to see
that a new man had arrived. Sobers took only six wickets in 93.5
overs. But Valentine in 140 had taken only five. Ramadhin in 139
had taken the same paltry number. Sobers was second in the bowling averages and in batting, in eight innings, had scored 38.50
runs per innings. One began to hear details about his style as a
batsman and as a super slip more than as a bowler. In the last Test
in Jamaica he made thirty-five not out and sixty-four. I was informed that from all appearances he would have gone on to the
century in a partnership with Walcott which added seventy-nine
runs. Sobers was completely master of the bowling but not of himself. Lindwall with a new ball bumped one short at him, Sobers
could not resist the hook and found deep square leg waiting for
the catch.

Then came a setback that startled. Sobers went to New Zealand
as one of the bright stars of the junior Test players. In four Tests
his average was sixteen runs and with Valentine doing all that was
needed from a lefthander he took only two wickets. In first-class
matches his batting average was below thirty and in all first-class
matches he took four wickets: far below the boy who had done
so well against the full strength of Australia before he was twenty.
But for a West Indies team in Port of Spain against E. W. Swanton's team, Sobers had three for eighty-five and three for forty-

nine, and made seventy-one, second only to Weekes with eighty-nine. New Zealand was a distant dot on the Sobers landscape.

West Indies came to England in 1957 and obviously Sobers was someone I had to see as soon as possible. I went down to Lord's to see the team at the nets but this was my first glimpse of the three Ws and I don't remember noticing Sobers, except for his fine physique. I missed the Worcester match but found myself at Northampton to see the second game. Curiously enough, as he did often that year, he played second fiddle to Worrell, in a stand of over a century of which his share was only thirty-six. But great batsman was written all over him, and I think it was Ian Peebles who referred to him in terms of Woolley. I remember noting the stroke off the back foot that sent the length ball of the pace bawler past cover's right hand. There was another stroke, behind point off a pitched-up fast ball. The ball was taken on the rise and placed behind point to beat the covers, now packed. Here obviously was that rare phenomenon, in cricket or any other form of artistic endeavour, someone new, who was himself and like no one else. There are vignettes in 1957 that are a permanent part of my cricket library. There was an innings against MCC at Lord's in which Sobers came as near as it was possible for him to look like Constantine in that with monotonous regularity the ball flew from his bat to all parts of the field. In the first Test at Birmingham, he made over fifty in little more than an hour and I remember in particular my being startled at the assured manner in which he glanced — I think it was Bailey — from the middle stump to square leg and so beat the man at long leg. The same determination to thumb his fingers at the covers lifted Lock or Laker overhead to drop in front of the pavilion for four; batsmen didn't do these things in 1957.

In the last Test at the Oval West Indies collapsed before Lock and Laker and there came fully to the surface the element of stubbornness which Sobers had shown in the last innings at Kingston in 1953 in his partnership with Walcott, and which I had glimpsed at his batting with Worrell at Northampton. Out of a total of eighty-nine he made thirty-nine and in the second innings out of eighty-six, forty-two. I believe I saw how famous men of old made runs on impossible wickets. To Laker in particular Sobers played back, always back. When Laker had him playing back often enough, he would drop a ball just outside the off-stump going away from Sobers to cut: there was a long list of West Indian casualties to this particular disease which appeared most often in the records as "Walcott c. Evans b. Laker". Sobers, however, it would appear was waiting for Laker. Time and again he could get across and cut the ball down past third man.

In a review of the season Skelding, former county fast bowler and now umpire, was reported in one of the annuals as saying that the Sobers he saw in 1957 would be one of the greatest batsmen who ever lived. I could not go quite so far but I have it down in writing of 1958 that if Sobers developed as he promised in 1957, he would be the greatest of living batsmen. So that the 365 which exceeded Hutton's 364 and the tremendous scoring which followed filled out a portrait whose outlines had been firmly drawn. No need to go through 1963. I saw and felt what I expected to see and feel. However, there was one piece of play in the field which I have seen mentioned only in *Wisden* and not commented upon elsewhere. That was his bowling in the Oval Test. The famous feat of fast bowling in 1963 was Wesley Hall at Lord's in the second innings when his figures read forty overs, nine maidens, four wickets for ninety-three runs. He bowled during the three hours and twenty minutes which play was in progress on the last day. I believe that on that last day he bowled thirty-five overs.

Now in the Oval Test Sobers bowled in the first innings twenty-one overs, four maidens, for two wickets, forty-four runs. I remember these two wickets. He had Bolus caught by keeper Murray (thirty-three) and Edrich, caught Murray, for twenty-five. Hall and Griffith had tried in vain to break that partnership and Sobers, struggling mightily, dismissed both of them well set. In the second innings he did even better; again he dismissed Bolus at fifteen, again well set, and Dexter when at twenty-seven he seemed poised for one of his great innings. Sobers bowled thirty-three overs and took three wickets for seventy-seven runs. At the time and to this day I measure that performance and Sobers as a fast bowler by his approximation at the Oval to Hall's far more famous feat in the Test at Lord's.

There is one episode on the field which for some reason or other sticks in my mind as representative of Sobers. He came out to bat at the Oval against Surrey early in 1963. He came to the wicket and some Surrey bowler bowled him a short ball. It went to the square-leg boundary. A dead metaphor can sometimes be made to live again: that ball went like a flash. As far as I remember the same over saw another ball, short, but this time outside the off stump and rising higher than usual. That ball streaked to the off boundary. Sobers had not scored any runs in the South and everybody including myself believed that here was the beginning of one of the great innings. It was not to be. Two or three balls later he was out to the almost audible lamentation of the crowd which had been keyed up to a pitch in the belief that we were going to see what we had come forth to see.

Sobers today is a captain and I believe it would be worthwhile to give some hint of what I have been able to detect of the personality behind the play. I do not know Sobers as well as I knew Constantine, George John and Headley and the men I have played with. But there are certain things that one can divine. I saw Sobers in 1957 make twenty-seven at Leeds and then get run out not through anybody's fault but by some superb fielding by Tony Lock. Finer batting it is impossible to imagine and that day nothing was more certain than a century before lunch in a Test. But this is not why I remember that day. What remains in my mind is the fury, the rage of Sobers at having been dismissed when he obviously felt that history was in his hands for the making. His walk back to the pavilion made me think of those hurricanes that periodically sweep the Caribbean. I caught a glimpse, by transference so to speak, of the aggressive drive which expresses itself in his batting and fast bowling. I have already referred to the demonic hits with which he greeted Hall's attempt to bowl him out in a practice game. In the Test which followed that practice game Sobers drove too early at a wide half-volley and was caught for 0. Again on his way back to the pavilion I saw the gleam of the damped-down furnace that raged inside of him. Therefore when I read his detailed protests against what he considers the unfairness of British reporters and commentators in their diatribes against his team of 1966 in general and Griffith in particular, I take it much more seriously than most. The protest is not a formality, or something that ought to be put on record, parliamentary fashion. He feels it personally, as a man feels a wound. I suspect that that is the personality which expresses itself as ubiquitously as it does on the field because it needs room. A man of genius is what he is, he cannot be something else and remain a man of genius.

I think of Sobers walking down the pavilion steps at Lord's, captain of an international cricket team. Sixty years ago it would have been Pelham Warner, another West Indian, and thirty years before that it would have been Lord Harris, yet another cricketer of Caribbean connotation. Whoever and whatever we are, we are cricketers. Garfield Sobers I see not as a fortuitous combination of atoms which by chance have coalesced into a superb public performer. He being what he is (and I being what I am), for me his command of the rising ball in the drive, his close fielding and his hurling himself into his fast bowling are a living embodiment of centuries of a tortured history.

1969

18

The Olympia Statues, Picasso's Guernica and the Frescoes of Michelangelo in the Capella Paolina

[*James's broad view of the continuity of human culture emerges in this lecture, originally prepared for television, on the links joining these works of art from different epochs, a theme which James has touched on in other writings. It is published here for the first time.*]

A few necessary words about the observer. I am a West Indian who grew up in the West Indies during the important years of my life. During those years there were not many motor cars in the West Indian islands. Most transport was either by rail or, more often, by horse. Chiefly horses. I used to ride, and when I came to England in 1932 I continued to ride. I went to Ireland and regularly rode in Phoenix Park. The horse meant a great deal to me. There were lots of fields and open spaces to be crossed in a Caribbean island in those days, and we were very careful always to look for and to avoid the fearsome bull. Finally, remote as we were from Italy, from early on I was very familiar with the frescoes of Michelangelo in the Sistine Chapel and with the Pietas of Raphael, because reproductions could be seen in many of the books in the public library and which we in the West Indies bought and exchanged.

Now to look at our subjects. First of all there are works of art intended for public display. The two Olympia pediments were the front and back of the roofs of a Greek temple. They were eighty feet long and ten feet high, and were placed in the Temple of Zeus at Olympia. The two Michelangelo frescoes are also parts of a religious structure, a small chapel specially devoted to a particular Pope, Paul, in the Vatican. They are twenty feet six inches by twenty-one feet eight inches, not too far from square, but obviously nothing to be hung on a wall. The *Guernica* was an exhibit specially commissioned for the Spanish Pavilion of the World's Fair in Paris in June 1937. It measures twenty five feet eight inches by eleven feet six inches.

The two Olympia Pediments are not unrelated to each other. Also related are the two Frescoes in the Capella Paolina. I want now to add to our consideration another work by Picasso which can be associated to the *Guernica*. In his most famous etching, done in 1935, *Tauromachy*, Picasso as we can see anticipates not only the structure but many of the images that are so striking in

Guernica. As is inevitable in an etching, *Tauromachy* appears in structure quite opposite to how Picasso actually etched it. The photograph of what Picasso actually did shows how close it is to the structure of *Guernica.*

Before we go into further details, let us see what are the immediate impressions, or rather facts that strike us as we examine these works, the five with which we began but, now that we have added the *Tauromachy,* six.

The ones with which Western civilisation and this age are most at home are the two Frescoes by Michelangelo. We know the story that they tell. The first, on the left as you go into the chapel, is the Conversion of Saul, a representation of Saul being struck blind from heaven because of his persecution of Christians, the episode being the means by which he was converted to Christianity to become one of the greatest figures in the history of Christian religion. It is a fresco full of intense dramatic movement.

Its counter is the Crucifixion of St Peter, where Peter is crucified with his head down because he did not wish to be crucified in the same way that Jesus was. Despite the fact that there are a number of people in the fresco, many of whom are moving, the primary impression of the fresco is one of immobility, the only sense of actual movement being the people who are moving the cross to stand it upright. So that we understand immediately in these two frescoes a portrayal of violent action contrasted with a picture of striking immobility.

But if we look now, first at the Pediments in Olympia, we shall see that the Pediment on the East of the Temple, which faces the sun, portrays also a scene of absolute immobility. The story need not detain us long. The Greeks would have known it well. King Oinomaos is just about to begin a chariot race with Pelops, the suitor for his daughter Hippodameia, whom he intends to murder as he has murdered thirteen previous suitors. He and his wife are to one side, Pelops and the girl are to another, and in the centre stands Zeus. But all are absolutely immobile.

The Western Pediment on the other hand shows a violent struggle between Peirithoos, Prince of the Lapiths, who had invited his kinsmen, the Centaurs, to his wedding feast. The Centaurs got drunk and tried to carry off the bride, the guests and boys. The Pediment shows the struggle at its most desperate, while behind the violently contending figures stands Apollo, not taking part but by his very presence and attitude showing what the outcome is going to be.

Now, when we look at the *Tauromachy* and the *Guernica* we see pretty much the same attitudes artistically expressed. In the *Tauromachy* we have the Minotaur, an eviscerated horse, a girl holding a light up to the Minotaur, and a woman toreador who lies dead on the horse. The point is that although the Minotaur seems to be resisting the light held in the hands of the girl, nevertheless the general feeling given by the etching is immobility. And just as in the other two, in the *Guernica* we see much the same cast of characters engaged in violent struggle.

It would seem then that in these works of art at such different periods in history and in such different social organisations, that the artist found himself constrained to presenting much the same type of artistic struggle. I do not think that is accidental and it is on this that I intend to lay my greatest emphasis. To continue looking at the works themselves, the East Pediment at Olympia, although immobile, yet has no fewer than eight horses represented on it. In the Pediment the central figure divides the Pediment into two parts, and the centre of each wing, so to speak, is the four horses which are to play the leading role in the fateful chariot race. We know in passing that the Centaurs who play such an important role in the West Pediment are themselves half horse and half human. When we look at the frescoes, in the Conversion of Saul for me the most striking image is that of the horse tearing into the attendants of Saul. In both the *Tauromachy* and the *Guernica* a horse is at the centre; and in the *Guernica* we can say that the horse dominates the mural entirely, everything is centred around the horse.

Let us look again at the Olympia Pediments. In the Western Pediment the extended right arm of Apollo dominates the Pediment both structurally and psychologically. In the Conversion of Saul the right arm of Jesus dominates the upper part of the structure. In the *Tauromachy*, the version which actually appears, the right arm of the Minotaur dominates the whole structure; and in the *Guernica* the woman with the right arm holding a light is an unmistakable figure.

To the horses and the extended right arm we can add one more distinctive feature. In the East Pediment there is a bearded figure, an old man deeply disturbed about the catastrophe which he foresees. In the Crucifixion of St Peter, on the extreme right, is a huge striking figure, an old man with a beard, who is also overwhelmed by what is taking place. In the *Tauromachy*, on the extreme left, is a half-clothed man with a beard escaping from the crisis that is taking place below him but looking on and, although not in such crisis as the other two of his counterparts, is obviously a similar type of figure.

Before we go further into establishing similarities of imagery and structure, we can get nearer to what the artists are trying to do by reminding ourselves first that these works of art, except for the *Tauromachy*, were all intended for public exhibition. The Olympia statues were carved probably between 468 and 456 B.C. They celebrated the victories over the Persians at Marathon and Salamis. The Persian Wars, with the victories of Marathon and Salamis, had ended in the decade after 480 B.C. and there was a tremendous feeling in Greece that one age had finished and another one had begun.

The frescoes in the Capella Paolina were not dissimilar in origin.

They were started in 1544 and both were probably completed in March 1550. Rome had been sacked in 1527, an event from which that generation never recovered. Michelangelo, in the fresco of The Last Judgement in the Sistine Chapel, had painted the end of an age. These two frescoes were his last paintings and can be looked upon as representative of the tremendous crisis from which the papacy and all Italy was suffering in the middle of the sixteenth century. The *Guernica* we know was a response to the bombing and destruction of the Spanish town of Guernica in 1937, but the imagery used, particularly the eviscerated horse, the bull and the general sense of crisis, had been apparent in Picasso's paintings, if not actually from the beginning, at least during the thirties. To repeat, the works were all produced at a time of universal crisis.

Now, still pursuing the extraordinary similarity between them, we shall look for a moment at the structure. First of all the pediment in a Greek temple was not only a basic artistic form with the Greeks but it has lasted to the present day; and therefore, although they may have begun because it offered a certain shape from the structure of the temple, we can presume that they kept it because they found that it offered opportunities of artistic presentation which were unrivalled. Let us remember that the two pediments were triangular in shape, eighty feet long and ten feet high in the centre. Curiously enough, having to be viewed at a distance by the worshippers, they were closer to relief than monumental sculpture. Although the pediments were eighty feet long, they were only three feet deep, and what is noticeable in particular about the Olympia pediments is that within that narrow space and unchangeable structure the sculptor, or more probably the sculptors, were able to produce dramatic examples of monumental sculpture. Take for instance the example of one of the women fighting against the Centaur.

But we appreciate the triangular structure not only of the Olympia but of the Greek pediment as a whole when we look at the Michelangelo frescoes, particularly the Crucifixion of St Peter. Here we shall see that Michelangelo has cut off the left side of the picture with two spears which together form such a straight line that it is quite impossible that this is accidental. He intended to cut off that side of the picture. Now on the right hand side I have drawn in another line which shows that Michelangelo had also cut off the characters on the right-hand side of the fresco. And it would appear that if we looked at the picture from the two soldiers at the bottom left right over to the big man with the beard who is leading a company at the bottom right, there is there a triangular shape also. On this basis cut out of the picture are the horsemen on the left and the figures on the top right, which are the highest peak of the fresco and which we shall come to in time.

When we look at the *Guernica* it is quite obvious that the woman on the right, the horse in the centre and the broken statue on the left form a central triangle.

On other words, the shape of the pediment remains a fundamental structure for these artists separated by so many thousands of years. Furthermore in Michelangelo's fresco of the Crucifixion of St Peter there is a pedimental structure at the centre and upright figures at the sides; and in the *Guernica* the structure is the same but even more sharply so. There is the triangular figure at the centre and two vertical shapes on the right and on the left.

In the second fresco — the Crucifixion of St Peter — there is a group of horsemen at the top left, and they occupy a very important place in the images which constitute that fresco, although, despite the fact that they are a body of cavalry, they do not play the dominant role that the horse does in the Conversion of Saul. From there it is only a step to look again at the horse in *Guernica*, which is unquestionably the centre of the picture and the most striking image.

Let me continue with the similarities in these three works, in which women play a very important role. In the West Pediment at Olympia the women are being attacked. There have for long been attacks upon the Greeks for the subordinate role played by women, even in the Democracy. But the sculptor here — as we can see, for example, in the presentation of Hippodomeia — makes no distinction between the women and the men. Look, for example, at Theseus and at Peirithoos, and at Hippodomeia. In nobility of feature and determination to struggle there is no difference between the women and the men. There are no women among the attendants disrupted by the Conversion of Saul; but there are six women in the Crucifixion of St Peter, four of whom are in the bottom right hand corner and they are obviously second and even third rate citizens in the social structure that Michelangelo presents to us. But Michelangelo does not stop there. Just above and to the right of the women are a group of demoralised people but among them a very militant young woman. While on the extreme right at the top, among to me the most significant personages in the fresco, is a woman listening to what is being explained to her by a male figure who, in my opinion, is the most remarkable male figure in all the paintings of Michelangelo. Women dominate the *Guernica*. There are those who suffer from the chaos, and the extended right arm which holds the lamp is the right arm of a woman who at any rate is in open opposition to the total chaos.

It is worthy of note that except for the horse tearing into the centre of the Conversion of Saul, all of these works tend to be closer to relief instead of pictures and statues of notable depth. However, it seems that the Crucifixion of St Peter that we see in the Capella Paolina has suffered from age and retouching, because the drawing of the Crucifixion made by G. B. de Cavalieri in 1567 shows the people to the right and the people to the left walking down on steps. In addition, one of the few remaining cartoons of the Crucifixion shows the three soldiers at the bottom left to be walking on steps. There, for the moment, we will have to leave it.

We have to proceed a little more closely to look at the bull in the *Guernica*. *Guernica*, after all, is our picture, that is to say, it is a picture of our time, and we need not only to know as much as we can about it but, by understanding as much about it as we can, it will enable us of this generation to understand more the previous works of art which in structure and in images have so much in common with it. There is lot of debate about the bull and Picasso has said contrary things about it, and finally has said quite plainly that the public has to decide. The bull is a bull, the horse is a horse, and the public has to decide. Let us begin by looking at the drawings which Picasso made in preparation for *Guernica*. These four show that we wavered as to what the bull should represent, and one of those preliminary drawings is very striking because it shows the bull with a completely Greek face. And these drawings are symptomatic of Picasso's uncertain and, one may say, antagonistic ideas about the Minotaur.

It is impossible to go into that here, but in his drawings of the Minotaur over the previous decade he showed that the Minotaur at one time was a rabidly lustful character and at other times was craving for sympathy and appreciative of kindness. These drawings that he did just before he finally did *Guernica* showed that Picasso at the time was wavering between these alternative conceptions of the bull. There is something that demands particular notice and which as far as I know has never been noted by any critic or commentator. On 19 April 1937, when Picasso was already thinking about what form or forms the *Guernica* should take, he did a drawing that he calls *Negro Sculpture before a Window, 19 April 1937*. He had already done *The Dream and the Lie of Franco*, in which the bull plays a dominating and revolutionary role against Franco and his counter-revolutionaries. And it seems to me that, uncertain about what he would do with the bull, he decided to make it what it always was in Spain and what he always had had in mind — an image of unconquerable power — and at the same time to make it as human as possible, and in doing so he went back to that drawing *Negro Sculpture before a Window* which he had done only a few weeks before. The only proof can be by looking at them, and not only is there in my opinion a close artistic relation between the two but, as often happened, Picasso went further with the ideas that he had worked out when doing *Guernica* and told us more about the bull.

In two paintings we see the bull on one side, and art and the candle on the other. In them the bull is not hostile to the representation of the paint and palette and the candle. It seems to me that there is sufficient evidence to prove that up to the time when he began *Guernica*, Picasso had not come to any definitive conclusion about the Minotaur and the bull which he had been working at for well over a decade, and that it is legitimate to believe that he began with one conception of the bull as a bull but later, as he worked at the painting, because he has always insisted that as you go on you find out what the painting should be, he felt the need to make the bull a figure which structurally was in opposition to the movement from right to left, which is the main movement in *Guernica*. And having decided that this was the bull that he had to present, he made the bull as human as possible, whereby the human side of the Minotaur he had formerly been so uncertain about comes out with extreme power but the bull remains a bull.

I don't think there is any point in arguing as to what the bull represents. Kahnweiler, who has been associated with Picasso for so many years, states emphatically that the bull represents the invincible Spanish people. Maybe it does. There was a time when I would have thought so. But today I see the bull as one figure in the structure of the painting by which Picasso insists that there is, in addition to the intellectual resistance of the woman with the lamp, a solid, material living figure which stands for the eternal human value of survival. I believe that those who feel, and there are many who say, that the bull represents defeat and darkness, are making the picture out to be what Picasso never intended and what millions of people who see the reproductions do not think.

We can now sum up (leaving other points to be added if convenient). In the West Pediment at Olympia the Ancient Greeks saw, and we see today, the human fighting the animal instincts in man. The magnificent figure of Apollo shows that the Greek is very certain that civilisation will win. We today, after over two thousand years, can see and feel much the same. In the *Guernica*, a contemporary mural, the human is stripped to the elementary need to survive, and, in the presentation of the bull, the need to propagate the species. Everything else is complete confusion, crisis and catastrophe. The mural bears the name of a small town in Spain which was bombed to destruction by German planes during the Spanish Civil War. There is nothing in the mural to represent or symbolise Guernica. What the mural does, and it was recognised at the time, is to say that all mankind is now subjected to destruction from bombing planes, an imaginative glimpse of the future which World War II was soon to justify. Furthermore, I believe that although a Greek would not have been able to understand the technical significance of the electric light, which symbolises machinery carried to its most destructive pitch, he would have been able to understand what was taking place if he were looking at *Guernica* on the basis of his own social experience.

It would be idle, however, to deny that one has preferences, and I conclude by saying that for me it is the frescoes of Michelangelo in the Capella Paolina which are the most fascinating. We must remember that he had already done the Judgement, in which it is agreed today he painted a picture of the catastrophic breakdown of the society in which he and his fellow Italians lived. Now he has to paint these two frescoes. The first one shows the breakdown of the society, and its most powerful elements are visited by Jesus and told to change their way of life. In the St Peter, Michelangelo does what in my opinion is a most remarkable and lasting picture of the society which he envisaged as arising from the chaos and disaster of the Judgement.

Peter is a hero, a leader who is prepared to suffer for the principles that he advocates. Around him, lifting the huge cross, are some working men. Michelangelo knew them well because he had worked with them, digging slabs of marble and transporting them. On the left of the circle of men lifting the cross is the foreman, the one who is in charge, and he is quite a remarkable figure. He has not got the slightest interest in what is happening to Peter. All he is concerned with is the job for which he is responsible. Another man who has no interest whatsoever in Peter is the one who is digging the hole. He has no interest in anything except what he has to do, for which he will probably get some small sum of money. He is a certain type. Then there is the circle of soldiers and beginning at the left are two who are presented to us chiefly with their backs, and then we go up; and as we go towards the peak of the triangle we see some soldiers, two soldiers in particular with spears who are interested in what is happening to Peter to an astonishing degree. They are really bewildered and horrified by what they are looking at. At the centre of the mural is a body of men whom we will call intellectuals, or maybe they were apostles of Peter. One of them is protesting and the others are telling him to keep quiet. If we continue, just next to the four men at the bottom are a group of people headed by the giant with folded arms. They are a very interesting group. The giant is an older man who does not know what to do. Behind him are people in much the same situation, except one girl who is one of Michelangelo's long list of rebellious women. She leans out of the group to look more closely and interestedly at what is happening to Peter. The others do not wish to involve themselves in what they cannot help, but she is bold enough to intrude herself into what is taking place. That leaves us with two groups of people. The horsemen at the left symbolise the State, authority, those who are in charge. Behind them, as in Velasquez's painting of the Surrender, Michelangelo has placed some spears to show what they are. But their leader does not seem to know what is taking place. He is pointing and seems to be quite uncertain. That to me is not surprising, because Michelangelo seems to be saying this is what now remains, or this is what we have after the Judgement and those are the elements of the new society that is shaping around us. That the men in charge do not know exactly what is taking place is not surprising.

And then we have to look at what it seems to me are the most striking people in both frescoes. If you look at the top right of the Conversion of Saul you will see a man and a woman together, who in style and in the position they occupy are quite separate from the somewhat commonplace group of angels who surround Christ. If you look at the Crucifixion of St Peter you will see that in the top right-hand corner these two people who were so distinctly

separated from the angels in the Conversion of Saul are reproduced again. The man is talking to the woman explaining what is
going on. She is listening eagerly to him. Behind them both is an
old man who, it is obvious, has been in battles all his life. And to
the right of the central figure, eager to get into the fray, is a youth
of about sixteen or seventeen. I will end this note by saying that I
do not find it difficult to show that the figure who occupies the
dominating position in the St Peter fresco is a repetition of famous
images of Michelangelo, the man who is being stirred to life by
the right hand of God in the Sistine Chapel and, in feature, the
statue of Brutus which Michelangelo did not many years before.

1970

19

The Atlantic Slave-Trade

[This essay was first published in volume 1 (1970) of Amistad, *a journal on black history and culture edited in New York by John A. Williams and Charles Harris, under the full title of "The Atlantic Slave-Trade and Slavery: Some Interpretations of their Significance in the Development of the United States and the Western World". According to James, "It is impossible to think of anything more important in regard to world history as a whole than the fact that the slave trade was the centre of the economic development which finally exploded in the industrial revolution."]*

Every people, every race, has passed through a stage of slavery. That which ought to be a commonplace of history has been obscured, corrupted and ignored by the injection of slavery into a modern and advanced society like the United States. It would be not only inextricably confusing but impossible to attempt any summary of the infinite varieties of slavery in past ages. However, it is useful to bear in mind two of these varieties. The first is the systematic breeding and selling of their own children into slavery by the backward peoples of Northern Europe. They traded with the highly developed civilisation of Rome, even when Rome was ruled by the papacy. The second is the oft-repeated sneer that the magnificent civilisation of ancient Greece was based on slavery. Slavery did not help to build the social order of the Greece that laid the foundations of Western civilisation in so many spheres. Rather, it was the growth of slavery which ruined ancient Greece. Furthermore, the term "slave" did not then have the meaning it has had since the African slave-trade to the Americas. The slaves in the mines of Greece were cruelly exploited, but in Athens itself slaves could become educated and officials of the city administration, and could attend the ritual performances of the dramatic festivals. As late as the fourth century BC, when the democracy was on the decline, Plato complained that the concept and practices of democracy were so deeply engrained in Athenian society that not only the slaves, but the very horses and dogs walked about in the streets of Athens in a manner that proclaimed their democratic rights.

Today it would be impossible to examine the most important of all phases of slavery, African slavery in the American continents, without having some view of the slavery in Africa itself before the Europeans established the Atlantic slave-trade, and the African slavery whicht was the result of that trade. African slavery before the European slave-trade was internal. For the most part it was also patriarchal. Thirty years ago, I summarised African civilisation and the effects of the European slave-trade as follows:

> "In the sixteenth century, Central Africa was a territory of peace and happy civilisation. Traders travelled thousands of miles from one side of the continent to another without molestation. The tribal wars from which the European pirates claimed to deliver the people were mere sham fights; it was a great battle when half-a-dozen men were killed. It was on a peasantry in many respects superior to the serfs in large areas of Europe, that the slave-trade fell. Tribal life was broken up and millions of detribalised Africans were let loose upon each other. The unceasing destruction of crops led to cannibalism; the captive women became concubines and degraded the status of the wife. Tribes had to supply slaves or be sold as slaves themselves. Violence and ferocity became the necessities for survival. The stockades of grinning skulls, the human sacrifices, the selling of their own children as slaves, these horrors were the product of an intolerable pressure on the African peoples, which became fiercer through the centuries as the demands of industry increased and the methods of coercion were perfected."

Within recent decades an immense amount of research has been done on pre-European Africa. Not only does that analysis still hold its ground, but there has been added to it a conception of pre-European African history which stresses the intellectual achievements of the postwar world. In a study done for UNESCO on *Race and History*, Claude Lévi-Strauss, after a recognition of the "richness and audacity of the aesthetic invention" of primitive peoples, turns to Africa:

> "The contribution of Africa is more complex, but also more obscure, for it is only at a recent period that we have begun to suspect the importance of its role as a cultural melting pot of the ancient world: a place where all influences have merged to take new forms or to remain in reserve, but always transformed into new shapes. The Egyptian civilisation, of which one knows the importance for humanity, is intelligible only as a common product of Asia and Africa and the great political systems of ancient Africa; its juridical creations, its philosophical doctrines for a long time hidden from the West, its plastic arts and its music which explored methodically all possibilities offered by each means of expression are equally indications of an extraordinary fertile past. The latter besides is directly attested to by the perfections of the ancient techniques of bronze and of ivory which surpass by far all that the West was practising in those spheres in the same period."

Neolithic man tilled the soil, domesticated animals, invented and used tools, and lived a family life subject to certain social regulations. Claude Lévi-Strauss believed that this was the decisive moment in the history of human civilisation. However, he is prepared to admit that there has been one other fundamental change in the life of civilised man. The Industrial Revolution, bringing mechanical power into use, altered the conditions of life and created a new type of society.

We can see this most dramatically in the two most important concerns of civilised man, war and revolution. Alexander the Great, Hannibal, Julius Caesar, and Napoleon each would have understood what the others were trying to accomplish on the field of battle; their strategy and tactics would have been much the same. But the moment we examine the American Civil War, military conflict breaks entirely out of the limits in which it had remained for thousands of years. The reason was the introduction of mechanical power — in the form of the railway — into war. Armies could now be five times as large as before. This larger army, with its rapidity of movement, upset the industrial and the social structure of the nation. Today, a little more than a hundred years later, the development of industrial power imperils the very continuation of civilised life.

It is the move to large-scale industry and the accumulation of great numbers of men in factories which is the starting point and the basis of Marx's theory of socialist revolution, and the contemporary nightmare of social destruction. There is no question today that the resources which initiated and established this epoch-making change in human life resulted from the Atlantic slave-trade and the enslavement of Africans in the Americas. Jean Léon Jaurès, in his history of the French revolution, a work which is a landmark not only in the history of the revolution, but in the writing of modern history, comments wistfully: "Sad irony of human history. . . . The fortunes created at Bordeaux, at Nantes, by the slave-trade, gave the bourgeoisie that pride which needed liberty and contributed to human emancipation." But Jaurès, whose thought represented the quintessence of social democracy, was here limited by his preoccupation with parliamentary politics. Gaston-Martin, in his *L'Ere des Négriers*, makes it clear that nearly all the industries which developed in France during the eighteenth century had their origin in goods or commodities destined either for the coast of Guinea or for America. It was the capital gained from the slave trade which fertilised what became the industrial revolution. Though the bourgeoisie traded in many things, everything depended on the success or failure of the traffic in slaves. In *Capitalism and Slavery*, Eric Williams has demonstrated that it was in slavery and the slave trade that the power originated which created modern industry in England, making it the workshop of the world.

The overwhelming majority of historians show a curious disinclination to deal with the seminal role played by the slave trade and slavery in the creation of what distinguishes Western civilisation from all other civilisations. As far back as 1847, Karl Marx stated in very aggressive terms what modern civilisation, and in particular the United States, owed to the enslavement of black people from Africa. Karl Marx, in 1846 in his polemical work *The Poverty of Philosophy*, made slavery in the United States the centre of his comprehensive uncovering of the fires which stoked Western civilisation:

> "Direct slavery is just as much the pivot of bourgeois industry as machinery, credits, etc. Without slavery you have no cotton; without cotton you have no modern industry. It is slavery . . . and it is world trade that is the pre-condition of large-scale industry. Thus slavery is an economic category of the greatest importance.
>
> Without slavery North America, the most progressive of countries, would be transformed into a partiarchal country. Wipe North America off the map of the world, and you will have anarchy — the complete decay of modern commerce and civilisation. Cause slavery to disappear and you will have wiped America off the map of nations.
>
> Thus slavery, because it is an economic category, has always existed among the institutions of the peoples. Modern nations have been able only to disguise slavery in their own countries, but they have imposed it without disguise upon the New World."

Fifty years after Marx's statement, an American historian, a young man twenty-four years of age, tackled the question. In 1954, looking again at his doctoral dissertation written for Harvard University in 1896, *The Suppression of the African Slave Trade to the United States of America, 1638-1870*, Dr W. E. B. Du Bois, in an apologia of two and a half pages, three times expressed his regret that when he was doing the work he had not had the benefit of any acquaintance with the works or theories of Karl Marx. Yet with his own independent, if youthful, judgement Dr Du Bois here showed himself as far in advance of American historiography as he was to show himself in other spheres of American life.

First of all, the title of the book could be misleading. The actual attempt at suppression (1807-1825) is treated as late as chapter eight. What we have here is a history of the slave trade and slavery in the United States. It is true that the very first sentence of the monograph, as he calls it (197 pages of text and 98 pages of appendices), declares that he proposes to set forth efforts from early colonial times until the present to limit and suppress the trade in slaves between Africa and America.

He first separates the planting colonies (the South) from the farming colonies (New Jersey), and then moves into the period of the revolution. He notes that from about 1760 to 1787, there is a "pronounced effort to regulate, or totally prohibit the traffic". Chapter six deals with the Federal Convention and the spirit of compromise leading each state (i.e. in the South) to deal with the question of slavery as it pleased. Then comes a most interesting chapter where we see at work the same mind which in *Black Re-*

construction in America linked the emancipation of the slaves in 1865 to the Paris Commune in 1871, and the black struggle for freedom in 1935 to the world-wide struggle against fascism and for colonial emancipation. Young Du Bois heads the chapter "Toussaint L'Ouverture and Anti-Slavery Effort, 1787-1807". The Haitian revolt sharpens the debate for and against slavery in the USA. It is "the main cause of two laws" and soon was "the direct instigation to a third". But despite the combined efforts of fear and philanthropy, the profits of trade won in the end.

Du Bois is pretty certain that it was the Haitian revolution and its influence which was one of the main causes of the suppression of the slave trade by national law. But to the apathy of the federal government is now added "The Rise of the Cotton Kingdom, 1820-1850". He concludes with a chapter on "the lesson for Americans". The Constitutional Convention had avoided the issue when it had been possible to do something about it. "No American can study the connection of slavery with United States history and not devoutly pray that his country will never have a similar social problem to solve, until it shows more capacity for such work than it has shown in the past." The last sentence of the text is even more clearly a product of moralistic thought. "From this we may conclude that it behooves nations, as well as men, to do things at the very moment when they ought to be done."

We can only estimate the numbers involved, but it is certain that the slave trade shifted many millions of Africans from their homeland. A conservative estimate is that 15,000,000 Africans landed after crossing the Atlantic; but some estimates give 50,000,000 and some go even higher. Further, the mortality rate on the voyage to the Americas was often high, and in addition some were killed in Africa in the raids and wars conducted to get slaves, and some died while waiting to be sold or shipped.

Effectively (and officially) the slave trade lasted three centuries, from about 1550 to 1850. Its period of greatest activity began after the middle of the seventeenth century. There have been many arguments about the effects of the trade on the African economy and population. We know it led directly to nineteenth-century colonialism in Africa and the accompanying degradation of the Africans. But an important area of research remains uninvestigated, which we can only mention here. What were the social and moral effects of slaving on the Africans who bought and sold slaves — what did they think of it themselves? What have been the long-term effects on the African peoples who remained on the continent? Our sources and scholarship are almost entirely Western, and Western thinking has governed our assessment, regardless of whether our standards have been overtly racist or antipathetic to slavery. But surely one of the most important areas of study is what Africans themselves thought of the trade, and what effect it had and perhaps lingeringly continues to have on Africa itself.

Scholars continue to argue about the effects on those taken into slavery. A plateau was reached in 1959, when Stanley Elkin examined the basis for what he called the "Sambo" stereotype of North American slave character. One of the most important bases of his argument is that the capture, voyage, sale, and adjustment to the new environment of the Africans may have created a "shock" that stripped them of their former personalities and rendered their cultural background meaningless.

Most revolts came either at the point of embarkation or between that time and actual sailing. Gaston-Martin catalogues several slave revolts on board ships, and says that he discovered fifty references to revolts, or about one every fifteen trips, in his studies of Nantes slaving. (Nantes is a French seaport.) He adds that there were almost certainly many revolts which were never recorded, and he comments that they were very likely accepted as a normal hazard of the trade. Some revolts even took place at sea, where the slaves would perish even if they overcame the crew, for they had no idea of how to steer the ships. Ships' logs record the ferocity of these revolts. Usually they failed, with only a few slaves and crew members dead; sometimes the death toll went as high as forty or fifty. Rather than be taken again some blacks drowned themselves. Many crew members died. A few revolts did succeed, in which case the crew was usually massacred, sometimes merely taken captive.

In these revolts, captains accessed the most Europeanised slaves as the leaders — for some slaves had been to Europe at one time or another. Informers among the slaves existed from time to time; but when they were discovered by their fellows, they were killed.

One writer quotes a 1788 account saying the blacks were always on the lookout to rebel or escape. "Insurrections are frequently the consequence, which are seldom suppressed without much bloodshed. Sometimes these are successful and the whole ship's company is cut off." Basil Davidson himself adds, "When they failed in revolt before they reached the Americas, they revolted there." Of the slaves, he writes, "The best and strongest took the first or second chance to resist or revolt: the rest endured. But endurance did not mean acceptance."

Revolts might also take place in co-ordination with attacks by Africans on the ship or shore "warehouse". Around 1760, the *Diane* was attacked by Africans while the captives revolted. The French crew was captured and ransomed by Europeans who later handed them over to a French ship. The *Diane* was lost. The *Concorde* underwent two revolts. During the first, forty-five blacks disappeared; in the second a co-ordinated attack between revolting slaves and a party from land destroyed the ship and killed all the crew but one.

Once the ship had sailed, the danger of revolt was greatly diminished. Suicides were frequent among slaves who could not bear their misery or stand the idea of enslavement. Some slaves threw themselves overboard during the voyage, and there are many reports of slaves dying of nostalgia either en route or in the Americas. To combat nostalgia and simultaneously give the slaves an early recovery period from the first stage of the voyage, which was invariably the worst stretch for them, about one fifth of the Nantes slavers out of Guinea would stop off for four to six weeks at islands in the eastern Atlantic. Here the slaves could rest, get fresh food, and rebuild the strength they had lost during the first stage of the voyage. Sometimes a high rate of sickness would prompt a ship to make a stopover. "Already isolated from the continent, the Negroes, in spite of a few examples of revolts, seem less antagonistic than on land; returned to good physical condition, they better endured the two or three months at sea separating them from the American islands."

Epidemics were frequent and could kill up to half to two thirds of the cargo. The most common illnesses were scurvy, diarrhoea, and various skin diseases. Insurrections, as we have seen, were still an occasional threat, and if the attempt failed masses of slaves might commit suicide together rather than submit to recapture. The mortality rate varied considerably from voyage to voyage and year to year. This is reflected in a list of mortality rates among slaves traded by Nantes shippers between 1715 and 1775. The rate ranged from five to nine percent in sixteen years, from ten to nineteen percent in twenty-two years, twenty percent to twenty-nine percent in fourteen years; and was thirty-four percent in 1733. In 1751, the year of the greatest slaving activity on the records, 10,003 Negroes were traded and 2,597 died, giving a mortality rate of twenty-six percent. For the total period from 1715 to 1775, 237,025 slaves were shipped and 35,727 died, giving a mortality rate of 15.1 percent.

After leaving the African coast and any stopovers, the "middle passage" began, lasting normally two or three months, though large ships might occasionally make the trip in forty days. The slaves could still die or commit suicide, though if there had been a stopover for "refreshment", the number of these deaths declined. But other dangers and the length of the middle passage eclipsed the earlier problems. Storms and calms were equally dangerous — the former because it could sink a ship, the latter because it could extend a voyage beyond the range of provisions. Pirates were a constant threat, and the frequent European wars put many enemy ships on the main sea lanes. As with the gathering of captives, a slaver's life, from this point of view, was not an easy one, and expenses could be disastrous. The degree of profit had to be calculated after several voyages, averaging out likely single losses against long-term gains. Whatever the problems, the trade was so extensive that it surely must have been profitable overall.

Treatment of the slaves on board depended a great deal on the captain. But if slavers were not systematically cruel, they were not at all benevolent.

A few writers emphasise that captains were normally not excessively cruel, for it was in their own interest to bring into port as large a live shipment as possible. But when we say "excessively", we are certainly speaking in relative terms. The slaves were never well treated; they were crowded into pens too small to stand up in. The slavers' basic doctrine was that the blacks would obey only in the face of force and terror. Fear of the slaves was the permanent psychological feature of slaver, slave trader, and slave owner. The captives were kept in irons throughout the voyages; the whips would be used for the most trivial purposes. And revolts were brutally punished. Normally only a few suspected ringleaders and examples were executed; but the manner of execution involved torture.

Upon arrival at his destination, the slaver first had to be cleared with health authorities. The inspectors were often bribable — indeed, they often refused clearance unless bribed. Sometimes they would demand that the captain disinfect his ship — buying the disinfectant in the colony, of course. A local governor who feared the captives might be dangerous could quarantine the ship under pretext of fearing a health problem. And genuine epidemics existed often enough to make genuine quarantine a necessity.

Next came port taxes. In the French colonies, Louis XV decreed that the island governors should receive a two percent ad valorem gratuity, half for themselves, half to be split by the two lieutenant governors. In fact this gratuity system was often used as the basis for extortion of much higher demands. Captains who protested too much could find themselves in jail.

Official cheating of slaving captains was common, even when forbidden by royal edict. Large fees could be extorted for such things as anchorage, legal costs, registration of documents, and so on. And of course if the captain had to make calls at several ports, these expenses all were multiplied.

Captains normally tried to give their slaves refreshment to prepare them for sale. When they did not have time, they doped the slaves to give them as healthy an appearance as possible. Slavers would first get rid of their worst-looking slaves at a low price. Many speculators were prepared to take a chance on buying such slaves and hoping they would survive, reckoning a one-third survival rate as satisfactory. The slaver would receive about what he had originally paid for them.

Sometimes the sale might be held up until a propitious moment, especially if there was a glut on the slave market. Either the captain or the company's agent would handle the sale, sending out leaflets to announce the time and place, and the time when the "merchandise" could be inspected. The seller would divide his slaves up into lots of about three or four, grouping them in a way that would bring the highest bidding. The auction would either be done in the usual way — taking competing bids until the highest was reached; or else bidders would be allowed each to make one bid for an entire lot.

If the sales were transacted on board, there was a reasonable chance of suicide by some of the slaves; if on land, there was a reasonable chance of escape. Here, again, we have evidence that at least some of the slaves were not so shattered at this point that they had lost all sense of personality.

Payment was rarely in cash. Often it was on credit, and defaulted payments were frequent. Apparently noncash payments accounted for over half the sales of Nantes slavers. At the start of the French and Indian War, they were owed £15,000,000. In order to stay on in the islands and collect their money, captains would frequently send their ships home under command of their first mates.

A second method of payment was either in merchandise or by deposit transfer at home. Most French planters kept bank accounts in France, and captains seem to have been good judges of which ones to trust. The most common method, certainly, was exchange of commodities. Either the buyer would give his goods to the seller directly, or else the buyer would write out IOUs which the captain would quickly spend on the island, buying up goods to bring home. The captains suffered some loss on the merchandise in this way — but presumably they more than made up for it when the commodities came to be sold in Europe, where they commanded very high prices.

This, then, was the slave trade. It was not easy on the slavers or on the slaves. It is notable that probably as many crew members as slaves died during the voyages. African leaders, if not ordinary free Africans, often willingly collaborated in the trade; and if they and the Europeans were out to get what they could from each other, and prepared to cheat each other where possible, it remains those who were actually enslaved who suffered the greatest miseries and hardships, and who died in vast numbers.

Who were the slaves? They came for the most part from West Africa, these slaves who had been stolen and taken from their homes and brought virtually nothing with them, except themselves. The slaves not only could not bring material objects with them, they could not easily bring over their older social institutions, their languages and cultures. Coming from a large area of West Africa in which dozens upon dozens of distinct peoples lived, with their own languages, social relations, cultures, and religions, these Africans were jumbled together on board the slave ships, "seasoned" by the middle passage and then seasoned again in their first years in the New World.

For the slave brought himself; he brought with him the content of his mind, his memory. He thought in the logic and the language of his people. He recognised as socially significant that which he had been taught to see and comprehend; he gestured and laughed, cried, and held his facial muscles in ways that had been taught him from childhood. He valued that which his previous life had taught him to value; he feared that which he had feared in Africa; his very motions were those of his people and he passed all of this on to his children. He faced this contradictory situation in a context into which he was thrown among people of different African backgrounds. All Africans were slaves, slaves were supposed to act in a specific way. But what was this way? There was no model to follow, only one to build.

The slave from Africa was denied the right to act out the contents of his mind and memory — and yet he *had* to do this. How was this contradiction resolved? What were the new forms created in the context of slavery?

A new community was formed; it took its form in the slave quarters of the plantations and the black sections of the cities. In the United States, this community developed its own Christian church, one designed to meet the needs of slaves and Afro-American freedmen in the New World. It had its own system of communication based on the reality of the plantation. It had its own value system, reflective of the attitudes of African peasants, but at the same time owing its allegiance to dominant American modes. It had its own language patterns, because of the isolation of the plantation system from steady European linguistic influences. West African words and speech patterns were combined with the speech of the eighteenth-century Scotch-Irish.

This black community was the centre of life for the slaves; it gave them an independent basis for life. The slaves did not suffer from rootlessness — they belonged to the slave community, and even if they were sold down the river they would find themselves on new plantations. Here, people who shared a common destiny would help them find a life in the new environment.

Each plantation was a self-sufficient unit. The slaves worked at all the skills necessary to maintain the plantation in working order and keep at a minimum the expense of importing necessary items from England. Slave blacksmiths manufactured everything from nails to plowshares. Coopers made the hoops around the tobacco barrels. The clothing they wore was turned out by slave shoemakers, dyers, tanners, and weavers. The slave artisan moved from one task to another as the need arose.

Skilled labour also took the slave off the plantation. Black pilots poled the rafts laden with tobacco from the tributaries of the river to its mouth, where the ship was anchored; black seamen conducted the ferries across Virginia's rivers to transport new settlers. Many planters found it more profitable to hire out their skilled black workmen for seventy-five to two hundred dollars a year. This black craftsman living away from the plantation was allowed seventy-five cents a week as his allowance for food and board. When the colonies engaged in their war with England for independence, all imports from the mother country ceased. Crude factories were started and slaves were used to work them; also, out of the mines they dug lead, a necessary ingredient in the manufacture of bullets.

The tedium of tobacco cultivation was worse than the exhaustion of simple physical labour. Cotton, which succeeded tobacco as the plantation's output, had to be chopped with great care when the young plant had no more than three or four leaves.

Overworked field hands would take off to the nearby weeds or swamps where they would lay out for a time. At night they would steal back to the slave quarters for food and information about what the master intended to do about their absence. In the swamps of the eastern section of North Carolina, runaways were employed by black lumbermen or the poor whites and could raise their own children for a time. The master, who didn't know the hideouts as well as the slaves did, let it be known through a word passed on to the slave quarters that he was prepared to negotiate for less work and no whippings if only his precious labourers would return.

The slaves fought to set their own tempo and rhythm of work. Says Frederick Douglass:

> "There is much rivalry among slaves, at times, as to which can do the most work and masters generally seek to promote such rivalry. But some of them were too wise to race each other very long. Such racing, we had the sagacity to see, was not likely to pay. We had times out for measuring each other's strength, but we knew too much to keep up the competition so long as to produce an extraordinary day's work. We knew that if by extraordinary exertion, a large quantity of work was done in one day, the fact becoming known to the master, the same would be expected of us every day. This thought was enough to bring us to a dead halt whenever so much excited for the race."

There was very little of the slave's life that he could call his own. In the slave quarters at night there was a lowering of the mask that covered the day's labours. Bantering and mimicry, gossiping and laughter could be unrestrained. House servants regaled other members of the "row" — some of whom had never set foot in the big house — with tales of "master" and "missus", would "take them off" in speech and gesture so faithful that the less privileged would shake with laughter.

Besides the oppression of the master himself, his laws and his overseers, the slaves were oppressed by their limited knowledge of the world outside the plantation. Masters felt that a slave who learned how to read and write would lose his proficiency at picking worms off tobacco leaves or at chopping cotton, so thoroughly had slavery separated thought and feeling from work. But the capacities of men were always leaping out of the confinements of the system. Always with one eye cocked toward the door, the slaves learned how to read and write, thus they attained that standard — besides the accumulation of money, tobacco, cotton, and lands — by which society judged the standing of its members. The Bible was the most readily available book; its wide and varied use by the slave would have made the founders of Christianity proud. It was a course in the alphabet, a first reader, and a series of lessons in the history of mankind.

The capacities of men were always leaping out of the confinements of the system. Written passes, which slaves were required to carry on their person when away from the plantation, could be made up by those who had learned how to read and write. Deciphering the alphabet opened new avenues to the world. A primary achievement of the slaves as a class is that they fashioned a system of communication — an illegal, underground, grapevine telegraph which would stand the test of an emergency.

When hostilities broke out between the thirteen colonies and the King of England, the British field commander in the South offered freedom to every slave who would enter his army. In Virginia alone, thirty thousand fled their labours; the bitter comment of a slaveholder points up this situation: "Negroes have a wonderful art of communicating intelligence among themselves; it will run several hundred miles in a fortnight." There was such a large proportion of slaves in the state, that South Carolina did not even dare enter the War of Independence for fear of what its labouring force would do. It lost twenty-five thousand nevertheless. Across the South every fifth slave fled toward the British army.

An independent national state was being set up by an American Congress. The very air became filled with expressed passions of human rights, liberties, dignity, equality, and the pursuit of happiness. One of its effects on the slaves was seen on the night of 30 August 1800. Over one thousand slave rebels gathered some six miles from Richmond, capital city of Virginia, the state which was to produce four of the first five American presidents. All through the spring of that year the slaves prepared their own arms, including five hundred bullets, manufactured in secret. Each Sunday for months, Gabriel Prosser entered the city, noting its strategic points and possible sources of arms and ammunition. Their plan was to proclaim Virginia a Negro state. If the merchants of Richmond would yield their fortunes to the rebels their lives would be spared and they would be feted at a public dinner.

On the night appointed for the march a heavy rain had fallen, making the road into Richmond impassable. The delay gave the stunned authorities an opportunity to mobilise themselves. Some forty slaves were arrested and put on trial. They revealed no names of other participants. Some estimates placed the extent of the rebellion at ten thousand slaves, others put the figure as high as sixty thousand. The demeanour and remarks of the prisoners on trial? Gabriel: "I have nothing more to offer than what General Washington would have had to offer, had he been taken and put on trial by them. I have adventured my life to obtain the liberty of my countrymen."

In this early period the slave who ran away was most often

a skilled craftsman, a man with confidence of making his way in the world. As described by a newspaper advertisement of the day:

"Run away from the subscriber's farm, about seven miles from Anapolis, on the 8th instant; two slaves Will and Tom; they are brothers. Will, a straight tall well-made fellow, upwards of six feet high, he is generally called black, but has a rather yellowish complextion, by trade a carpenter and a cooper, and in general capable of the use of tools in almost any work; saws well at the whip saw, about thirty years of age. When he speaks quick he stammers a little in his speech. Tom, a stout well-made fellow, a bright mulatto, twenty-four years of age, and about five feet nine or ten inches high; he is a complete hand at plantation work and can handle tools pretty well . . . they have a variety of clothing, and it is supposed they will not appear abroad in what they wear at home. Will writes pretty well, and if he and his brother are not furnished with passes from others they will not be lost for them, but upon proper examination may be discovered to be forged. These people it is imagined are gone for Baltimore as Tom has a wife there."

Except in a general way he could not be sure of the direction of his travels, guiding himself by the stars and by the moss which grew on the shady side of the trees. In earlier days the safest places of concealment were the nearby swamps, the neighbouring Indian tribes and Spanish Florida. The long military arm of the slavocracy eventually reached into all these temporary outposts of freedom and incorporated them into slavery. Then soldiers returning from the War of 1812 brought the news that slavery was outlawed in Canada. The route of flight began to cut across the Kentucky mountain ranges and the Atlantic seacoast.

John Parker, a free black man from Ripley, Ohio, considered it below his dignity to ask any white man how to conduct slaves to freedom; he was responsible for the successful passage of one thousand runaways, but left no memoirs as to how he carried out his work.

In later years the work of the scout took him into the Deep South rather than await the knock on the door. On her expeditions, Harriet Tubman would take the precaution of starting on Saturday night so that they would be well along their journey before they were advertised. Harriet often paid another black person to follow the man who posted the descriptions of her companions and to tear them down. The risks of taking along different types of people in one group had to be considered. Babies were sometimes drugged with paregoric. She sometimes strengthened the faint-hearted by threatening to use her revolver and declaring, ". . . you go on you die . . . dead [N]egroes tell no tales."

As with practical people everywhere, everything was done with the materials at hand. An iron manikin in front of the home of Judge Piatt marked an interrupted station; the judge was hostile to the activity, but his wife was an enthusiastic undergrounder. A flag in the hand of the manikin signaled that the judge was not home and that his house had become a temporary station on the road. For disguise one runaway was provided simply with a gardening tool placed on his shoulder. He marched through town in a leisurely way like a man going to work somebody's garden, left the tool in a selected thicket at the edge of town, and proceeded on his way.

The Underground Railroad in the period of the 1840s grew so saucy that it advertised itself publicly as the only railroad guaranteed not to break down. Multiple routes were the key to the practicaly success of the railroad. It all came into being after the period of the Founding Fathers had definitively come to an end. The men of education, the leading figures of the revolution, Washington, Jefferson, Adams, Hancock, Hamilton, Lafayette, and Kosciusko, all expressed opposition to slavery in their private conversations and correspondence. But their chief fear was that pushing antislavery to the fore might permanently divide the country into antagonistic sections.

Washington accurately described the sentiment in certain parts of the country after he himself had lost a slave in New England. "The gentleman in whose care I sent him has promised every endeavour to apprehend him; but it is not easy to do this when there are numbers who would rather facilitate the escape of slaves than apprehend them when they run away."

In the early formation of the Underground Railroad, another group whom the runaway touched with his fire was the Quakers. When they arrived in America to escape persecution, the prosperous trade in slaves corrupted even the most tender of consciences. Not being interested in politics, and prohibited by religious belief from being diverted by the theatre, sports, or drink, the Quakers became highly successful businessmen and farmers. The Quakers were prominent and influential people and could afford to rely on the letter of the law which in Northern states had declared slavery illegal.

Having established the principle, effective organisation for antislavery work came naturally to a group whose life had been drawn tightly together for hundreds of years as a religious sect. By 1820 there were some four thousand fugitive slaves in the Quaker stronghold of Philadelphia and all advertisements for runaways disappeared from Pennsylvania newspapers.

Free blacks, Quakers, and New Englanders, linked up to each other, conducted the Atlantic coast route of Underground Railroad operations. Men of a different stamp initiated a section of the western route. At the turn of the century the back-country farmer of Virginia and the Carolinas suffered much from the poverty of his land. The state legislatures were in the control of coastal planters and their lawyers; new government taxes and old debts magnified his poverty. He freed himself of all these burdens by migrating westward into the wilderness.

The slaves who accompanied this first great tide of migration, which depopulated Virginia of two hundred thousand people, were as scattered as their masters. On the early frontier there was less consciousness of their slave status. They helped in the household chores, building cabins and protecting them from Indian attack. Ofter they were the boatmen, whose arrival was as welcome in the settlement as the ringing of a postman in a modern apartment house.

The runaway slave heightened the powers of the popular imagination. Here was a figure who not only fled oppressive institutions, but successfully outwitted and defied them. And his flight was to the heart of civilisation, not away from it; he was a universal figure whose life was in turn adventurous, tragic, and humorous.

The runaway, freed from the disabilities of slavery was in the second and third decades of the nineteenth century coming into close contact with another highly specialised group of people — the intellectuals. The thinking of intellectuals is characterised by the fact that they view matters whole and in general, however one-sidedly and abstractly. This jamming up of two diverse elements — the black man who supposedly had no civilisation in the range of his existence, and the white intellectual in whom society had placed the whole heritage of civilisation — produced those works that reminded people who gave thought to the slave held in bondage that they were themselves intimately bound with him for life.

The antislavery movement was produced by the specific relation of blacks and whites during the first third of the nineteenth century. It is a fantastic phenomenon climaxed by the central phenomenon of all American history, the Civil War. Writers offer various explanations, but after a certain amount of reflection it becomes clear that abolition must be seen as an absolutely necessary stage in making America a distinct civilisation, rather than just one more piece of boundaried territory in the mosaic of the world's geography.

Abolition is the great indicator of parallel movements before the Civil War and after. History really moves when the traditionally most civilised section of the population — in this case New Englanders representing the longest American line of continuity with the English tradition of lawful sovereignty — joins as coequals with those without whose labour society could not exist for a day — in this case the plantation chattel. Otherwise, history stays pretty much the same, or worse yet, repeats itself. Such was the case of the independent lay preachers in the great English revolution, who joined with the apprentices and day labourers; the French intelligentsia in conjunction with peasants and slum proletarians of royalist France; the Russian intellectuals meeting on certain grounds with factory workers under a Tsar. In all these instances history moved forward with lasting impress.

Abolition, itself an important instance of democracy, took upon itself the extension of a certain practice and mode of national behaviour. Much of the mode of national behaviour was based upon regional considerations — the great potential for abolition was the Southern slave in flight to freedom from plantation labour. Then there was the firmest base of abolition extant, the free black communities of Northern city and town. New York City, for a time, provided heavy financing. Garrison's Massachusetts was becoming an antislavery fortress and the rest of New England followed, in various degrees. Children of New England had settled in the fine agricultural flatlands of Ohio and upstate New York; a momentous development as "free soil" was prepared to clash with slave expansion appetites. Pennsylvania housed an antislavery diffused with quakerised quietist feelings.

Without the self-expressive presence of the free blacks in the cities, embodying in their persons the nationally traumatic experience of bondage and freedom, antislavery would have been a sentiment only, a movement remote and genteel in a country known as impetuous and volatile. The bulk of subscribers to Garrison's *The Liberator* were blacks in New York, Boston, and Philadelphia. It was the publicity surrounding the revolt of Nat Turner which guaranteed that Garrison, the white advocate of immediate abolition, would become a household word. The independent conventions of free blacks were anterior to the rise of Garrison and his friends. The succession of slave personalities delivered by the Underground Railroad would eventually lead to black political independence from Garrison himself.

Ohio was the scene in the 1840s of the "Hundred Convention" — political life as daily fare, with regional figures turning into nationally representative ones. Douglass, the self-emancipated slave by way of Baltimore; Garrison, who hardly had left New England before except to visit neighbouring New York or far-off merrie old England; these two together spoke themselves hoarse and into general exhaustion. This now-settled middle frontier, this venerable Old Northwest, was clamouring to hear about the state of the nation from true figures of national stature, since nothing more was heard from the doughfaces in Congress sitting on the hundreds of petitions pleading for justice to the slave, and discussing the role of free settlers in a democracy.

Impending war with Mexico was a spur to far-reaching conclusions. The revived National Negro Conventions listened to a proposal for a general strike by the slave labourers of the South, who would act as a human wall barring the United States Army from invading Mexican territory and turning it into a slave planting domain. The proposal lost by one vote.

Sophisticated prejudice tells us that *Uncle Tom's Cabin* by Harriet Beecher Stowe is another vast mistake! In impact and implications marking off the hour and the decade of its arrival it rang true; in universal aspect, clear. The average worker competing with the free black man for a job and a place to live, and wrestling with his prejudices all the while, went to see the play and wept upon his identification with the slave runaway. Where formal government failed on the slavery question, people reached for a government which the Greeks had introduced so very many years earlier: that of popular drama — which the city-state then made sure everyone could see for free — so that whatever they thought of politics they could see, through the form of dramatic representation, principles, conditions, and resolutions, and sense from that emotional experience where a whole society was going. Mere political representation was succeeded by a more intense social reproduction, a more popular accurate representation, in book form. *Uncle Tom's Cabin* circulated more widely through the whole of the nineteenth century than any other book, with the sole exception of that book of books, the Bible.

And if it was the running debates with Stephen A. Douglas which elevated Abraham Lincoln from the legislator's semi-obscurity to national star-fire, who or what besides abolition had initiated the debate, fixing free discussion of nearly obscured cruelties on a Mississippi cotton field as the nation's prime business; set forth the concrete choices, which no mere election could decide, on the future of mid-nineteenth-century America? And if the abolitionists' method had so elevated Lincoln, what shall we say of their achievement in turning each runaway slave, now threatened with kidnapping under a new and permanent sectional compromise, into a monument either to the American's love of liberty or acquiescence to captivity? Before abolition enabled Lincoln to hallow his name, it inscribed Shadrach and Anthony Burns and Dred Scott on to the heavens for the whole world to read the American future through them.

The leading charge against abolition in the 1850s was aimed at its nearly absolute trust in the uninterrupted process of civilisation. The main critique centred upon Garrison and Phillips' endorsing — before Civil War broke out — the secession of the South, confident that slavery, separated from federal protection, must die.

The Civil War was a corrective of the notorious nineteenth-century optimism which trusted free speech and free press and the industriousness of unchatteled labour to push authoritarianism of every familiar type over that same cliff where the vestiges of feudal relations had been shattered or left to hang for dear life.

Confronted by preslavery compromises which were a source of infinite corruption, abolition gave obeisance to certain eternal principles, themselves corollaries of the civilising process at a certain stage. Growing transcending morality titled "the higher law" would overwhelm all momentary deviousness, nullify all expedients and prearrangements disguising themselves as pillars of the Federal Union.

Belief in the morality of "the higher law" was hardly an empty absolute, devoid of content and barren of result. It was a driving impetus separating democracy in politics from the growing "hunkerism", mere hankering after public office and governmental seat-warmings which dulled the very sense of social accountability and paled before the historical momentousness of American existence.

The years of Civil War show what might have been done much earlier during the War for Independence itself when this nation was first born, and egalitarian feelings were at a zenith. But then there had been no antislavery organisation. The unity of the young nation, monarchies all, had taken a certain turn at the Constitutional Convention and elsewhere, indicating that the semblance of national solidity could be maintained only if the slave kept his back bent to his labour; then North and South, East and West would not divide, and foreign enemies would wait in vain for internal weakness as the signal to spring upon their prey, the New World as distinguished from the old. But national unity excluded the black from independence; national prosperity was guaranteed by subordinating the labourer to his labour. The very existence of abolitionists during the next climatic phase of this very same question — Civil War — simply insured that the slave would not be lost sight of no matter how much the government tried to lose sight of him.

The destruction of the colonisationists earlier was the main factor staying the hand of the government which wanted to colonise blacks, freed men, even in the midst of, and because of, the tensions of Civil War, to avoid disputations as to their American destiny.

On the universal effect of American abolition: it helped free the Russian serf on the other side of the world — but not directly. Indirectly, it is clear enough if we go by stepping-stone geography. Harriet Beecher Stowe's book was banned in Italy as an incitement to the peasantry. But the leading Russian publication of the intellectual exiles translated the whole work as a free supplement for all subscribers. Keep in mind, too, that from the time of Peter the Great, Russia had been trying to make its way through the front door of world civilisation. Add to this a fact of international power politics: when England and France threatened to join the South, Russia shifted its weight to the North. In the middle of the Civil War the Russian fleet showed up in New York harbour, a great ball was thrown and a festive time was had by all. Abolition of serfdom there and of slavery here occurred almost simultaneously.

Something should be said about the white American worker in regard to abolition. Some were antislavery, some were not. Skilled workers, proud of their craft which brought them a measure of independence, were by and large antislavery. The unskilled, fearing possible competition from the blacks, inclined toward neutrality or gave in to caste prejudice. However, skilled or unskilled, the worker in America was an ardent democrat. No matter how much he suspected another man might take his job, he could not develop a great affection for plantation life as the prototype of American life as a whole.

Abolitionists were not only concerned with the rights of blacks, free and slave, they were concerned with their education. The abolitionist created the first integrated education in the United States — including higher education. And when they did not create integrated education they conducted classes and schools for the ex-slaves, schools partially staffed by black teachers. The abolitionists were at the centre of the educational reforms and changes of this period in the United States. In schools for Negro children they experimented with improved methods of education.

But more. They fought not only for the emancipation of Negroes and the improvement of the lives of freedmen. They fought for the emancipation of women, their education, and their own self-development. Oberlin College, the first college to accept Negroes in the United States, was also the first college to accept women in the United States, becoming the first co-educational institution of higher learning.

In their struggle for women's rights, a struggle that went on inside and outside of the movement, abolitionists set in motion the liberation of women — and consequently of men. What Margaret Fuller and other great female abolitionists were trying to establish was their right to create relations with men in which they were not in effect the chattel of their husbands through the marriage contract, as slaves were chattel in the grip of property holders.

The abolitionists were involved in a crucial way in the most significant struggles for human emancipation that were going on in the United States: the abolition of capital punishment, prison reform, attacks on established religion in the name of a purified religion, work for the rights of new waves of immigrants and better treatment of American Indians, and the movement to abolish war. Though they often differed among themselves, and were very often confused in the way that people are who are going forward, there is a very direct development from the Declaration of Independence to the abolitionists' efforts to Lincoln's understanding that the Civil War was about whether government of the people, by the people, and for the people would perish from the earth.

It must be said that the slave community itself was the heart of the abolitionist movement. This is a claim that must seem most extraordinarily outrageous to those who think of abolitionism as a movement which required organisations, offices, officers, financiers, printing presses and newspapers, public platforms and orators, writers and petitions. Yet the centre of activity of abolitionism lay in the movement of the slaves for their own liberation. The general impact of the abolitionist movement upon the slave communities was profound. It gave the slaves the hope that enabled them to survive, and to engage in the day-by-day struggles that won for them the amount of extra room in which to live that made more than mere continued existence possible.

The abolitionist movement led to a change in the climate of American life. The reaction after the American revolution had led to a period in which a profound pessimism touched the lives of all those who lived by the ideals of the Declaration of Independence, that clarion call for a new birth of freedom for mankind. Abraham Lincoln, a son of the Declaration, had in 1837 felt that all that could be done was to defend the gains of the revolution, and to hope that in the future gradual forward motion could be made. The work of the abolitionists, of black slaves changed all that. By the end of his life Lincoln could see the path of the Declaration, of human freedom, open once again. This was a mighty achievement for the movement.

The spontaneity and universality of feeling which accompanied the antislavery movement indelibly stamped itself on the opening days of the Civil War. The people arose. When the people arose in the North it was a self-mobilisation of men and women. Of the 700,000 total Union Army, half a million were volunteers. This was, perhaps, the last great voluntary war in the history of mankind. Savour the following words:

> "So large an army as the government has now on foot was never before known, without a soldier in it but who has taken his place there of his own free choice. But more than this: there are many single regiments whose members, one and another, possess full practical knowledge of all the arts, sciences, professions, and whatever else, whether useful or elegant, is known in the world; and there is scarcely one from which there could not be selected a president, a cabinet, a congress, and perhaps a court, abundantly competent to administer the government itself. . . .
>
> It is worthy to note that while in this, the government's hour of trial, large numbers of those in the army and navy who have been favoured with the offices have resigned and proved false to the hand which had pampered them, not one common soldier or sailor is known to have deserted. . . .
>
> The greatest honour, and the most important fact of all is the unanimous firmness of the common soldiers and sailors. To the last man, so far as known, they have successfully resisted the traitorous efforts of those whose commands, but an hour before, they obeyed as absolute law."

This is from Lincoln's absolutely sober message to Congress, 5 July 1861.

One of the great underestimations in the whole sphere of historiography is undoubtedly the contribution of the slaves to the making of America as a civilisation. Some of the justifications for such an underestimation are quite elementary. It is said that all civilisation rests upon city life; the bulk of slave labour was on the countryside. The actual documentary works by which much of early

America lived are those of the Anglo-Saxon heritage with some bow to Plutarch and perhaps Rousseau, Montaigne, and Demosthenes. The slaves produced little of this kind of literature. They are therefore to be left on the fringe of the matter.

But a New World view of the old question of slavery induces a greater wisdom. For one thing the triangular trade in sugar, rum, and slaves in an instance of programmed accumulation of wealth such as the world has rarely seen. "American slavery," says one author, "was unique, in the sense that, for symmetry and precision of outline, nothing like it had ever previously been seen." The element of order in the barbarism was this: the rationalisation of a labour force upon which the whole process of colonisation depended had the African at its most essential point. If he had not been able to work or sustain himself or learn the language or maintain co-operation in his social life, the whole question of America as a distinct civilisation could never have arisen. We might be then talking about a sort of New Zealand or perhaps Canada.

The native American Indian was migratory in his habits and a hunter in his relation with nature. But the slave had to be an African labourer, a man accustomed to social life, before he could ever become a profitable grower of cotton or tobacco — the vital element required before America could claim that it had salvaged something from the wilderness. Something which could be extended to the point where it would win recognition as a landmark in man's emergence from subservience to any·laws of nature.

The man who made it possible, and we do not know if he knew he was making it possible, was the transported African. Rationalisation of the labour supply was tied in with rationalisation of production itself. Planters in Louisiana would weigh the pros and cons of working slaves to death in the hazardous work of the rice paddies as against protecting the slave from excessive labour in order to maintain the interest in him as property. The long letters George Washington wrote on the organisation of labour on his plantation represent merely one side. The exchange of letters between Thomas Jefferson and Benjamin Banneker, the surveyor of what was to become Washington, D.C., about the propensities and capacities of black people enslaved and otherwise is the other side of the same phenomenon: the recognition that for reasons both clear and obscure the fate of America had depended upon the blacks as labourers. This was to be argued out in the antislavery movement at a higher level, and in the midst of the Civil War and Reconstruction. It is also a seemingly inescapable fact to everybody, but historians have managed to escape it. That is not altogether a surprise. The writing of history comes about at a period when men think about their activity so as to record it in a more permanent form. To give the slave his actual historical due is to alter one's notion about the course of civilisation itself. If, for example, each plantation had to strive to be self-sufficient as a unit, it was the skilled and semi-skilled black who would make it so.

The runaway slave fled to the North without compass or definite point of destination, without being blessed like Columbus by Queen Isabella selling her jewels for the voyage, or like the pilgrims to Plymouth Rock — members of a church soon to make a revolution affecting all of England and Ireland; or like pioneers into the wilderness, trying to set a distance between themselves and civilisation. If, as can be later demonstrated, the flight of the runaway slave from the South is seen as setting in motion a whole series of forces, which no other class of people, no mere party or political sect, no church or newspaper could succeed in animating, then the whole configuration of America as a civilisation automatically changes before our eyes. The distinguishing feature of the slave was not his race but the concentrated impact of his work on the extensive cultivation of the soil, which eventually made possible the transition to an industrial and urban society.

The triumph of slavery, the negative recognition that the slave received in every work sphere shows how little the South or skilled workers themselves sometimes could tolerate the black as an artisan. In prebellum America he had to be driven out of trade after trade before the assertion could be demonstrated that the black man is fit for nothing more than brutish labour with its inevitable consequence.

Historically one can now begin almost anywhere to show what civilisation meant to the slave as a preliminary to showing what the slaves meant to civilisation. The natural form of organisation was the work gang during the day and the slave quarters at night. The large scale of cultivation required for a profitable export crop guaranteed social connections for the slave even if he was isolated from the centres of "civilisation" by the rural surroundings.

But the first specific form of slave organisation was the fraternal association which was organised to accompany to their permanent resting place those caught up in life's mortal coils. Small coins were saved for accomplishing that occasion in at least minimal style. The slave was no more afraid to die than is or was any other mortal; he was fearful of dying unaccompanied by those with whom he had associated in the fullness of his life.

Given a holiday, that is, an occasion, the slave was, like most working humans up to this day, his own person. It was for naught that the defenders of the planter's way of life feared the effect of Fourth of July oratory. They might just as well have feared the Christianity in Christmas. It was not only intellectually that everything universal in sentiment panicked the "peculiar institution". It was the concentration of people all experiencing the unbridgeable gap between their arduous daily toil and the exceptional holiday from work — with the to-ing and the fro-ing from plantation to plantation, the arrival of guests and the spreading of news — which brought about the system of slave patrollers and written passes across the South.

We are dealing with matters of individual skill and social impulse.

Small equivalents of the strike action took place at work. Flight to the neighbouring woods, followed by messages trailed back to the work area showed that the blacks knew above all that, even if despised for race, they were necessary — vital to a labour process geared to the agricultural season. Feigning of illness was a commonplace; indeed, one simple definition of the abolition of slavery is that a man or woman need not go to work when incapacitated. This absenteeism may seem of no great import by itself, but the diaries and records of the slavemasters show it to be a matter of grave concern. Everybody knew what was involved in the work process.

And the blacks knew what was involved in their day of rest. The growth of an autonomous black church draws up a balance sheet on historical Christianity. It is not finished yet, but if Christianity, as some assert, brought the principle of personality into a world that knew no such thing, and in the person of a simple carpenter who later recruited an equally simple fisherman and so on, the climax of that primitive church was the mass joining together of a population considered as so much flesh to be traded and hands to be worked and backs to be bent or broken under the lash. To the whites religion may have meant a buttress to conscience. To the blacks it meant a social experience out of which would come the active principle of personality: the black preacher.

In the more practical workings of the plantation, the slave owners themselves discovered that the position of foreman or driver was one which fewer and fewer whites measured up to in personal stature. So that in the decade before the Civil War there was a wholesale increase in the number of black overseers. Though it did not mean that race prejudice on the part of the slave owners had changed one whit, this problem of supervision was proof of the demoralising effect black labourers had upon those who not only considered themselves superior to the slave's lot but had the weapons and the authority to put their superiority into momentary practice. Most white overseers went even before the slave system fell into the dust of Civil War. And by a healthy process of circularity, the fictional summations of the type, the Simon Legrees of the world, were portrayed with such effectiveness that it stimulated the movement toward that system which produced such monsters wholesale. The important point of the slave's contribution to civilisation is that he recognised and did battle with the slavery system every day before, long before, white audiences would stare with horror at the representation on stage or in a book.

There is also the matter of the link-ups of the plantation to the outside world. Blacks were the boatmen and teamsters of that day in the South. They would have been the longshoremen as well, but were driven out. Simply by driving the master's coach around they learned of the outside world and brought back information to the slave community. It was known in some of the deepest haunts of

the South that there was some kind of underground which would
transport a runaway from one hiding place to another if he would
but risk the trip.

Indeed, if by virtue of the brutishness and isolation of his situation the slave were himself a brute, how then could he make
contact with such varying and even opposing sections of the population as he did? Harriet Tubman had a rapt listener in the philosopher Ralph Waldo Emerson, and Frederick Douglass in governor
— and later presidential candidate — William Seward. William
Wells Brown could speak to all size groups, from two hundred
to two hundred thousand people across Europe. It was not a matter
of dispute about the capacity of the Negro; it was not even the
great political debates about the future of America — slave or free.
It was something so concrete, so easy to overlook and yet so broad
in its consequences: the black man was a social being, in some
senses the most highly social product of the United States. This
was not necessarily due to skin colour, but to the close relation between labour and society that he experienced more than did
planters, ethnic immigrants, religious societies, pioneering settlements and their human products, political parties and their candi-
dates.

That link of labour and society took on national and even international proportions. Starting from obscure places which nobody
ever heard of or even wanted to hear, it became writ large as the
experience of slavery intertwined with everything else — politics,
diplomacy, commerce, migration, popular culture, the relation between the sexes, the question of labour and civilisation in the future
of America as a whole. The black man was not in any popularity
contest as to who most represented this new man — this unde-
fined American — who so intrigued the Europeans. He was something more: a self-appointed minister with nothing but experience,
social experience, to guide him toward those qualities most universally recognisable in the ordinary people — some of whom were
still tied to the land in Europe; some recently incorporated into
proliferating industry; some hearkening to the American experience;
some settling matters with crowns and courts in their Old World
countries. The black man was the supreme example not just of
how to rise in the world but of how to raise the world toward his
own level. He inherited the Declaration of Independence which
the plantation plutocracy mocked. In politics, Frederick Douglass
took the Constitution as an antislavery document when his own
abolition colleagues, Wendell Phillips and William Lloyd Garrison,
set the match to it. The runaway slave, Dred Scott, threw the Chief
Justice of the Supreme Court (and the country as a whole) into
confusion on whether slavery was a national or regional issue.
The black man was not afraid to declare war on war, for instance
the conflict with Mexico over Texas in 1846. He could link himself to movements for temperance in drink or for the right of
women to divorce or to the nonpayment of rents by upper New

York State farmers.

It was training in social labour which gave blacks the opportunity to increasingly affect all social questions of their day. It was their concrete ability to turn from the facilities used in physical work to the powers of speech and other forms of self-expression which made certain of the ex-slaves the astonishing figures they were. After he drew two hundred thousand people to hear him in Europe, William Wells Brown then returned to a port near the Great Lakes, between America and Canada, to help fugitive slaves across the water, unite families, violating the mere boundaries of national existence. In addition he printed a paper announcing the uniting of families, the successes and sometimes failures of the underground travellers, their adventures and misadventures; and denouncing the "peculiar institution" and all those who would compromise with it, thinking they could thereby escape compromising themselves.

The startling challenge to current notions about civilisation was presented by the slaves, as soon as they won the public's ear, on the familiar matter of conscience. The contribution of the blacks was that type of social experience — whether it was lyceum, church or Underground Railroad — which challenged one set of social institutions with a social impact of a most original kind. Doomed by slavery to impersonality, the ex-slave responded with a personality and personal force that had the most obvious social implications and conclusions. Condemned to seasonal labour, and the rhythm and routine determined thereby, the blacks carried on agitation in and out of season until the body politic came to recognise that the country could no longer survive as it was, could survive only by embarking on an uncharted course of slave confiscation and Southern reconstruction. After having been isolated by slavery in provincial fixity, the runaway traversed national boundaries and oceanic waters. Graded by the abolition movement itself as fit only to tell slavery as an atrocity tale, Frederick Douglass and others insisted on publishing their own political policies. This is a long way from the reflex response to slavery by a disturbed conscience. It is a social impact on all media that distinguishes civilisation from barbarism. The impact of the slave labour system upon the South as a distinct region has a number of aspects clearly visible to this day.

The plantation was an organised community that was part of a larger regional configuration, but given the isolation concomitant with the rural character of slave society, the social stamp upon the individual, particularly the slave himself, guaranteed certain results. The internal economic principle of the plantation was self-sufficiency. To the slavemaster this meant insularity: foreign immigration mainly excluded; missionary society activity suspect (including the riding preachers who would as likely as not be anti-slavery); no lyceum or lecture circuit on any extensive scale; no compulsory elementary or secondary education; little exercise of the faculty of logical speculation. For a break in the routine of plantation life there were visits to the North, often no further than the river port city of Cincinnati; or politics in the state capital or in Washington, D.C., actually a Southern city.

To a large extent, certain of the above characteristics were true of America as a whole, or at least of its western part. Especially the smaller Southern planters had certain characteristics in common with the yeomanry of the American Northwest: the need to create isolated pockets of white habitation in a land belonging to the Indians, the establishment of paths into the wilderness, the harsh life for the women of the family, the back-breaking toil in wrestling some socially productive result from the natural surroundings, and the independence of habit and speech that is the inevitable result in people living under these conditions.

The dialectical set of connections of the South to the old Northwest is both genuinely subtle and profound. Both were agrarian areas, with the Mississippi and other rivers serving as the turnstiles to ports and citified places. Other similarities were the suspiciousness toward all those outside the isolated region where one's house and cultivated areas and perhaps hunting grounds were located; the tightness of the family and usually its patriarchal basis; the shortage of monies and credit, such that life frequently remained, generally according to the season, on a subsistence level, with only the holiday season to punctuate with some enjoyment above the everyday standard.

Further, there is the historical connection. All of American settlement, at its origins, proceeded in the same manner for both inland planters and Northern yeomanry, and their pioneering ways continued right up to the Civil War. In that sense Southern rural inhabitants were "these new men", the Americans who so intrigued the European observer often sceptical of America as (1) a civilisation and (2) a viable nationality. Thus if the black man has been left out of so many history books, if the controversy over the significance of slavery to the South seemed until very recently a matter of no great moment, it is because a certain aspect of American historical continuity seemed to justify itself and no mere racist conspiracy of silence could accomplish what seems to have been embedded within that historical aspect. To which must be added the fundamental matter of political organisation and the effect of the South on certain basic institutions by which an organised society emerged out of the natural wilderness. The individual planter was conditioned not only by pioneering inland to new territories; he had to become an individualist with a social authority larger than the boundaries of his plantation. The reasons are as follows. The South had been originally colonised by British trading companies licensed by the Crown. The Northern settlements were more likely to be religious colonies or fur-trading outposts. So that from the very start the planter, who had to be in charge of the practical and hazardous work of founding some lasting economic basis in the New World, was thrown into conflict with the concentrated mercantile capitalism of the metropolitan colonising land. To put it succinctly, the anticapitalist bias of the Southerner was there from the day of his birth. It was no small thing. The former slave — the supposedly emancipated black — became, for lack of credit, a sharecropper. This happened because all of Southern history had prepared somebody for that role, and the people at the bottom of the social ladder fell into it and remained there, some unto this day. To make up for their embattlement as regards the shortage of capital, the Southerners would compensate with (a) their geography, strategically considered, (b) the fixed position of the main section of the labouring force — the slaves, and (c) a type of politics which would guarantee the viability of (a) and (b).

All these things add up to a "nativist" outlook that is not that of country bumpkins, but one characterised by a sophistication that was constantly changing by the very reason of its taking place in a nineteenth- and late eighteenth-century setting that was becoming rapidly modernised. Slavery is a peculiar institution not only because of its horrors but because it was something-unto-itself. The Southern attitude seems so often a matter of temperament — unformed character expressing itself against a general trend in worldly affairs which opposed the fixed investment of wealth in land and human chattel. In other words, the South produced "personality" rather than minds of singular or original power. But the personalities are of a singular and sustaining force: Patrick Henry, Jefferson, Jackson, Calhoun, Clay, Stonewall Jackson, Tom Watson, Huey Long are personae who will interest the public imagination until possibly they are surpassed by the characterisation of the lives of the obscure slaves and indigent blacks. This tends to be the ongoing matter of interest in our own day.

There is a material basis for the Southern production of men and women of outstanding temperamental force. (The fictional Scarlett O'Hara or Blanche DuBois convey that the matter is not limited to the male gender.) Despite all geographical rationalisations, the commodity crops — tobacco, rice, sugar, cotton, and hemp — were not limited to the South by climate. The planters were a class capable of taking over matters of national interest: they had warred against nature, against the Indian; they had warred against the blacks on the plantation, against the British, the French, and the Spaniards. Their experience had a certain cast by virtue of the international nature of their products — human flesh and large-scale commodity crops. Such large-scale experiences do not lead to the production of small-minded men. So they participated in the formation of an original American nationality. The historical claim can be substantiated that they produced more figures of national distinction than did, say, by comparison. the robber barons. All this combines to make the controversy about the impact of slavery on American civilisation such a pregnant and vital intellectual confrontation.

Certain mundane matters have to be mentioned at least in a preliminary way. It was the boredom and harshness of plantation life that ensured that not general activity, but politics was the only matter of universal interest and appeal. If the rural character of their life induced in the planters, or at least in some of them, a certain respect for plebeian democracy in other sections of the population, it had to be by the nature of the planter's own setting, an abridged version of popular participation in decision-making. The father of the political party of any mass status in American life was the planter-political philosopher, Thomas Jefferson. The father of popular participation in political office, apart from mere suffrage, was the planter Andrew Jackson. The head of an army having the popular militia as a section of its base was the planter George Washington. Yet the halfway houses to genuine democracy which each of these figures created remain America's bones of contention unto this day.

What of social vision? The early accomplishments of these men corresponded to the formative period of American nationality. They could not go beyond. The results were embedded in the American mentality but not anywhere in self-generating institutions. The popular militia is now the not-very-progressive National Guard. The political parties resting on mass suffrage are now in a state alternating between paralysis and crisis. The spoils of office distributed to members of the population are now a source of perpetual scandal and parasitism.

The Southern figures of the mid-nineteenth century vacillated between accommodation and hopeless fanaticism. Clay was a genius of the first order. He could never win actual leadership of the country as a whole, though he was persistent and colourful enough to engage the political attentions of his countrymen. Calhoun was a different sort. He sought to make the American Constitution a protector of the South's position in national life, invulnerable to changing national majorities. And of Jefferson Davis it can perhaps best be said that though he failed in the Southern rebellion, he was saved from hanging by the long tradition of Northern-Southern accommodation — a tradition punctured only by the actualities of the Civil War.

Some of the bobbling of the minds of the planters was due to the very fact that they stood on a tripod of vital revolutions in the then-known Western world: the Puritans in 1642, the War of Independence in 1776, and volatile France of 1789. The Clays and Calhouns lived to consider the realities of the continental-wide European Revolution of 1848. Their situation was one of Anglo-Saxon nativism turning against itself. Immigrant New York might celebrate 1848, Puritan New England might relate revolutionary antislavery sentiments to the wars between Cavaliers and Roundheads, the democratic yeomanry of the western territories might enjoy the sight of crowns falling all over Europe. The Southern planters had no comparable frame of reference. They stuck by

Constitution and Compromise.

And when that did not last they went to war to protect geography. It was not all that simple. The border states which did not produce commodity crops but which had domestic slaves were the geniuses of accommodation right up to the last moment and beyond. The idyllic notion of domestic servitude, patriarchal chatteldom, originates from those Kentucky, Tennessee, upper Virginia, Maryland, and even Delaware manors. If American politics became entwined with a style of life rather than a manner of thought, we have no difficulties discovering why. In short, the Southern position was that of a provincialism entwined with American nationality as a whole, but defenceless against the universal trends of revolutionary democracy of the nineteenth century.

Nevertheless the effects of the planters were immense: the location of the nation's capital in the borderline South; the creation and manipulation of national political parties; the fielding of armies and the tradition of militant armed conflict; the specialisation of the South in politics as manoeuvre and divagation; the bias in favour of the nation that agricultural wealth was real, and commercial wealth always fraudulent; the sense of the manor not as parasitic but as a centre of human community; the assertion that the concreteness of the manorial community was superior to the impersonality of the large Northern city; the impulsiveness of the Southern personality as more appealing than the social discipline seemingly inherent in industry and commerce; the general link-up with the rural-romantic character of America's past — all of this seems irrevocable and untouchable by general intellectual argument.

The only way to deal with it is by taking up its foundations. The Southern planter could engage in politics on a much larger scale than many Northerners or Westerners because he was of a leisure class, born and bred — a commander of the fate of men, women, and children of a different colour with a more permanently fixed status. Suckled by a black nurse, attended by black servants, often encouraged to sexual experiments in the slave quarters, accustomed to the sight of blacks caring for all business involving manual labour; encouraged, even inspired, by the succession of Southern presidents, the ambitious Southerner could see politics, even statesmanship, as destiny's decision, and cast himself in the role of fortune's darling. Furthermore, for the isolated manorial communities, politics was the prime form of social communion, whereas in the North religious revivals swept all before them in periods in between political excitement. In today's parlance, the pre-bellum white planter gives the impression of having found an early answer to the problems of the "lonely crowd" in the solidity of his native tradition, the fixity of his social status and the values of an inherent and irrevocable individualism.

The availability and accessibility of having things always at hand extended itself to the vast virgin lands and the supply of slaves. If capital and credit were in short supply, then the curse was on the head of the mercantilists — be they tyrannical Englishmen or grasping Boston Yankees. Social status had taken on an over-weening importance; but even greater was the display of public personality — elections as jousting contests, a codified individualism rather than the self-expansive effluvia of the Northern transcenden-talists.

The rationalisations for the Atlantic slave trade and American slavery, whether borrowed from the Bible or the instances of Greece or Rome, raise a compelling challenge to the whole matter of what indeed constitutes a civilisation. It is safe to say that the majority of Western scholars seem to have placed a gloss on the manner and the matter of this case.

                                                                 1970

20

George Jackson

[*This short article, appraising George Jackson and establishing the links between his generation and that of people such as Du Bois and James himself, was written for* Radical America *and appeared in the November-December issue of 1971, a few weeks after the murder of Jackson at San Quentin prison.*]

It would be quite stupid, if not ridiculous, to attempt to give some sort of brief or concentrated account of black struggles in the United States. To do that properly would require a book or a series of lectures. Instead I shall continue, in fact intensify, the method that I have been raising so far. The most important name in the history of black struggles in the world at large or in the United States is Dr W. E. B. Du Bois. All thinking about black struggles today and some years past originates from him. Here, however, I have to take one single quotation from his work. In *Black Reconstruction in America, 1860-1888,* Dr Du Bois sums up his future of black struggles in the world at large. He concludes with a picture of the frustration suffered by blacks in the United States. He writes on Page 703:

> "Such mental frustration cannot indefinitely continue. Some day it may burst in fire and blood. Who will be to blame? And where the greater cost? Black folk, after all, have little to lose, but civilisation has all. This the American black man knows: his fight here is a fight to the finish. Either he dies or he wins. If he wins it will be by no subterfuge or evasion of amalgamation. He will enter modern civilisation here in America as a black man on terms of perfect and unlimited equality with any white man, or he will enter not at all. Either extermination root and branch, or absolute equality. There can be no compromise. This is the last great battle of the West."

That is where in 1971 we have to begin. In 1938 I visited the United States, and by 1948, speaking on the platform of the Socialist Workers' Party (trotskyism, which I left three years afterwards), I introduced a resolution on the Negro question. In the course of it I said as follows:

> "We can compare what we have to say that is new by comparing it to previous positions on the Negro question in the socialist movement. The proletariat, as we know, must lead the struggles of all the oppressed and all those who are persecuted

by capitalism. But this has been interpreted in the past — and by some very good socialists too — in the following sense: the independent struggles of the Negro people have not got much more than an episodic value, and as a matter of fact, can constitute a great danger not only to the Negroes themselves, but to the organised labour movement. The real leadership of the Negro struggle must rest in the hands of organised labour and of the marxist party. Without that the Negro struggle is not only weak, but is likely to cause difficulties for the Negroes and dangers to organised labour. This, as I say, has been the position held by many socialists in the past. Some great socialists in the United States have been associated with this attitude.

We on the other hand say something entirely different. We say, number one, that the Negro struggle, the independent Negro struggle, has a vitality and a validity of its own: that it has deep historic roots in the past of America and in present struggles; it has an organic political perspective, along which it is travelling, to one degree or another, and everything shows that at the present time it is travelling with great speed and vigour. We say, number two, that this independent Negro movement is able to intervene with terrific force upon the general social and political life of the nation, despite the fact that it is waged under the banner of democratic rights, and is not led necessarily either by the organised labour movement or the marxist party. We say, number three, and this is the most important, that it is able to exercise a powerful influence upon the revolutionary proletariat, that it has got a great contribution to make to the development of the proletariat in the United States, and that is in itself a constituent part of the struggle for socialism."

The reader will have to note* that not only was the black question given an independent role, with its own role and its own leadership, he must note also the great step forward that was made in point three. Previous to 1948 the whole marxist movement, including myself, had always thought that on the whole and also in particular it was the proletariat, the marxist party which had to educate all the elements of society on the fundamental reality of political struggle for socialism. A careful reading of point number three will show that a sharp break was made with this traditional policy. There it was made quite clear that the black struggles in the United States would be the education of the whole society in the realities of contemporary politics. That is precisely what is happening today and the best proof I can give of it are two quotations from the letters of a young man, George Jackson, published under the title *Soledad Brother*. Jackson was in prison at the age of eighteen and was shot and killed in prison at the age of twenty-

---

*The document referred to is "The Revolutionary Answer to the Negro Problem in the USA", see pp. 119-27.

eight. Of the ten years that he spent in prison, seven were spent in solitary confinement. The letters are in my opinion the most remarkable political documents that have appeared inside or outside the United States since the death of Lenin. Here is the first quotation:

"There is an element of cowardice, great ignorance, and perhaps even treachery in blacks of his general type. And I agree with Eldridge and Malcolm, we are not protecting unity when we refrain from attacking them. Actually it's the reverse that's true. We can never have unity as long as we have these idiots among us to confuse and frighten the people. It's not possible for anyone to still think that Western mechanised warfare is absolute, not after the experiences of the Third World since World War II. The French had tanks in Algeria, the US had them in Cuba. Everything, I mean every trick and gadget in the manual of Western arms has been thrown at the VC, and they have thrown them back, twisted and ruined; and they have written books and pamphlets telling us how we could do the same. It's obvious that fighting ultimately depends on men, not gadgets. So I must conclude that those who stand between us and the pigs, who protect the marketplace, are either cowards or traitors. Probably both."

The second quotation explains and historically places the first. Jackson claims that all the prisoners in his prison who are specially confined and specially punished think exactly as he does. He says that words like "honkey", a word that is commonplace for abuse of white people by black revolutionaries, these young men never used. Here is what Jackson says of them:

"All of these are beautiful brothers, ones who have stepped across the line into the position from which there can be no retreat. All are fully committed. They are the most desperate and dauntless of our kind. I love them. They are men and they do not fight with their mouths. They've brought them here from prisons all over the state to be warehoused or murdered, whichever is more expedient. That Brother Edwards who was murdered in that week in January told his lawyer that he would never get out of prison alive. He was at the time of that statement on Maximum Row, Death Row, Soledad, California. He was twenty-one years old. We have made it a point to never exchange words with these people. But they never relent. Angela, there are some people who will never learn new responses. They will carry what they incorporated into their characters at early youth to the grave. Some can never be educated. As a historian, you know how long and how fervently we've appealed to these people to take some of the murder out of their system, their economics, their propaganda; and as an intelligent observer you must see how our appeals were received. We've wasted many generations and oceans of blood trying to civilise the elements over here. It cannot be done in the manner in which we have attempted it in the past. Dialectics, understanding, love, passive resistance — they won't work on an atavistic, maniacal, gory pig. It's going to grow much worse for the black male than it already is — much much worse. We are going to have to be the vanguard, catalyst, in any meaningful change."

It is quite obvious that where Du Bois and myself were observing a situation, taking part, organisationally in our various ways, but guided by theoretical, that is to say intellectual development, the generation to which Jackson belonged has arrived at the profound conclusion that the only way of life possible to them is the complete intellectual, physical, moral commitment to the revolutionary struggle against capitalism. They are a stage beyond all historical and theoretical writing, and I add here an opinion that in my travels about the United States I have met or been aware of many thousands of young black people who could not express themselves in this manner, for Jackson is a born writer. But that is how they think, those are the principles on which they act, and as blacks they are not alone. It would take too much to show that their attitude is not confined to blackness, but that for the time being is enough. The reader of this must now go and for himself read all about Malcolm X, Martin Luther King, Angela Davis, Huey Newton, the Black Panther Party, and the whole list of other names and persons who fill the political life of the United States today. But unless he has some clear grasp of the historical development which I have outlined he will not only be wasting his time but corrupting his understanding of what is taking place in the United States today.

1971

INDEX OF NAMES